The Moral Mappings of South and North

Annual of European and Global Studies

An annual collection of the best research on European and global themes, the *Annual of European and Global Studies* publishes issues with a specific focus, each addressing critical developments and controversies in the field.

Published volumes:
Religion and Politics: European and Global Perspectives
Edited by Johann P. Arnason and Ireneusz Paweł Karolewski

African, American and European Trajectories of Modernity:
Past Oppression, Future Justice?
Edited by Peter Wagner

Social Transformations and Revolutions: Reflections and Analyses
Edited by Johann P. Arnason & Marek Hrubec

www.edinburghuniversitypress.com/series/aegs

Annual of European and Global Studies

The Moral Mappings of South and North

Edited by Peter Wagner

EDINBURGH
University Press

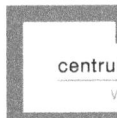

centrum im. willy brandta
willy brandt zentrum

Edinburgh University Press is one of the leading university presses in the UK. We publish academic books and journals in our selected subject areas across the humanities and social sciences, combining cutting-edge scholarship with high editorial and production values to produce academic works of lasting importance. For more information visit our website: edinburghuniversitypress.com

Edinburgh University Press Ltd
The Tun – Holyrood Road
12(2f) Jackson's Entry
Edinburgh EH8 8PJ

Typeset in Minion Pro and Gill Sans by
Servis Filmsetting Ltd, Stockport, Cheshire,

A CIP record for this book is available from the British Library

ISBN 978 1 4744 2324 3 (hardback)
ISBN 978 1 4744 4441 5 (pbk.)
ISBN 978 1 4744 2326 7 (webready PDF)
ISBN 978 1 4744 2327 4 (epub)

Contents

List of Figures   vii

Notes on the Contributors   viii

Acknowledgements   xi

1   Finding One's Way in Global Social Space   1
    Peter Wagner

2   Does the World Have a Spatio-political Form? Preliminaries   18
    Gerard Rosich

3   The BRICS Countries: Time and Space in Moral Narratives
    of Development   51
    Cláudio Costa Pinheiro

4   Russia between East, West and North: Comments on the
    History of Moral Mapping   72
    Maxim Khomyakov

5   Digging for Class: Thoughts on the Writing of a Global
    History of Social Distinction   107
    Jacob Dlamini

6   North–South and the Question of Recognition: A
    Constellation Saturated with Tensions   127
    À. Lorena Fuster

7   On Spaces and Experiences: Modern Displacements,
    Interpretations and Universal Claims   161
    Aurea Mota

8   The South as Exile   183
     Nathalie Karagiannis

Index   217

Figures

Figure 6.1 The Centaurus constellation, in Johann Bayer, *Uranometria: omnium asterismorum continens schemata, nova methodo delineata, aereis laminis expressa*, Augsburg: Christoph Mang, 1603   134

Figure 8.1 William Kentridge, drawing from 'Felix in Exile', 1994, charcoal and pastel on paper, 120 × 150 cm / 47-1/4 × 59-1/16 in. Courtesy of the artist and Marian Goodman Gallery. Copyright: William Kentridge   183

Contributors

Jacob Dlamini is Assistant Professor of History at Princeton University. He obtained a PhD from Yale University in 2012 and is also a graduate of Wits University in South Africa and Sussex University in England. Jacob held a postdoctoral fellowship at the University of Barcelona, Spain, from November 2011 to April 2015, and was a Visiting Scholar at Harvard University from August 2014 to May 2015. His research interests include the intellectual history of pre-colonial Africa, the social and political history of modern Africa, comparative histories of violence and political collaboration, and the environmental history of Africa. His is the author of *Askari: A Story of Collaboration and Betrayal in the Anti-Apartheid Struggle* (2015) and *Native Nostalgia* (2009).

À. Lorena Fuster holds a PhD in Philosophy from the University of Barcelona, where she works as a postdoctoral researcher. On the one hand, her research is focused on the conceptualisation of political imagination, especially from the perspective of contemporary philosophers, and in relation to the historical genealogy of social imaginaries or collective self-understandings. On the other, she makes contributions to the field of gender studies and is a specialist in the work of women philosophers. She has published several papers on these topics in books and scholarly journals.

Nathalie Karagiannis is a sociologist who also holds degrees in law and political science. Her interests have included the relation between the social and the political, the ambiguities of solidarity, and democracy. She has published *Avoiding Responsibility: The Politics and Discourse of European Development Policy* (Pluto Press, 2004); *European Solidarity* (ed., Liverpool University Press, 2007); and *Varieties of World-Making: Beyond Globalization* (co-ed., Liverpool University Press, 2007). In

2014, she published *Saranta* (Athens: Agra), a book of poetry, together with the artist Christina Nakou, and in 2016, *Exorismos* (Athens: Melani) and *La búsqueda del Sur* (Barcelona: Animal Sospechoso). She also translated Peter Wagner's *Sauver le progrès* (Paris: La Découverte, 2016) into French.

Maxim Khomyakov is Vice-President for International Relations and Director of the BRICS Studies Centre at Ural Federal University, Ekaterinburg, Russia. He is author of more than sixty publications on the history of medieval philosophy, the history of Russian philosophy and on contemporary political theory. His most recent English-language works include 'Toleration and Respect: Historical Instances and Current Problems', *European Journal of Political Theory*, 12: 3 (2013), 223–39; 'Building a World-Class University and the Role of the University Rankings: A Russian Case', in K. Downing and F. Ganotice (eds), *World University Rankings and the Future of Higher Education*, IGI Global, 2016, pp. 396–422; and 'Mastering Nature: A Russian Way in Modernity?', *Social Imaginaries*, 2: 2 (2016), 165–81. His works in Russian language include *Deus ex machina: Rationalism i mysticism v philosophii obshego dela Fedorova* (Rationalism and Mysticism in Fedorov's 'Philosophy of the Common Task') (Ekaterinburg, 1995); and *Problema tolerantnosti v christianskoy philosophii* (The Problem of Toleration in Christian Philosophy) (Ekaterinburg, UrGU-press, 2000).

Aurea Mota is an interdisciplinarily oriented sociologist whose main research interests lie in social theory and comparative historical sociology. She studied Sociology at the Federal University of Minas Gerais (UFMG), Belo Horizonte (BA in 2004, MA in 2010), and her PhD is from the Institute for the Study of Society and Politics (IESP, formerly IUPERJ) in Rio de Janeiro (2012). She is a member of the Political Philosophy Group of the Latin American Council of Social Sciences (CLACSO) and an associate researcher of the 'Participatory Democracy Project' (PRODEP) at UFMG. Aurea was a Visiting Researcher in the Department of Sociology, Sussex University, UK (2010). She was the recipient of two awards from CLACSO in 2006 and in 2010. Her publications are about Latin America, social participation in contemporary Brazil and social theory.

Cláudio Costa Pinheiro is Professor at the Institute of History of the Rio de Janeiro Federal University and Chair of the Sephis Programme

(South-South Programme for the History of Development). His research interests include sociology of knowledge and epistemological frameworks in contemporary human sciences, with concerns to colonialism, postcolonialism and aspects of the institutionalisation of power, comparing Asia (particularly India) and Latin America. Recent research projects involve the dynamics of the international scientific production developed outside the hegemonic centres, analysing academic dependency at peripheral areas in relation to the international academic mainstream. He has been a Visiting Scholar and/or Professor at the Bukkyo University (Kyoto, 2001–2), the University of Lisbon (Lisbon, 2003), the Center for the Study of Developing Societies (New Delhi, 2005), the University of Delhi (2005), the University of Calcutta (Kolkata, 2005), at Goa University (Panjim, 2006) and Free University (Berlin, 2012–13).

Gerard Rosich holds a PhD in Philosophy. Located in the areas of conceptual history, historical sociology and political and social theory, his present work is centred on the current reinterpretations of the modern foundations of politics, focusing on the concept of collective autonomy and evaluating its conceptual and normative adequacy in terms of understanding the current global/local transformations. His research interests include modern theories of autonomy, cosmopolitan studies and theories of historical injustice. His most recent publication is the book, co-edited with Peter Wagner, *The Trouble with Democracy* (Edinburgh University Press, 2016).

Peter Wagner is Research Professor of Sociology at the Catalan Institute for Research and Advanced Studies (ICREA) and at the University of Barcelona and has been Principal Investigator of the European Research Council Advanced Grant project 'Trajectories of Modernity' (TRAMOD, 2010–15). His recent publications include *Progress: A Reconstruction* (2016; French edition: *Sauver le progrès*, 2016; German edition forthcoming 2017) and *Modernity: Understanding the Present* (2012) as well as the (co-)edited volumes *The Trouble with Democracy* (with Gerard Rosich, 2016), *African, American and European Trajectories of Modernity* (2015) and *The Greek Polis and Democracy: A Politico-cultural Transformation and Its Interpretations* (with Johann Arnason and Kurt Raaflaub, 2013).

Acknowledgements

The research that has led to this volume has benefited from funding by the European Research Council (ERC) as Advanced Grant project 'Trajectories of Modernity: Comparing Non-European and European Varieties' (TRAMOD, 2010–15; grant no. 249438). All contributors have in various ways been associated with the TRAMOD research group. We would like to thank ERC for the generous funding that has made our work possible and the other members of the TRAMOD group for extended discussions about the topic of this book. The final stage of research and writing coincided with the beginning of the project 'The Debt: Historicizing Europe's Relations with the "South"', funded by the consortium Humanities in the European Research Area within the framework of its Joint Research Programme 'Uses of the Past' (HERA JRP UP, 2016–19), with which some of the contributors are associated. Some of the early reflections on 'The Debt' entered into this volume, and we would like to thank HERA for support for this new research endeavour.

English is the main language of global communication in the social sciences and the humanities today, but not everyone grows up with it. Once again, we would like to thank Samual Sadian for his careful editing of the contributions.

Finding One's Way in Global Social Space

Peter Wagner

1. Faraway, so close: the South

THE TERMS 'GLOBAL South' and 'Global North' are the latest in
a long series of conceptual distinctions that serve as attempts at
world-interpretation and world-ordering. By now they are widely used
without further explanation, in particular the term 'Global South',
showing that they have entered common language in global public
debate. A recent bibliometric study showed that the use of the term
'Global South' in the social sciences and humanities has been steadily increasing from 19 in 2004 to 248 in 2013 (Pagel et al. 2014; for
general reflections on this rise, see Hylland Eriksen 2015). There are
now scholarly journals that carry the term in their title, such as *The
Global South*, published by Indiana University Press and already in its
tenth year, or the open access online journal *Bandung: Journal of the
Global South*. Higher education institutions have started to honour the
concept by institutionalising it, such as through the Global South Unit
at the London School of Economics and Political Science or the Global
South Studies Center at the University of Cologne. If rapid diffusion is
a measure, the apparently geographical distinction between South and
North is a great success.

At the same time, this distinction is problematic in numerous
respects. Indeed, the stream of publications in which the term 'South'
is used as a concept – or, some might prefer to say: in place of a concept
– as if it had an evident and generally accepted referent keeps being
accompanied by a debate about the very meaning and usefulness of
the term, in which numerous and not at all consonant voices can be
heard. To give just a few illustrations: conceptually, the distinction
between North and South has multiple – overlapping, but not identical
– meanings. North/South may be taken to be a distinction between the

rich and the poor, the dominant and the dominated, the centre and the periphery, the 'advanced industrial societies' and the 'developing' ones, among others. Empirically, the Global South is not identical with the southern hemisphere, in which societies of the Global North, such as Australia, are located, and vice versa. Beyond the spatial appropriateness of the terms themselves, there are also important cases of societies that cannot easily be placed into these categories: is China, the second-largest economy in the world, part of the Global South; or is Russia, highly dependent on exportation of raw materials, part of the Global North? Finally, and maybe most importantly, these concepts may also be just another misplaced attempt at conflating conceptual signification with bounded geographical space. This has always been problematic, one of the most widely discussed cases being the conflation of 'Europe' and 'modernity' (see Stråth and Wagner 2017). In the contemporary world, marked by unprecedented degrees of interconnectedness, often called 'globalisation', such an attempt may be even less fruitful than at other moments.

Concept-formation is always open to objections. Given that the South/North distinction fails on so many counts, however, it may be more flawed than other, earlier attempts at world-ordering. On first reflection, one may just conclude that South and North are useless categories in the work at understanding the contemporary world within the social sciences and the humanities. This book, in turn, suggests that one should not arrive at such a conclusion prematurely. Rather than decreeing uselessness, it is worthwhile to explore the uses to which these categories are actually put and to see whether they are useful for certain purposes. In the social sciences and the humanities, concepts are not meant to 'map' empirical reality – even though confusion may easily arise when concepts use geographical terms. Rather, they interpret experiences and suggest ways of acting in the light of experiences. The interesting question, therefore, is not whether a South exists, but from and to which experiences the coining and acceptance of this term speaks and what avenues of action it opens up. This book intends to contribute to answering this question.

Doing so, the contributors to this volume pursue two different avenues of investigation. Some of them stay close, at least to start with, to the recent conceptual transformation in ways of world-interpretation, as sketched at the outset. They explore the usefulness as well as the limits of the South/North distinction by looking at the varieties of ways in which it has been cast: by emphasising its performative character

(Cláudio Pinheiro on BRICS); by widening the historical context for specific world-regions (Jacob Dlamini on Southern Africa, Maxim Khomyakov on Russia); and by elaborating elements of a political philosophy of planet and world (Gerard Rosich). In contrast, the other contributors approach the current debate from afar, to continue on the spatial metaphor. They identify and retrieve features that underlie this topical debate and are crucial for understanding it, but are normally not visible. Thus, they suggest: that that which was to be called the South is at the origins of political modernity, thus is constitutive of the North and of the very distinction (Lorena Fuster); that, going beyond opposing a Southern epistemology to the colonial imposition of Northern knowledge, world-interpretation is better advanced by displacements than by staying within locations (Aurea Mota); that South is a term for the place from which one is not but has to go to or intends to go to, South as exile and as a remedy for exile (Nathalie Karagiannis).[1]

This short introductory chapter will follow the contributors on this dual trajectory, looking at the distinction between South and North from close and from afar. In the first part, the current use of Global South and Global North is investigated by looking contextually (2) at its *conceptual* implications, by testing in how far it supports (3) a *critical* analysis of our present time, and by exploring and questioning (4) the *claims* that are often associated with its use. In the second part, the South is seen in longer and wider perspective. The argument about (5) the co-originality of the South and political modernity is mirrored in a reflection about the possible *end of the South* in our time. In the time in-between, which is and will always be our time, the place of the South has never been stable: with changing socio-political constellations, the South kept being restructured; however, the South also turned out to be (6) a *moving target*, escaping from any fixation. Thus, in conclusion, we will find that (7) the South is *ubiquitous*, but also *always elsewhere*.

2. The disappearance of the other North

As a conceptually driven attempt at world-ordering, the distinction of Global South and Global North is an updating of the distinction between a First, Second and Third World after the implosion of the Second World. The three-world distinction was arguably the first one in a long time in which the globe was provided with a comprehensive conceptual mapping, only preceded by the distinction between the Old World and the New World that emerged in the early sixteenth century at the moment when more geographical sense was made of the so-called discoveries. Other distinctions were also intended to signal the most significant boundary, often in binary terms, such as between 'Hellenes' and 'barbarians' or between 'Orient' and 'Occident'. But they were less comprehensive given that they either acknowledged areas of the globe that were not covered or displayed such a lack of knowledge about the other that any conceptual use was impeded. The term 'Third World', in contrast, first coined in 1952 by Alfred Sauvy with broader connotations (see Pinheiro in this volume), acquired a clear conceptual meaning when it was connected with theories of economic development in the course of the following two decades. When the term 'South' first emerged in a global-institutional sense in the report of the Brandt Commission in 1980, headed by the former West German Chancellor Willy Brandt, it was used in exactly the same sense: the South was composed of countries that failed to base their economies on high added-value manufactured products and, thus, to overcome widespread poverty. For global justice and security, they should benefit from resource transfers from the North. In line with Brandt's earlier foreign policy, the report eliminated what for three decades had been seen as the most significant distinction, the one between Western democratic capitalism and Soviet socialism, between First and Second World. Brandt's credo in 'peaceful coexistence' did not foresee the disappearance of Soviet socialism, but was based on the expectation that the gap between the two underlying world-views would shrink, not least due to functional requirements to which he added politico-moral demands.

When Soviet socialism collapsed a decade later, the ground had therefore already been prepared for a new comprehensive conceptual distinction, now a binary one. But it is necessary to review the use of the earlier triple distinction to understand the variety of meanings that can be associated with the new set of counter-concepts, Global South and Global North. Conceptually, the three-worlds image was based on an economic view of society with industrialism at its centre, in the First World seen as advanced predominantly by market exchange and embedded within moderately democratic politics and in the Second World steered by a state apparatus acting in the name of the working class. Importantly, there was a clear view of progress, namely steadily better satisfaction of needs due to industrialisation, only disagreement as to how such progress was to be brought about. The Third World related to the First and to the Second Worlds in equally asymmetric ways. In current terminology, the South had two Norths to which it was

4

oriented. The question then is what changes when one of those Norths disappears.

The conceptual consequences are ambiguous. The coexistence of democratic capitalism and state socialism meant a limited plurality of viable modes of socio-political organisation. The disappearance of one of those modes can be seen as entailing the evidence that only one of those was truly viable in the long run. This conclusion was readily drawn by evolutionary thinkers in the social sciences who thought to identify in these processes the selection of the functionally superior model. But rather than the end of plurality, this transformation can also be seen as spelling the end of the limits of plurality. In this sense, the flourishing of the debate about 'multiple modernities' (Shmuel N. Eisenstadt) after 1990 is closely connected to the fall of existing socialism. These varieties of modernity have either been seen as rooted in long-term civilisational legacies, under the heading of 'multiple modernities', or they have been identified with projects for societal organisation, not least in the face of a hegemonic model of liberal-capitalist modernity, then more typically described as 'alternative modernities' (Dilip Gaonkar). In both these versions, the idea of a linear trajectory of societal development is aban-doned. Following these approaches, the end of the other North entails the end of all possible North.

But can there be a South without a North? The reflections above sit uneasily with the rise of the term 'Global South'. To consider the latter's usefulness further, we need to add its critical and normative purposes to the conceptual ones.

3. Beyond globalisation?

Critically, the proposed terminology objects against the idea of a 'flattening' of the earth through processes of globalisation and indi-vidualisation, as sociological theories used to see it, or through the finally global diffusion of the universal principles of human rights and democracy, as political theory and political science tended to put it. These scholarly discourses have had wide impact on public debate for some time. They have provided elements for a novel reinterpretation of the global socio-political constellation with very characteristic features. The theorem of globalisation and individualisation combined with the discourse on human rights and democracy in suggesting that there is – and: should be – little or nothing between the individual human being and the globe. Every social phenomenon that stands in-between tends, in sociological terms, to be annihilated by the ever more widespread use of new information and communication technology and, in political terms, to be considered as having freedom-limiting effects. Significantly, the notion of democracy, which presupposes a specific decision-making collectivity and thus appears to stand necessarily in an intermediate position between the individual and the globe, tends to be redefined. Rather than referring to a concrete, historically given collectivity, processes of democratic self-determination are, on the one side, related to social movements without institutional reference, and on the other side, projected to the global level as the coming cosmopolitan democracy. We can characterise this conceptual tendency as the erasure of meaningful space. In a second step, we can identify a similar tendency towards the erasure of historical time. The individual human beings in question are seen as free and equal, in particular as equally free. Thus, their life-histories and experiences are no longer seen as giving them a particular position in the world from which they speak and act. And political orders are seen as associations of such individuals who enter into a social contract with each other, devoid of any particular history (for more detail on the above see Wagner 2015).

This imagery provided significant orientation for much political action after the implosion of the Second World. And, arguably, it is against the hegemony of this imagery that the coining of the term 'Global South' critically reacts. Rather than only one world, it appears to suggest, there are two worlds on the globe. Against the conceptual erasure of space, in particular, it proposes a dual spatiality. In the political and intellectual context of the late twentieth century, it was highly important to insist on the fact that something that one used to call social structures persisted even under the new conditions. The question, however, is how well the South/North distinction serves this purpose.

It is useful to recall the sites of debate. The heyday of globalisation has been monitored and interpreted by the World Economic Forum since 1987, having been preceded by the European Management Forum since 1974, at the moment of the first serious economic crisis of the post-Second World War order. As a critical alternative, the World Social Forum started to meet in 2001, first in Porto Alegre, having been preceded by *encuentros* in Latin America since 1996. The two fora can be seen to embody – or: as having for some time embodied – the major sites at which reflection about the current global socio-political constellation takes place, the one in deliberate contrast with the other.

Can the one be seen as representing the North and the other the South? At a closer look, the alternative forum works with a critical conceptualisation that is quite at odds with the two-world image. According to its principles, the participants in the World Social Forum 'are opposed to neoliberalism and to domination of the world by capital and any form of imperialism'. Thus, the starting assumption rather is that a single world has already been created under the auspices of capital. The answer to this challenge, so the principles continue, is the commitment 'to building a planetary society . . .' (World Social Forum 2001). Thus, the social structures that are identified are planetary structures of domination that have to be overcome by building 'another world' that, or so it appears, has similarly a planetary dimension. If the forum were to present the Global South, this would be nothing but the other half of the Global North, coinhabiting not only the same planet, but also the same world (for a nuanced discussion of 'world' and 'planet' see Rosich in this volume).

In such understanding there is little room for a 'South' as being involved in a process of world-making (Karagiannis and Wagner 2007) nor for one that truly has a significant spatial meaning. If it is the case that neo-liberal global capitalism imposes itself in a homogenising way across the planet, then it will destroy any South that may have existed and, broadly following Marx's critical attitude, resistance to it will rebuild a world after the complete erasure of meaningful space (for a critique of such a view of history, see Chakrabarty 2000). And indeed, in recent debates about the Global South one can recognise that the link to a concrete spatiality becomes more and more tenuous – and this now no longer merely for reasons of the very imperfect geographical mapping, mentioned at the outset, but also because of the difficulty of matching spatial reference with a critique of domination (see recently Trefzer et al. 2014).

4. The South as an alternative

Obviously, one does not have to follow this particular approach to the critique of domination. But the preceding reflections underline the necessity to reflect carefully on the link between spatiality and conceptuality. When emphasising the economic aspect in terms of a critique of capitalism, the supposed South is nothing but a mirror image of the North, it has no features of its own (unlike the mirror image created by William Kentridge, discussed by Nathalie Karagiannis in this volume).

In contrast, when the focus in understanding the emergence of the Global South has been particular claims for Southern knowledge, they have regularly been associated with some notion of otherness of the South, an otherness, furthermore, that can be considered as an alternative to the North. It will suffice here to discuss three contributions to this debate as examples each for one approach to the question: Raewyn Connell's *Southern Theory* (2007); Boaventura de Sousa Santos's epistemologies of the South (see most recently the collection Santos 2014); and Jean and John Comaroff's *Theory from the South* (2012).[2]

Southern Theory is a work in retrieval. Against the background of a contextual analysis of the rise of European social theory, Raewyn Connell rediscovers authors from other continents whose works have been eclipsed by the dominance of 'Northern' theory. Underlining the socio-theoretical nature of these works, she provides a corrective to the implicitly – and sometimes explicitly – still dominant view that 'Northern' theory prevailed because it offered superior conceptualisations and explanations of social relations and their transformations. What she cannot fully do is to reconnect the theoretical work from the South with the one in the North and to confront the two with each other (see Aurea Mota in this volume). This is indeed a huge task for two main reasons: first, even though the world-regional strands of theorising did not develop in complete isolation from each other, they evolved in rather pronounced separation, the only exception being the closer relation between Latin American and European theorising. Thus, conceptual connections would need to be carefully constructed through analyses of contextual specificities. Second, the greater continuity from nineteenth-century European social theorising to late-twentieth-century 'Western' social theory created an asymmetrical relation to the various strands of Southern theory that can hardly be undone. For these reasons, the retrieval makes a strong case for recognising greater plurality of world-interpretations and serves as an inspiration for overcoming blind spots of Northern theory, but it cannot provide the contours of an alternative to the latter.

Theory from the South has a rather different agenda. Focusing on the present, its analyses are set in a context of a high degree of world-regional interconnectedness. Where Connell's starting assumption is one of differences in experiences that lead to varieties of forms of knowledge, Jean and John Comaroff presuppose a degree of similarity between world-regions that permits transfers of knowledge and insights. This is a standard assumption of theory from the North, a key example being the sociology of modernisation and development during the 1950s and 1960s. The originality of the book lies in the inversion of the perspective: rather than African societies evolving towards Europe and North America, the Comaroffs see the North following the recent social transformations of the South. Furthermore, there is also what we may call a perversion of the traditional Northern perspective: rather than things getting better over time, indeed through processes of modernisation and development, the Comaroffs see them as getting worse as the North keeps following the South. What has changed is the vantage point from which global social change can best be observed and analysed and the direction of such change, but the change itself keeps being considered as global and rather unidirectional.

Epistemologies of the South makes a much stronger claim. In contrast to the Comaroffs, the difference between North and South lies for Boaventura de Sousa Santos not in that which can be observed but in the ways of observing and interpreting. In earlier works, which made do without spatial connotations, he had distinguished between knowledge for domination and knowledge for emancipation. These were two basic epistemologies, both of which were at work in the North, the former dominant in the service of power and the latter expressing resistance against domination. Associating now such epistemological reasoning with a history of capitalism and colonialism, the knowledge for domination comes to be seen as predominantly located in the North and the knowledge for emancipation as prevailing in the South. This spatialisation of epistemology goes along with a second shift: while knowledge for emancipation had earlier been seen as one epistemological approach, Southern epistemologies are now based in the plurality of experiences of oppression and resistance, thus occurring themselves in a plural form. In this latter sense, Santos connects more closely with Connell and envisages varieties of alternatives emerging from the South, and importantly: positive alternatives, not merely an inversion of direction of a linear history.

As different as these proposals for Southern theories or epistemologies are, they all have in common that they link the generation of knowledge back to experiences made. Saying this, they do not oppose experience to theorisation. They rather suggest that what they call Northern theories or epistemologies are the historical crystallisations of specific experiences, made at the neglect or suppression of other experiences. As a consequence, false claims to universality or generalisability are made that can be challenged by theorising in the light of different experiences. But to be effective, such challenge needs to overcome exactly those claims to universality or generalisability that insulate Northern theory from any impact of new experiences. While this move is to be strongly appreciated, a major question remains: all three proposals for reopening practices of knowledge generation in the social sciences had already been made before within the North, so to say, but without attaching spatial significance to them. The question thus is: what is so specific about Southern experiences that new theories and epistemologies arise from them? And in what sense are those experiences truly Southern; in what way does the concept 'South' link these multiple and different experiences to each other?

5. Origins and end of the South

As stated at the outset, the current distinction between South and North can be seen as the latest of a comprehensive conceptual mapping in view of world-ordering, with the distinction of the New World from the Old World in the early sixteenth century as the first one. In the preceding section, furthermore, we have seen how claims for Southern knowledge were inscribed into the history of European global domination that started with the moment of 'discovery' of the so-called New World. This domination is characterised with different terms such as colonialism, capitalism, imperialism, often without making clear distinctions, which is not a minor problem. But before touching on this issue, it is important to underline that the South is thus given a history, and significantly a history that is different from other histories. Thus, it is possible to relate conceptuality to historicity, and to delineate a certain trajectory of the South.

For a long time, the crucial debate about 'the rise of Europe', the onset of modernity, and the beginning of a basically linear process of modernisation was focused on the world-historical transformations around the year 1800, namely the cumulated effects of the scientific revolution and the Enlightenment, the French Revolution and the Industrial Revolution. The period that historians of Europe call 'early modern times' only stood in the background; it had little significance of its own. What happened between 1500 and 1800 was 'early' because it gained meaning only as events in preparation of modernity. Furthermore, these centuries were analysed in terms of largely endogenous European developments, sparked by the Renaissance. The rest of the world had only a minor role in the rise of European modernity (see Jacob Dlamini, in this volume, bringing historical social structures in Africa into world-history and into sociological theory). Ironically, however, it is exactly this account in which Europe is isolated from the rest of the world and, subsequently, imposes itself on it, that lent itself to the elaboration of postcolonial and decolonial theories that reason against the background of a caricature of European modernity.

The more recent focus on the period between 1500 and 1800 allows to alter the picture. It helps recognising that European self-understanding was transformed as a consequence of the encounter with the unknown others in America, with human beings whom one did not expect and about whom one did not know anything, not even whether they are human. That way of thinking that is often called the European political philosophy of modernity, elaborated by scholars such as Las Casas (often forgotten in standard accounts), Hobbes, Locke, Rousseau and Kant, drew its main questions and conceptual inspirations from the encounter with the New World other (Dussel 2003). It is in this sense that the South is most fruitfully seen to constitute itself during this period (Lorena Fuster in this volume). As a consequence, this moment also sees the origins of the distinction between South and North. We cannot understand the history of the North and Northern epistemologies without its origins in the South and in the encounter with the South.[3]

While highly asymmetrical in many respects, the moment of origins is an encounter that is faced in the absence of adequate tools for cognition and recognition by both sides. Fundamental questions are without an answer but in need of an answer, most clearly acknowledged in the Valladolid–Salamanca debate of 1550–1. Even though the debate remained without conclusion, further practice denied native Americans equal treatment as full human beings. This was an orientation that prevailed, with considerable variety, during all of the colonial period until the late twentieth century. It justified the denial of the right to self-determination to the Southerners, and it justified the domination of the North over the South. In the Marxian tradition, 'reification' is the term used for the process in which relations between human beings transform into relations between things. The North/South relation is a case of what one may call unilateral reification: the dominated others are considered as if they were things, but not the same is true the other way round. Keeping the reciprocal uncertainty of the first encounter in mind, we may apply to the relation between North and South what Axel Honneth (2005) said in more general terms: reification is the forgetfulness of the original act of recognition.

If reification is forgetfulness, what happens when one remembers, or better: when one is reminded? The anti-colonial struggle has been highly successful, even though it has taken a long time and caused many victims. Most of the territories that were governed at some time between the sixteenth and the twentieth centuries by Northern powers have gained independence. Within those territories, the relation between descendants of settlers, of indigenous peoples and of slaves is mostly governed by formal equal freedom. This has been a struggle that has moved close to its final point only very recently. The end of apartheid in South Africa marks the moment at which any domination of one category of persons over another one has become utterly unjustifiable (which is not to say that it does not exist any longer at all). Elsewhere I have referred to this moment as the moment of the end of formal domination (Wagner 2016). As we have seen before, however, the concept of the South has mostly been used as an 'asymmetrical counter-concept' (Koselleck 1979) that helped to grasp the relation of domination between North and South. The end of formal domination between North and South then will necessarily have consequences for the persuasiveness of a concept that is built on the notion of such domination.

Thus, one may have reason to assume that the South will turn out to be an only temporarily significant concept for world-ordering. The moment of its explicit emergence already contains the signs of its imminent demise. The Global South was needed to express and criticise the restrictedness of 'Northern' world-interpretations and to underline the transformative potential of the 'Southern' alternatives, but also the latter's lack of actual power of transformation. Currently, the rise of BRICS (as discussed by Cláudio Pinheiro) is part of a new interpretation that draws on the tradition of 'the South' but radically alters it. In the centre of this reinterpretation, the BRICS alliance includes key societies of the former South, but also former embodiments of Northern world-interpretations. Furthermore, BRICS refers to states of considerable power, and the BRICS discourse is no longer one of dependence and powerlessness. One may say that, despite topical doubts, BRICS is more powerful than any former 'South', but at the same time considerably less 'Southern'.

6. The South as a moving target

Nevertheless it is unlikely that the South will disappear even in the case of a further rise of BRICS and the emergence of what is now called multi-polar world-politics. What is currently referred to as the Global South and what Southern theories and epistemologies claim does not exhaust the meaning of the South. In a first step we can approach the broader significance of the term by looking at a case that still stays close to issues of global politics.

During the immediate aftermath of decolonisation, the European Economic Community, the predecessor of the European Union, acknowledged its historical responsibility towards the former colonies and made this debt and duty the underlying rationale for its development policy. Already during the 1980s, however, the policy orientation changed, and the responsibility of each society for its own fate under conditions of market exchange was increasingly emphasised (Karagiannis 2004). With the formation of the European Union, the particular nature of the relation between Europe and its former colonies was further de-emphasised. The EU as a new actor positioned itself more neutrally, devoid of any historical burden, in the field of global politics and global commerce. This shift can be analysed as a move from a paternalistic self-understanding as promotor of modernisation and development abroad, consonant with the domestic Keynesian democratic welfare state, towards a view of oneself as a market actor guided by self-interest, consonant with the enterprise culture of neo-liberalism. Furthermore, though, it has consequences for what one means by South.

During the colonial period, the South was closely connected with Europe. This is visible, for instance, in the fact that integration of metropole and colonies on equal terms was considered in Portugal and France at the moment of decolonisation, even though this proposal never came close to realisation except for small territories. The immediate postcolonial arrangement was a relation between formally equal states with the former coloniser assuming debt and responsibility towards the former colonies. The more Europe started to consider itself as a unit, rather than an alliance of nation-states, however, the more distance was taken from the South. The acceleration of European integration after the Maastricht Treaty also was an attempt to finally shed the moral debt towards the former colonies entirely. The South was from now on clearly seen as outside Europe in territorial terms; it became a Global South allegedly without particular historical relation to Europe.

By now one recognises, though, that the establishment of a boundary of moral responsibility did not succeed. The South re-emerged within the territory of Europe: through urban protest by descendants of immigrants from the former colonies; through refugees; and through the widening of politico-economic heterogeneity in the current Euro crisis creating an intra-European South.[4] These recent developments can be seen as an act of intended domination of the North over the South, which significantly tried to fix the South in space. However, that which was to be dominated escapes from control; it cannot be fixed in space, rather becomes a moving target.

7. The South is elsewhere: space, direction and movement

Thus, it may be wrong to ask *where* the South is. Looking for the South may not – or at least, not necessarily – entail looking for a geographical space, it may mean asking for directions (Karagiannis 2016). North and South are categories of direction as much as of space, thus lend themselves to analysis of both place and movement. A comprehensive analysis of the rise of the distinction between South and North as social categories, therefore, needs to widen the perspective and consider movement and direction beyond location in space.

A first observation concerns the change of connotations compared with preceding related terms. Terms such as 'modern' and 'traditional' or 'developed' and 'developing' emphasised social change over time. 'North' and 'South', in turn, privilege space over time. This has several consequences. The apparent symmetry of spatial terms, on the one hand, eliminates some of the evaluative intentions: the North is not as such 'advanced' over the South; but neither do the terms 'North' and 'South' contain a hint of domination, in contrast to the centre/periphery distinction, for instance. On the other hand, the abolition of evident asymmetry allows for novel uses: the South can become a site of conceptual superiority and innovativeness or greater adequacy, in terms such as 'Southern theory' or 'epistemology of the South'. As seen above, however, the case for linking geographical space closely to conceptual claims cannot entirely convince. As Aurea Mota (in this volume) argues, the advance of knowledge may arise from displacement between spaces rather than from location in space.

As corporeal human beings can only be in one space at a time, any such displacement is always both a movement in space and in time. The conflation of temporality and spatiality has a long history in socio-political thought. 'In the beginning all the world was America', as John Locke famously and erroneously claimed, referring to presumed life before the social contract (see Jacob Dlamini in this volume). A key example is the conceptual relation between individual and community, guided by the notion that individualisation is a dominant historical trend and that culturally strongly integrated communities are a phenomenon either of the past or of a different space. Claiming to state the inevitable, this assumption has often also led to nostalgic longings for a past place or utopian expectations of a future place. Significantly, disputes over these interpretations show normative ambiguity: individualisation is supposed to increase freedom and possibilities for self-realisation, but it also leads to conformism, anomie and disorder.

While not without validity, most such conceptualisations suffer from two problems: they work with some teleological notion of social change (for a forceful critique, see Sewell 2005), and they conceptualise social change as an aggregate of supposed experiences that are not actually researched and reflected upon. Looking at the latter by other means, from poetry, philosophy and psychoanalysis, one recognises in the condition of exile a loss of one's space and a movement towards another space that create a quest for a return that cannot happen as such, because it would entail a move back both in space and in time. The South, as Nathalie Karagiannis (in this volume) shows, is indeed imagined as a return from such exile. It provides direction at a time when the coordinates of global social space have been upset so that to find one's way has become difficult.

Notes

1. Most of the contributors address more than one of the aspects mentioned. Their names are here given as an indication for the key appearance of these themes. Overall, the volume may be seen as a self-exercise by the contributors at finding their ways in global social space (paraphrasing Boltanski and Thévenot 1983), an exercise that has become more difficult not only owing to recent social change but also to the authors' own contradictory spatio-temporal locations (to paraphrase Wright 1978).

2. The authors of these works are kindly asked to excuse the somewhat schematic presentation of their reasonings for present purposes.

3. An observation of a different kind needs to be added: recent debates tend to deny or overlook that a great variety of South/North constellations – of colonial constellations, we may say – were forming between the sixteenth and the twentieth centuries and that it is this variety that makes it difficult to conceive of a single South opposed to a homogeneous North. If we consider for a moment the so-called Brandt line, the implicitly most often used way to geographically define South and North, two main outliers are immediately visible. The more recent one is Russia whose association with BRICS locates it today sometimes in the South,

but which has placed itself historically much more clearly in the North, indeed in its own context of colonisation (Maxim Khomyakov in this volume). And the much more familiar one is Australia, geographically clearly in the South, a society emerging from colonisation, and nevertheless unequivocally seen as part of the North. Comparing Australia with colonised or so-called settler societies in Africa, America and South Asia, its condition for becoming Northern is arguably the near extinction of the indigenous population. This is what it has in common with North America, which becomes Northern for the same reason (for a related comparative reasoning, in different conceptual terms, see already Hartz 1964).

4. The latter has been reflected in attempts at looking at Southern Europe in terms of versions of Southern theory. See Dainotto (2011); Cassano (2012).

References

Boltanski, Luc and Laurent Thévenot (1983), 'Finding one's way in social space', *Social Science Information* 22: 4–5, 631–80.

Cassano, Franco (2012), *Southern Thought, and Other Essays on the Mediterranean*, New York: Fordham University Press (1st Italian edn, 1996).

Chakrabarty, Dipesh (2000), *Provincializing Europe*, Princeton: Princeton University Press.

Comaroff, Jean and John L. Comaroff (2012), *Theory from the South: How Euro-America is Evolving Towards Africa*, Boulder, CO: Paradigm.

Connell, Raewyn (2007), *Southern Theory: Social Science and the Global Dynamics of Knowledge*, Cambridge: Polity.

Dainotto, Roberto M. (2011), 'Does Europe have a South? An essay on borders', *The Global South*, 5: 1, 37–50.

Dussel, Enrique (2003), *Política de la liberación*, Madrid: Trotta.

Hartz, Louis (1964), *The Founding of New Societies*, New York: Harcourt, Brace and World.

Honneth, Axel (2005), *Verdinglichung. Eine anerkennungstheoretische Studie*, Frankfurt am Main: Suhrkamp.

Hylland Eriksen, Thomas (2015), 'What's wrong with the Global North and the Global South?', in Andrea Hollington, Tijo Salverda, Tobias Schwarz and Oliver Tappe (eds), *Voices From Around the World: Concepts of the Global South*, Cologne: Global South Studies Centre.

Karagiannis, Nathalie (2004), *Avoiding Responsibility: The Discourse and Politics of EU Development Policy*, London: Pluto.

Karagiannis, Nathalie (ed.) (2016), *La búsqueda del sur*, Barcelona: Animal Sospechoso.

Karagiannis, Nathalie and Peter Wagner (eds) (2007), *Varieties of World-Making: Beyond Globalization*, Liverpool: Liverpool University Press.

Koselleck, Reinhart (1979), *Vergangene Zukunft. Zur Semantik geschichtlicher Zeiten*, Frankfurt am Main: Suhrkamp.

Pagel, Heike, Karen Ranke, Fabian Hempel and Jonas Köhler (2014), 'The use of the concept "Global South" in social science & humanities', presented at the conference *Globaler Süden/Global South: Kritische Perspektiven*, Humboldt University Berlin, 11 July 2014, available at <http://www.academia.edu> (last accessed 10 October 2016).

Santos, Boaventura de Sousa (2014), *Epistemologies of the South*, Boulder, CO: Paradigm.

Sewell, William H., Jr. (2005), *Logics of History: Social Theory and Social Transformations*, Chicago: University of Chicago Press.

StrÅth, Bo and Peter Wagner (2017), *European Modernity: A Global Approach*, London: Bloomsbury.

Trefzer, Annette, Jeffrey T. Jackson, Kathryn McKee and Kirsten Dellinger (2014), 'The Global South and/in the Global North: interdisciplinary investigations', *The Global South*, 8: 2, 1–15.

Wagner, Peter (2015), 'Understanding the present: a research programme', *Social Imaginaries*, 1: 1, 105–29.

Wagner, Peter (2016), *Progress: A Reconstruction*, Cambridge: Polity.

World Social Forum (2001), *World Social Forum Charter of Principles*, available at https://fsm2016.org/en/sinformer/a-propos-du-forum-social-mondial/ (last accessed 10 January 2017).

Wright, Erik Olin (1978), *Class, Crisis, and the State*, London: New Left Books.

Does the World Have a Spatio-political Form? Preliminaries

Gerard Rosich

1. Framing the question

FROM A GLOBAL perspective, democracy seems to be nowadays the political regime that in discursive terms is implicitly considered the sole legitimate political order. Now, in contrast to the past, whenever democracy is not acknowledged as the only suitable regime to institute an order, either explicit ad hoc justifications have to be provided to show why temporarily democracy should not rule, or resistance to democracy is associated locally with resistance to domination.[1] Paradoxically, at the moment in history when the reputation of democracy is at its best globally, a series of elements seem to suggest that its workings are in trouble (Rosich and Wagner 2016). Or, in other words, the constitution of a new global order that connects *all* human beings, arising as a response to the crisis of the previous order and possessing a commonly understood need to be democratic in its outlook, appears as tension-ridden. It is the first time in history that a socio-political ordering of the totality of human beings has to be normatively justifiable on democratic premises. Thus, it is an urgent task to collectively reconstruct socio-political thinking in the light of this present challenge.

Nevertheless, in both intellectual and historical terms the challenge itself is not new. Cosmopolitanism is the intellectual tradition that focuses on this *problématique*, though until very recently it did so *only* from a normative point of view and addressed it as a politico-philosophical project. However, Immanuel Kant, who remains the most representative thinker of this cosmopolitan project, did not believe that it was reconcilable with democracy (Kant [1784] 1989).[2] From a historical point of view, the two 'world' wars of the twentieth century gave birth to two consecutive global political institutions, first the League of Nations and afterwards the United Nations. The failure of the Wilsonian utopia of 'making the world safe for democracy' after the First World War led the founders of the United Nations to envisage a much less ambitious political programme, putting human rights at the centre of their normative project and leaving to the principle of state sovereignty the political regime of member states. Additionally, both projects were still informed by a political theory that has conceptualised from time immemorial the political form in relation to that which was the source of power and to the question of *who*, *where* and *how* to rule. In this regard, political theory has assumed a deep connection between politics and spatiality that has shaped the way polities are self-understood. Moreover, our historical periodisations are largely done by identifying continuities, transformations and inventions regarding the form and the place of polities and how they interrelate.

Two intertwined present facts suggest that the assumptions and methods of this time-honoured approach are no longer appropriate to an interpretation of the political realm. First, the growing interconnectedness between human beings has reached a level in the present that unsettles the boundaries defining the internal and external relations of a polity, rendering indeterminate its substance and spatial dimension. Though a new ordering seems to be at the moment self-instituting, we still do not know how to best conceptualise it and if it will be democratically constituted in political terms. The emerging categories such as the Global South in relation to a still hegemonic North work on the assumption that the globe is '*a*' unified whole, though its constitution is conflictive and it is not democratically shaped (Connell 2011). In addition, the global or regional institutions that have been in place since the first half of the twentieth century have hitherto been unable to address this 'reordering' democratically because they are not able or do not want to self-transform. The Global North/South debate, a division spatial in origin, has the virtue of assuming new collective subjects but is unable to address the current reconfigurations because, as I will argue, it still works with a conceptual and empirical framework that is in tension with the democratic regime and that possesses a reductionist understanding of world-formation, as is also the case with the contemporary globalisation discourse.

Second, scientific evidence suggests that the biogeochemical conditions under which the life of *Homo sapiens* has flourished on planet Earth are transforming dramatically due to human-induced climate change and the mastery of 'nature'. The dialectic between nature and environment has always been considered a trans-historical condition for human political ordering. Historical change could be observed in the transformations of particular practices and interpretations of this relation, with nature being the independent aspect of the relation, and the environment the transformation of nature by human agency. The difference now is that we as species (still?) cannot adapt to it and it negatively affects the planet as a whole, not only regions of it. This transformation seriously jeopardises the continuity of the human species on this planet. The relevance of this fact in the context of this chapter relates to the kind of political action that has to be performed in order to address this challenge and the 'structural' conditions such action imposes on a world ordering. To be successful, this political action has to be global in nature, but it is far from clear that it can be democratic. Even more, democracy may have boosted the deterioration of the environment (Chakrabarty 2009).

Against this background, the aim of this chapter is to make a contribution to the reconstruction of socio-political theorising. First, I will succinctly introduce the basic theoretical distinction of spatial concepts used politically to refer to totality. This is a fundamental requirement that has to be met if the 'ordering of the world' is to have any meaning. These concepts will help us to think, in a second step, whether a new spatio-political ordering of human totality is gradually taking form and under what conditions. Assuming such a transformation can be identified, we also have to inquire into its basic contours in order to assess the challenges that tensions in the current political spatial reordering pose for democracy considered as a political regime.

2. Comprehensive spatial concepts

The concepts that have been used to refer to an 'ordering' which includes all human beings are spatial: the West/East opposition, centre and periphery, globalisation and now the Global South/North, at the moment a technical term of scholarship that has not reached the level of public opinion. The spatial representation of human totality has been a fact common to a wide variety of civilisations at different times in history, and it did not necessarily imply a political human ordering articulated in spatial terms, as the history of nomadic peoples attests. Moreover, in contrast to the past, nowadays all humans are considered 'humans' and there is no justifiable division among human beings that circumscribes totality to a particular qualitative interpretation of what makes a human being 'human':

'humanity' is the sum of all human beings, which corresponds with the 'human' as a biological category, namely to the human as a species or as a 'race'.[3] It is important to specify that I am not referring strictly speaking to the different cosmologies or representations of the structure of the universe that humans have produced, as old as rock art, but to the particular way humans have understood themselves spatially in relation to what today we call 'humanity'. True, both representations can intersect, as we will see later, but geography and the natural sciences devoted to the study of geological and astronomical phenomena are two different ways of representing totality: one includes humans and the other not.

One cautionary note is important in this context. The concepts to be discussed – world, globe and Earth – are used interchangeably, not only in ordinary language, but also in scholarly debate. The conceptual distinctions discussed below are analytical, insofar as this is possible, and are intended to denote significant ontological differences between these concepts that have an impact on the way we create/represent human totality. Though my discussion is excessively concise for the deep implications it triggers, the only purpose of the distinctions drawn here is to prepare the ground for the following section. The reasoning is conceptual, though I will trace back at some moments the respective cultural-historical lineages.

World

The concept of 'world' is central to metaphysics and to 'world' history from the comparative civilisational perspective. Indeed, the difference in both uses, despite disputes between schools of thought or intellectual traditions, relates to whether a more conceptual or empirical approach is adopted. The tradition inaugurated by phenomenology and hermeneutics, mainly initiated with the work of Martin Heidegger and Edmund Husserl and further pursued by Hannah Arendt and Maurice Merleau-Ponty, opened new avenues for rethinking the relation between the human being and the world. The concept of 'world' refers to one of the fundamental structures of human existence. It does not designate a constitutive element of the human considered as a living being or, insofar as this is possible, of the individual human being. A 'world' is possible wherever the existence of human beings is collectively constituted. From this angle, the main contours of what a world consists of are as follows: (1) a world makes relations possible;

(2) it is created by a collectivity of humans; (3) it is an incomplete, commensurable whole.

(1) Relations between human beings, and even the constitution of selfhood, do not take place without mediation and *ex nihilo*. When we come into existence, a framework upon which social significations, a meaningful language and attitudes and/or frontiers between the living and non-living beings hangs, is in place. Moreover, as Hannah Arendt has indicated ([1958] 1998: 136), the necessary work that has to be realised to adapt ourselves to nature and make it safe for human dwelling creates an 'objective' world that stands in front of us as if it were independent but nevertheless our own. This is the *immanent field* that implicitly or explicitly mediates any kind of reflexivity or social relation.

(2) This leads us to the second fundamental element, the fact that in spite of always preceding us, the world is a *human creation*. The world is neither atemporal nor necessary for human existence. It may occur or not. The fact that it is not atemporal means that the world can disappear, be created anew, or transform. It also means that there is the possibility of losing the world or 'worldlessness' in specific situations where the immanent field that mediates human relations disappears. As a human creation, the world is the work of human imagination, as Cornelius Castoriadis has pointed out, and is thus the result of a particular dialectical movement. It is created by human beings by means of 'social imaginary significations' and in turn it becomes the world within which human beings relate to each other. It points both to the creativity of human beings in shaping their own world, without assuming that meaning is given or preordained in the act of instituting the world, and to the impossibility of reducing or deriving the meaning human beings attach to the social world from any systemic logic (Castoriadis 1997: 359). Following Arendt, in creating the world, the human being creates something that will last beyond actual human lives: the world endures. The fact that the world will persist creates a particular relation between immanence and transcendence. The world is the collective creation of human beings but transcends the duration of actual human lives, thus it appears as if the world were independent of us.

(3) This dialectical condition is what makes the world *incomplete*. This may sound paradoxical given that the creation of a world aims also at stabilising the immanent field in order to reduce the degree of uncertainty and fragility to which human life is subject. A world is what holds together and sustains a collective self-understanding. It presup-

poses wholeness and unity (Castoriadis 1997: 149). However, contingency and the workings of human imagination make the aspiration to absolute completeness a hubristic ambition. A world is neither closed nor self-contained. The incompleteness of a world is also what allows for the experience of another world or other worlds, or the simultaneous coexistence of different worlds. All these elements together are what make communication and exchange between different worlds not only possible, but also a necessary condition for sustaining a world. A world closed to the unexpected and to novelty does not need the actual engagement of human beings in its *mise en forme*: it is a world driven by a self-propelled logic. A world is a historical creation of human beings, and as such it is subject to contingency. This historical contingency, together with the fact that a world is what mediates relations between human beings, is what makes commensurability and reciprocal interaction possible. And yet, since a world is an immanent field, there is no position of exteriority that allows for a universal form of comparability. The efforts to theoretically reduce this variability to a common and single matrix impoverish our comprehension of 'what there is'. Other worlds need to be interpreted and translated, and this can only happen, in the words of Hans-Georg Gadamer, if a 'fusion of horizons' of both worlds occurs, namely if a hermeneutical situation is created through their encounter, a situation which should not be taken for granted and also can lead to mutual indifference or conflict (Arnason 2006). This does not mean that both worlds are fused into one through the encounter.[4] From this perspective, each world-formation entails a concrete interpretation of human spatiality.

Globe

In contrast, the globe is a concrete imaginary signification of space produced very recently in historical terms and is at least as old as the invention of the armillary sphere by ancient Greek astronomy, placing a globe representing the Earth at the centre of the celestial sphere. The globe is the spherical representation of the surface of the planet where humans live. It is a geometrical reduction made by human imagination in order to represent on a human scale the space it occupies. It transforms the terrestrial body into a human-scale model. The 'actual globe', the planet Earth, cannot be represented by means of human perception (Husserl [1913] 2014: §27). Its three-dimensionality and its volume do not permit that humans grasp it completely. Scaling the planet into a globe allows for the fiction that one can master it. Indeed, our basic categories for geographical orientation are based on this assumption: the hemisphere, the poles, equators, meridians, parallels, and so on. The mastering of the globe is based on the superposition over the terrestrial surface of a mathematical construct that makes the horizontality of this surface legible independently of the observer's position. It converts the infinitude of the horizon into the finitude of the sphere. It allows for a radical change of perspective. What was unknown because it was beyond one's own experience, and therefore was limited by all sorts of constraints, now becomes knowable because it can be modelled in advance and is finite. In turn, it is the universe that becomes infinite. The mathematical modelling of the terrestrial surface has several conceptual implications. The planisphere, the projection of the globe onto a map drawn on the plane, radically transformed the continuity of plural world-cartographies.

Once the complete circumnavigation of the surface of the globe was achieved by Magellan–Elcano, the geometrical and the cartographical imagination began to merge. This was first achieved by the global map made by Diogo Ribeiro in 1529, considered the first 'scientific' map, whose main intention was to determine the exact position of the *raya*, the geometrical demarcation line that divided the globe into two hemispheres of imperial domination between Spain and Portugal. The map's aim was to settle territorial disputes between them. Global maps were incorporated as legal documents, for the first time, in the Treaty of Saragossa in 1529, which put an end to the disputes between both crowns arising from the 1494 Treaty of Tordesillas (Brotton 2013: 186–95).

The geometrical cartography of the globe, which permitted the abstraction of the actual surface of the Earth and the people living in it, was the first attempt at transforming the varieties of human interpretations of space into an empty and homogenous construct filled with points and lines that correspond to positions, limits and areas on the surface of the Earth. This understanding aims at overcoming the resistance of earthly matter to wilful exploitation through techniques premised on the physical and mathematical sciences. The Copernican revolution, the introduction of the coordinate system by Descartes together with his concept of *res extensa*, and the concept of absolute space by Newton radicalised this trend in making space an infinitely divisible and measurable scientific construct and positions within it relative and qualitatively indifferent (Rosich 2018).

Planet Earth

In opposition to world and globe, and despite the past association of the globe with the Earth as a planet, techno-physical 'progress' has emancipated the planet Earth from this connection. Today it has become a purely objective one. The planet called Earth would exist even if humans did not. The place of this planet is the universe. This representation was not evident to other comprehensions of the planet. In many civilisations, the 'planet' was a religious concept lying at the core of a cosmogony in which humans were an integral part. Indeed, the name 'Earth' refers to an imaginary with different historical meanings according to the various historical formations of worlds. It may indicate relations to soil, nurturing (as in 'Mother Earth'), rootedness and dwelling (Cosgrove 2001: 7). Until very recently, the heavens were above because we as humans were attached to Earth. Now, what is relevant is the fact that the Earth is a 'planet' as it is understood in astrophysics, and that its biogeochemical structure has made possible the evolution of living organisms.

There have been two major recent transformations in the representation humans have made of the planet Earth. The first one, as Hannah Arendt pointed out brilliantly, is related to the representation that humans had of the planet in relation to the universe. Once the first human-made object was launched into the universe and later humans travelled to space and landed on the Moon, humans were no longer bound to the Earth as a planet.[5] They could imagine themselves for the first time in history as no longer conditioned by a deep evolutionary and anthropological fact. Moreover, when a real photographic picture of the planet Earth was made from the Moon by the *Apollo 8* spacecraft in 1968,[6] it 'fuelled representations of the world as a distinct, unified global entity whose constituent parts are fitted together into a single whole' (Herod 2009: 27). This picture reinforced visions of eternal movement without time at a human scale and it miniaturised the planet. The human scale moved from the Earth to the entire universe. Units of cosmic time and distance were no longer measurable by human imagination.

The second development did not refer to the actual view of the planet from outside, but to biogeochemical internal processes that have transformed the Earth into a unified, single human environment.[7] The enormous potency of the instrumental mastery of 'nature' by humans and its effects on the Earth system have reached such a level that, in contrast with the past history of the Earth, natural processes are no longer independent of human agency. This means that humans have become a 'biogeochemical force'. Humans have been able to alter, by means of the mastery of nature, the structure of the Earth when considered as a planet. We no longer adapt ourselves to nature, but rather transform nature in order to adapt it to ourselves. Geologists and climatologists suggest that we are moving out of the Holocene, the historical epoch in which we have been living for the last 12,000 years from the perspective of Earth history, because the climate and the bio-geochemical conditions that defined it have changed radically and are transforming the Earth 'system'. They propose calling this new histori-cal epoch the 'Anthropocene' because it has been induced by human action. Paradoxically, this reintroduces imaginary significations of the Earth as a living being with agency (Latour 2014).

3. What, if anything, makes us a totality?

It is when we understand the concepts defined in the previous section historically that the frontiers between them become fuzzy and thorny. In order to keep the historical limits between them analytically clear, I suggest considering the history of civilisations as the history of how worlds are (trans)formed (Arnason 2014: 293–5), the history of the globe as the history of globalisation, and the history of the planet Earth as what is usually called in broad terms 'natural history'. This will help us to assess what kind of relations mediate the interconnectedness of human beings together with the intensity and quality of different layers at play in human interaction, that is, to investigate historically whether all such relations secure the same level of interconnectedness for all and do so in the same way. At the same time, it will offer ways to compare the different historical trajectories of such relations and relate them to the question of democracy.

The world is modern

At this point, we should admit that the concept of world, in contrast to the other two, is hardly a spatial one in spite of the spatial metaphors we use. It does not refer to a bounded unit identifiable in spatial terms and it cannot be apprehended as a substance. It is a metaphysical concept that forms the interpretative horizon that encompasses all the dimen-sions of social life. It is the 'horizon of all horizons' (Husserl [1913]

2014: 48–50). As such, it is a concept that does not refer to concrete collectivities or to a sum of them, to political entities or cultural formations or particular regions, but to a shared imaginary that informs the ways social, political and cultural formations are established. From this perspective, we should bear in mind that different worlds can coexist in singular spatio-temporal settings.

In historical terms, the research questions are: what are the basic constituents that shape a world, how does it transform, and to what level and degree is it shared among different social configurations? It is only having answered these that spatio-temporal settings can be established. From this angle, the history of civilisations seems to be the best empirical access to the study of this metaphysical dimension of social life.[8] As Martin Heidegger has suggested, we should not identify the world in relation to the concept of civilisation with the idea of world-view. A world-view presupposes the idea that representing the world is possible, that is, that the world is an object, even if it is the totality of what one stands in front of.[9] It also implies that there is a subject who has a view of the world. The idea of a world-view makes sense only within a particular historical constitution of a world.[10] For Heidegger, it corresponds to the scientific constitution of the world in the modern period. In the context of this chapter, what we have to ask is whether there is a shared social imaginary among all the different social formations that allows us to say that there is currently only one single civilisation. Indeed, the concept of civilisation, as it is here thought, implies a plurality of worlds. From this perspective, the idea of a single civilisation is tantamount to the existence of a single world, which is logically the same as saying that there are no longer civilisations given that we can no longer make synchronous comparisons between them because there are no other coexisting worlds.[11] In any case, 'modernity', regardless of whether it is a new civilisation or not, is the concept proposed for representing this new globally shared social imaginary.[12]

Modernity's fundamental constituents are reflexivity, in the sense of openness and uncertainty, autonomy and mastery. The signification of this social imaginary does not lend itself to being interpreted, either conceptually or historically, in a unidirectional way, since there are a variety of possible interpretations of this signification. The fact that the modern social imaginary is open to reinterpretation by human beings leads to the view that it cannot be interpreted univocally, therefore there will always be conflict surrounding the interpretations that are attached to the modern social imaginary. This multiplicity of possible interpretations is, in the words of Shmuel Eisenstadt, 'beset by internal antinomies and contradictions' (Eisenstadt 2003: II, 499) which, according to Arnason, constitute 'a field of tensions that can neither be absorbed by a system nor by a strategy of transformation' (Arnason 1991: 186); or, as Peter Wagner points out, the 'elements of this signification are ambivalent each one on its own and tension-ridden between them' (Wagner 2008: 10). Moreover, in order to empirically assess the varieties of modern imaginary significations while escaping from the unidirectional and convergent view, a distinction between economic, political and cultural/epistemic realms is suggested, without collapsing the content of these realms into specific institutional domains, or assigning any functional/structural capacities to them, or deriving the practices belonging to one realm from the others (Arnason 2003: 197; Wagner 2012: 74). This allows for the study of trans-historical human experiences while making it possible to distinguish between different civilisations, to separate modern and non-modern experiences, and to open up the historical question of whether the answers given to the problems arising in each realm differ and whether they represent different solutions to the modern constitution of the world. From this perspective, modernity in itself is not a spatio-temporal concept. Elements of it can be found in other historical periods and in different places of the globe (Therborn 2014).

North/South and the global spatialisation of the world

This approach to modernity allows us to escape from positivist institutional approaches, like the ones proposed by modernisation theories, and from reductionist and univocal interpretations of the commitment to modernity. However, answering the question of why we are *now all* modern, with its basic assumption of a world-ordering including the totality of human beings, becomes a hard task when proceeding to discuss historically the creation of the modern world, that is, where, how and when it is spatio-temporally instituted in such a way that a shared social imaginary can become 'global', irrespective of the plural spatio-temporal interpretations of this social imaginary. A quotation from Carl Schmitt's *Nomos of the Earth* will help me to outline in a clear and concise way the generally accepted hypothesis of the idea of a complete modern spatial ordering of human beings. This explanation is normatively bifacial. One can highlight the elements of domination, as critics of modernity do, or put the emphasis on the exceptionality of European civilisation in contrast to other civilisations:

> No sooner had the contours of the earth emerged as a real *globe* – not just sensed as myth, but apprehensible as fact and measurable as space – than there arose a wholly new and hitherto unimaginable problem: the spatial ordering of the earth in terms of international law [. . .] From the 16th to the 20th century, European international law considered Christian nations to be the creators and representatives of an order applicable to the whole earth. The term 'European' meant the normal status that set the standard for the non-European part of the earth. *Civilization* was synonymous with *European* civilization. (Schmitt [1951] 2006: 86)

In the terminology used in this chapter, Carl Schmitt's influential view can be translated as a theory suggesting that only in a context where the planet Earth was represented as a globe, namely as a spherical, physically divisible mathematical surface, a spatial ordering of totality could be envisaged. This understanding would correspond to a particular representation of a civilisation. Paradoxically, it is a civilisation that would connect a particular world-formation, the Christian one, to a particular region of the globe, Europe. What is at stake is that this particular civilisation has an understanding of world-ordering that is connected essentially with spatial ordering. When the planet Earth appears as a globe, the Christian world can be globalised, or in other words, European civilisation civilises the other 'civilisations' thanks to its particular understanding of law and science.[13] One singular world is extended to the whole Earth, that is, a world is globalised, which is the process by which one world becomes the globe. This process would merge the globe, the world and the planet Earth into a single imaginary.

What Carl Schmitt is suggesting is that if another civilisation had circumnavigated the globe, the question of a spatial ordering of the Earth would not have emerged because they did not have the same understanding of space, law and science. This particular explanation associates the history of globalisation with a particular world-formation, the Christian European one, and relates the current degrees of connectedness that sustain a view of the globe as a unified totality with the history of spatial *domination* of the 'non-European part of the globe'.

From this angle, the history of modernity starts with the domination of the other by means of the destruction of their own worlds through the imposition of the European world upon them (Fuster and Rosich 2015). It is a double process of wordlessness. First, it triggers internally a self-destruction of the European world by converting it into the globe, and second, to transform the world into the globe it needs to erase other worlds. As Hannah Arendt put it, 'World alienation, and not self-alienation as Marx thought, has been the hallmark of the modern age' (Arendt [1958] 1998: 254). This is the historical development that makes it possible to think of globalisation in totalising terms. The other side of the coin is that the social bond that connects all human beings *globally* is possible because it is based on a dialectic of domination and resistance to domination shaped by a modern social imaginary linked to the developments of European history.[14]

Before pursuing this line of reasoning, it is worth reminding the reader that Carl Schmitt's book is a theoretical landmark both for postcolonial scholars, like Enrique Dussel (2007) or Walter Mignolo (2012), and for American neoconservatives.[15] Thus, the modern world is linked to the history of globalisation: it began in Europe at the beginning of the sixteenth century and was spread to the rest of the globe by the modern domination of non-Europeans. Transformations within the history of modernity occur thanks to the progressive emancipation from domination, with the Enlightenment being a significant moment in this history (Rosich 2018). This particular kind of relation defines in a clear manner what constitutes a collectivity and its position in the social order, namely its 'identity', its spatial location and how domination is achieved. This extremely concise outline[16] helps me to illustrate what lies at the core of general theories that divide the globe politically in spatial terms. The division of the globe between a North and a South reflects in geopolitical terms the political relation that has created the globe as the absolute space from where social relations based on a dialectic of domination are established. The North–South divide allows for a hierarchical positioning of collective actors or for an all-embracing social stratification in spatial terms. The answer given to this spatial political ordering will depend on the normative standpoint of the actors, but both assume the view that the globe, as previously defined, is the framework for understanding an exclusive world-formation.

In spite of all the ideological and violent presuppositions, the previous political ordering based on the three-world model that disintegrated with the collapse of the communist bloc suggested the simultaneous coexistence, even at the same place and time, of a plurality of worlds not based on a binary distribution. Their interrelations were based on different, even opposed, social imaginaries, which for the most part were not signified in spatial terms. The assumption that there is one single world implies its globalisation, namely its absolute spatialisation. Depending on the emphasis, it is divided in a binary fashion if it is in conflict or it is represented as an aggregated whole if it is a network. In either case, its boundaries are spatial and, to put it ironically, they correspond to the atmosphere.

Confronted with the question of what makes us an interconnected totality, we have to boldly answer that we all as humans occupy space upon the spherical surface of the globe, which is politically shaped as the outcome of a history of modern domination.[17] In metaphorical terms, a new *raya* divides the globe into two separate but interdependent parts. Once the structure of past domination is over but its effects in the present are still at work, the struggle between North and South becomes a contest between opposing interpretations of how the globe has to be politically constituted in the present. This is the reason why the South has also become global: it aspires to challenge the current hegemony of the North in the globe, that is, of the past imperial powers. The main objective of the societies of the South is to achieve full recognition from the North by means of a redress of the historical injustice of global imperialism. Paradoxically, in order to attain this goal, the Global South has to work on the same assumption with which past imperialism worked: there has to be only one world that corresponds to the globe. This globalisation of the world is in radical conflict with the understanding of the world as suggested above: it looks for completeness and total unity. From this angle, a world-in-common that mediates relations between all human beings can only be sustained if a world is reduced to the globe.[18] Moreover, what mediates social relations is domination, not collective human agency. In this context, agency is only recognised as belonging to those that globalised the world, namely the European world and its different settler colonists.

Reinterpretation of the world

But with all its persuasiveness, and even if we share the view that domination is a key feature of the constitution of the modern world, this narrative is not sufficient for the purpose of understanding what elements of the European world, if any, triggered its transformation into the globe and why the rest (read: the Global South) succumbed, adopted it or reshaped it according to its own historical trajectory. Contemporary historical scholarship has provided enough empirical evidence to show that European civilisation was not modern according to its own criteria. In addition to these generally overlooked historical developments, world-historians are challenging in a radical way the view that the rise of Europe to world hegemony has to be equated with the birth of modernity.[19] They test and nuance the premise that the European world is the site of the birth of modernity. On the contrary, drawing on their empirical work one can make a conceptual distinction between the constitution of the social imaginary significations of the modern world and the power relations within it. Thus, to see relations of domination *within* modernity makes it possible to break with any substantive notion of modernity as domination and to invalidate the view that interprets the end of Western global hegemony as the end of modernity. Power relations are a trans-historical dimension of human existence that cannot erase any meaningful understanding of history, change and transformation and the different and plural historical human self-understandings that have constituted historical worlds. These historians situate European modernity in a global context and look at how modernity originally emerged as a phenomenon in response to the new level of interdependence and interaction between worlds (Stråth and Wagner 2017).

Additionally, a closer examination of the history of ideas shows that the social imaginary that constituted the European world during the sixteenth century does not lend itself to be interpreted univocally as triggering its own globalisation. On the contrary, different opposing imaginaries were at work and only further developments, which took place above all during the nineteenth century, can explain the expansionist model. The methodology consists in confronting the self-understanding of the European world with the empirical record that derives from its own interpretation of history (Wagner 2012: 84–90). The misleading assumption that the commitments to modernity were fully realised exclusively in Europe much before the Second World War is a kind of self-distorted understanding which was to some extent required to justify its role as global *hegemon*. This question points to a major problem when understanding why during Europe's hegemony Europeans misinterpreted their own history. In my view, this is not due to a problem of falsity, error or alienation, but rather to a particular hermeneutical and phenomenological difficulty. The question is why Europe did not comprehend what she was when the sufficient historical evidence and the conceptual apparatus to do so were already available. This tension makes it necessary to question the historical constitution, interpretative framework and actual availability of archives and canons from the perspective of the European *histoires des mentalités*.[20] In my view, the intellectual sources where we have to investigate the reasons for this self-distorted interpretation are precisely the same that have been used to explain why modernity appeared first in Europe and why it was diffused globally. I have no space to discuss in detail the ascendancy of these approaches, but the common root that lies at the core of the majority of them, critical or self-flattering, is based on the *two worlds* dualism and the associated conceptions of how these worlds interrelate.[21]

Three main intellectual traditions are singled out in this self-understanding: the constitution of philosophy in classical Greece, best represented by Plato's distinction between the visible and the intelligible world; the transition to Hellenism in combination with the creation of Christianity (Assmann 2008: 77), namely a particular interpretation of God as creator of the world, as exemplified in the Augustinian distinction between the City of God and the City of Man (Eisenstadt 2003: I, 45); and lastly, the transition to modernity understood as rationalisation and secularisation, which is generally associated with the Cartesian distinction between *res cogitans* and *res extensa* when questioning nature, in combination with the teachings of the Protestant reformers creating a gap between the 'worldly' world and the otherworldly world. The many versions of the philosophies of history that stem from the assumption of this dualism are a privileged site for investigating the origins of the distorted European self-understanding. This philosophy had to reconcile the outcomes of European agency in *this* world with the European comprehension of the contents of the *other* world.

This problem moves the discussion again to the level of world-formation in relation to the civilisational dimension. As stated earlier, I have to insist on the idea that the temporality, contingency and incompleteness that constitute the world are the elements that allow for its transformation, namely the idea that despite being a metaphysical concept, it is historical. In methodological terms, this imposes hard conditions when engaging in historical-interpretative analysis of worlds-formation.[22] However, even when 'the search for origins' is a futile activity (Wagner 2016b), or even if teleological assumptions necessarily have to be made in order to pursue this search, if we have to understand the historical relation between different worlds, we should look at those particular events that created the conditions for a global, not only regional, worlds-encounter and its codependent historical transformations. The problem here is not the study of the relation between intra-civilisational developments and inter-civilisational interactions, that is, whether the notion of encounter or entanglement is more fruitful to understand worlds-(trans)formation. The current historical evidence seems to suggest that this is a question that cannot be answered without making a priori anthropological conjectures.[23] What is relevant is that there has been only one event in the history of civilisations, as Carl Schmitt also points out, that created the conditions for a global, not only regional, worlds-encounter: the arrival of Europeans on American shores in 1492. Moreover, the nature of this event – radically contingent, novel, unexpected and unintended – had a huge impact, precisely because an encounter of that sort was completely unknown up to that moment. Only from then on is it plausible to interpret the history of civilisations and their transformations as interconnected while keeping at the same time a comparative operational concept of unit of analysis. This should provide a firm ground for the question of an eventual fusion, assimilation, conflict or parallel coexistence of horizons.

And yet, when it comes to the history of concepts and to the understanding of the modern imaginary as it is here defined, a major problem emerges insofar as the current historical sources suggest that the relation between what we call the European world and the modern imaginary, even if it is tension-ridden, seems to be different than with other worlds. This is still a major difficulty that has to be addressed even when one does not want to equate the history of modernity with the history of Europe. Regarding the question of the local context in which the modern imaginary emerges and the widening of its significance, even though the European developments that produced a radical conceptual rupture with its own past did not produce historical modernity and thus were not diffused to the rest of the world, it is true that some important conceptual transformations related to the modern imaginary occurred in Europe from the fifteenth to the seventeenth centuries. To avoid the classical explanations offered for the appearance of the modern imaginary, which are based on path-dependency and endogenous explanations, further historical and conceptual efforts should be devoted to investigating the interdependence between the inter-civilisational perspective – the 'discovery of America' – and the 'intra-civilisational' one – in the case of Europe, the Reformation.

These events have not been analysed as deeply interrelated because historiographical research agrees that the impact on Europe of the 'discovery of the New World' at the level of the imaginary was almost non-existent up to the seventeenth century (Ryan 1981). However, though this may be true, when approaching the ideas and concepts that inform the modern imaginary and register the significance and relevance of events, research is needed in the history of ideas which aims at looking into the context of their appearance as constituted simultaneously by the interrelation of these two events. From this angle, it is essential to question the archives *as if* the transformations produced by these two major historical events were interdependent in conceptual terms. One should investigate all the intermediate levels of interaction between the different categories of social actors and the social imaginaries at play during this period in relation to the onset of the globalisation of the world (Cheah 2016: 5), without assuming their substitution or assimilation to this totalising logic as postcolonial scholars do.

In sum, when interpreting what, if anything, interconnects all human beings, I have aimed at showing the need not to reduce the world(s) to the globe or the other way around. This approach requires interrelating both dynamics historically, conceptually and methodologically. This cannot be done without proposing ways of reading the connection between processes of globalisation and worlds (trans)formation. For instance, Osterhammel and Petersson (2005) distinguish between world-history, understood as the comparative study of civilisations, and global-history, which studies their interactions. Maintaining this distinction offers new insights when interpreting the history of human interconnectedness as driven by a dynamics of globalisation–deglobalisation–reglobalisation. Additionally, they do not identify one single globalising logic (either capitalism or imperialism), but rather identify different logics at work that can be mutually contradictory and produce different outcomes. The concrete periodisation, spatialisation and (de)structuring will depend on the concrete interpretation of the interrelation between world and globe, that is, between common or divergent answers to processes of globalisation of different civilisations, as well as different degrees of (de)globalising agency depending on the varieties of categories of social groups and their relation at the intra- or inter-civilisational level (such as elites, migrants, religious groups, economic actors, and so on).

From the critical perspective adopted in this chapter regarding the insufficient but inescapable globalist understanding of the world,

I consider Dipesh Chakrabarty's distinction between two different human histories – 'History 1' and 'History 2' is his labelling – a promising interpretative framework.[24] If I adapt his distinction for my own purposes – which I think can be done despite the logical dependence of his distinction on an interpretation of capitalism from a Marxist perspective – one can read History 1 as the history of globalisation and History 2 as the history of worlds-formation. These histories should not be read as 'past', but as belonging to the historical period where the idea of a socio-political ordering of the totality of human beings is meaningful, which is still the case. What is decisive in his analysis is that both histories are not independent of each other despite different temporal and spatial logics being at work. It allows for the simultaneous presence of two divergent ontological realms determining the same phenomena: a 'fact' can be seen as fitting at the same time and place either into a global order or the particular world order where the global is embedded. The codependence of both histories makes the aspiration of History 1 to override History 2 hyperopic and the other way around, myopic: a full achievement of globalisation would undermine the conditions that make it possible, and vice versa, acting as if globalisation were not a fact, one would be self-disoriented. In contrast to Dipesh Chakrabarty, who sees History 1 as parasitical on History 2 and History 2 as interrupting and deferring History 1,[25] we should not identify any particular logic between them, and instead leave open to investigation for each concrete world the shape of this dynamic. The aim of a world(s)-history, from this perspective, is thus the *comparative study of the interconnection of historical difference.*

Planet Earth and the geological turn

The 'Anthropocene' hypothesis is transforming our epistemic understanding of the relation between the planet Earth and humans as living beings. It is difficult to know at this stage whether its current relevance is a symptom of a paradigm shift, whether it is related to the functioning of the academic market, or whether both dynamics are at work. Paul Crutzen, the Nobel Prize-winning atmospheric chemist, coined the concept Anthropocene to suggest:

(i) that the Earth is now moving out of its current geological epoch, called the Holocene and (ii) that human activity is largely responsible for this exit from the Holocene, that is, that humankind has become a global geological force in its own right. (Steffen et al. 2011: 843)

This condensed statement has a wide range of implications in all the spheres of human life, which can be summarised with two main 'ideas': first, the 'fact' that it is not nature 'who' is progressively making the Earth inhospitable to human beings, but the same human beings through intensive use of fossil fuel for energy consumption and the mastery of nature,[26] *as if* it were self-inflicted; second, this agency would also have (self-)cancelled the modern gap between nature and, for lack of a better word, artifice (Chakrabarty 2009). That is, natural history and human History 1 and 2 will have to be read from now on as interdependent. The alleged difference between objective things independent of us, the natural realm, and what we create with the help of our own capacities and will, is no longer sustainable from the moment that we become a 'geological force'. From this perspective, we will have to complement History 1 and History 2 with a third history, that is, the history of the evolution of human beings into a geological force in relation to the history of Earth as a system.

From the perspective of the spatial ordering that connects *all* human beings, the Anthropocene hypothesis represents a strong challenge. This hypothesis appears extremely controversial when interpreting historically when and how the Anthropocene emerged as well as who the subject/object is; depending on the answers given to these questions, different orderings may appear.[27] That is, if we define this history as History 3, geo-archives and human archives will have to be read in conjunction. The idea that the frontier between natural and human history has been blurred due to anthropogenic transformation of the Earth is not very convincing. It corresponds to a very restrictive reading of the archives that constitute the intellectual history of modernity. The blurring hypothesis proceeds in a largely teleological fashion: it retrieves from the past one particular historical tradition among others – the one that created an insurmountable gap between natural and human history – in order to justify the hypothesis of a deep transformation in the present that has cancelled this distinction due to the effects of human agency. The question of the relation between nature and history has been very problematic from the beginning of modern times and is much more open and ambiguous than is affirmed in the philosophy of history of the Anthropocene.[28] The intellectual tradition that created such a gap between nature and history appeared during the so-called Age of Revolutions in connection to a particular strand of the Enlightenment and was already severely criticised from many perspectives during the second half of the nineteenth century.[29] Moreover, while it is true that in modernity nature is being constantly 'humanised' by an expansionist philosophy that constitutes nature, in the words of Martin Heidegger, as a standing-reserve, this does not imply that the distinction is completely blurred. For this to be true, one should prove that humans have not only become a 'geological force', but an 'all-encompassing absolute force', which means that there is nothing which does not depend for its existence on the existence of the human beings. This is the classical position reserved for God in theological understandings of the place human beings occupy in the universe. What today seems plausible is only to claim that we can no longer separate Earth history from human history because human agency is transforming the biogeochemical conditions that make life possible on Earth.[30] The delicate problem begins when interpreting this particular dialectical relation.

The question of subjectivity, of who is the 'anthropos' in the Anthropocene, has three dimensions: it refers to the question of who is responsible for triggering this process, who has in the present to respond to this challenge and who is affected by this process. These are not easy questions, and can by no means be answered from a 'scientific' point of view. The scientific account of the Anthropocene reintroduces a positivist philosophy of science as if 'facts' were independent of interpretations and as if 'scientists' have the qualitative differential knowledge required to address this situation (Bonneuil 2015). They read History 1 and 2 only as constitutive elements of History 3. They postulate an undifferentiated and ahistorical human subject in answering questions related to the agency problem: that is, humankind as a species. This kind of answer also does not allow for posing the question of the relation between concrete civilisations and their relation to nature as qualitatively different from others when understanding the instrumental mastery of nature, that is, what History 2 does. Furthermore, it evades the question of the asymmetrical relation between global actors, which History 1 approaches by looking at the relations of domination between different collectivities as mediated by the globalising process of expansion and the exploitation of nature. From this scientific perspective, the scientific hegemony in the interpretation of the Anthropocene erases any dimension of human spatiality. It makes it very difficult to read the Anthropocene as the outcome of a history of intra-species dominations, not inter-species. South and North, from this critical angle, are spatial layers that refer to the subjectivities involved in the Anthropocene, understood as a further step in the modern history of human domination. As Christophe Bonneuil has suggested (2015), the scientific view depoliticises and naturalises History 3. The destabilisation of the relation between nature and artifice provoked by the hypothesis is fixed by reducing the artificial to the natural. The vulgarised Gaia hypothesis, a metaphor for considering the Earth as a living being, or labelling the Earth as a 'system', are attempts to relocate the human as one of its fundamental natural elements and convey a sense of totality where living and non-living entities are structurally combined as a self-regulating device. Another strategy would be to consider the Anthropocene as an 'interpretative category by which contemporary societies reflect upon themselves and upon life itself . . . [that] contains strong normative elements, including imaginary significations' (Delanty and Mota 2017). This would allow us to avoid the dichotomy between facts and interpretations. However, there are as yet no empirical studies available that support this view. Additionally, as I will try to briefly explain, the Anthropocene framework does not allow too much room for thinking in terms of 'societies' and of the possibilities they have of acting upon themselves. On the contrary, it seems an interpretation of the current transformation that dissolves the possibilities of thinking individual or collective autonomy.

In contrast to world and globe, it seems almost impossible to refute the idea that the global deterioration of the environment affects literally all human beings. The history of becoming a geological force is thus the history of the actual interconnection of all past, present and future humans. There is no political, economic or epistemic escape from this condition that does not involve all human beings. Thus, to the question of what is the bond that equalises all human beings, the answer can only be the fact that all their lives are at risk because they are affected by climate change. Indeed, this bond equalises all living beings, not only humans. It is as if we are in the process of inventing a new collectivity, which is neither the sum of all individuals nor a new *humanitas*, but a sort of Leviathan that acts as unified species among others (Clark 2015: 15–16).[31] However, this answer becomes more problematic when we try to respond to the question of who has to face this challenge. Allegedly, if we are all affected, we should all act collectively to redress this risk. This answer suggests that the self who acts reflexively is the same self upon which the action is performed. This is the classical example of autonomous action. In historical terms, this view would be supported by what has been labelled as the Great Acceleration, that is, the geobiochemical indicators used to quantify the deterioration of the environment exploded exponentially in relation to human inputs, above all fossil fuel, affecting the Earth soon after the end of the Second World War. As Dipesh Chakrabarty suggests, this is the same period of decolonisation, developmentalism and the globalisation of democratic patterns of consumption (Chakrabarty 2014). This hypothesis suggests that the South and the North have to share the burden when interpreting who fostered the Anthropocene. Thus, if this is true, all human beings should be asked to collectively react at the same level. And yet, if we adopt the long-term perspective required when looking at epochal change from a geological angle, have all human histories actually contributed *equally* to the constitution of the human living entity, of our species, as a geological force?[32] Do we all have the same responsibilities even if all human beings act as a geological force? A recent article published in *Science*, which aims at justifying the Anthropocene hypothesis stratigraphically, dilutes plural human historicity into an evolutionary logic that starts with the beginning of agriculture. Significant moments are the Columbian Exchange, using the title of Crosby's book, and the Industrial Revolution (Waters et al. 2016). But how can one reconcile these extremely divisive social events in political, economic and epistemic terms with the view of a single and equal humanity assumed by the Anthropocene hypothesis?

4. Concluding overture: democracy and totality

The current historical constellation has brought into prominence an inescapable condition of our times. It is based on two observations. Historical injustice, in contrast to the past, has become an issue waiting for an answer now that non-European collectivities that in the past were dominated by Europeans are politically on an equal footing. As the history of globalisation aims to show, there are *no* humans in the present who are not heirs of this legacy of past domination: either as dominated or as dominant or both at the same time. From that angle, the distinction between a Global South/North aims at making visible the opposed subjectivities constituted by this legacy. This injustice was justified largely by the Global North on the grounds that they represented the interests of 'humanity'. What in the past was a justification based on mere normative-conceptual reasoning that could be mobilised at will depending on the context of domination, now appears to be a 'fact': a 'real interest'[33] of humanity exists which consists in the preservation of the geochemical conditions that allow the biological reproduction of human life. These two dimensions, as stated at the outset, have to be addressed democratically given that no other legitimate regime of political justification is in competition with democracy, at least *up to the present*. Past democratic action, as it was embedded in the former ordering of the world, did not have to explicitly face the challenge of political totality, precisely because colonialism was still a reality and knowledge of climate change was not yet available. Every time that political action targeted human totality it was undemocratic.

The relations between democracy and totality have been extremely problematic in historical and conceptual terms. This is due to the fact that democracy entails a double process of exclusion/inclusion, which occurs simultaneously during the (re)constitution of new democracies: first, it establishes an external boundary, even if it is porous and flexible – namely, if 'identity' is not given and fixed – between the *demos* and the *other*; and second, the internal workings of a democratic regime presupposes a division between *party* and *people*. This double process is tension-ridden: in order to constitute the *demos* as the collectivity that creates the necessary external boundary in order to determine *one*self, the internal division between *party* and *people* has to be cancelled and the *people* has to appear phenomenologically as *one*, as an *indivisible whole*. This representation creates an internal conflict because it imposes limits on the possibilities of the *self* to transform, that is, the self that is actually determining must correspond to the representation of the people-as-one, thus the possibilities of democratic action are restricted; and at the same time, *the political* division between parties is established as a contest to represent the people-as-one, the indivisible whole: a part aspires to become the whole. To make matters more complicated, when the *demos* is seen from the perspective of its interaction with the *others*, it appears as a *divided part* that excludes itself from the *whole* in order to self-determine. In sum, democracy presupposes some degree of wholeness but precludes totalisation. Or in other words, it requires divisiveness but posits oneness.[34] Against the background of the previous sections, this brief outline of the democratic form questions any straightforward democratic socio-political ordering of the totality of human beings. It is an ordering that, as I have tried to show, has three different historical and conceptual frames: world politics, geopolitics and Earth politics. If this is true, then the question of who is the collectivity that acts upon itself democratically becomes a complex issue with no clear answer. For lack of space, I will address the issue from only the perspective of Earth politics.[35] The following reasoning is only conceptual. This is partly due to the fact that the event to which it refers is currently taking place.

When we are confronted with this problem from the perspective of humans as a 'geological force', the answer to the question of *who* is the people-as-one seems simple: humanity considered as a living being, namely humanity as a particular species. Therefore, what constitutes us as a collectivity is the fact that our biological life is threatened. The first difficulty with this answer is that it assumes that no human collectivity is excluded from this *demos*: all human beings are included by the mere fact of belonging to the human species. If an exclusion is created through self-determination,[36] either a qualitative interpretation of the human species has to be provided that contradicts the idea that all 'humans' belong to this species, or on the contrary, the wholeness from which humans exclude themselves as a part is the totality of all 'living beings', of all species. Both solutions do not seem adequate: the former because it gives room to a eugenic politics that questions the ground from which it emerges from the moment it threatens the life of a part of humanity, and the latter because it assumes that all species can interact reciprocally on equal and democratic terms, which appears not to be the case. The Hobbesian paradigm seems to offer the best normative solution to this problem, but we can hardly say that it is based on democracy. Rather, it is based on the idea of absolute sovereignty whose purpose is the preservation of life: human beings cede their 'natural' force to the sovereign in order to protect their lives.[37]

If we look at the same problem from the perspective of *who* is the *self* that could act upon the human as a *species*, as Dipesh Chakrabarty contends, 'we humans never experience ourselves as a species' (2009: 220). If, nevertheless, we want to know what *party* would appear phenomenologically as the people-as-one in the contest for representing the human species, the problem would be what might happen to the other parties when the representation of the people-as-one is based on the idea of 'securing life'. Will they represent a threat to this attaining objective? The solution to this potential risk is already in place: it corresponds to the concept of human rights and their constitutionalisation. The problem with this solution is, first, that this constitution would have to be global; second, that individuals would be those protected by human rights; and third, that these rights could not be transformed by democratic action. Again, this may lead to the advocacy of a global state to confront this challenge, but it is mainly based on views of the state as having a global monopoly on the legitimate use of organised violence (Wendt 2003), not as the outcome of democratic self-transformation.

To conclude, and by way of illustration, I would like to quote one of the paragraphs of the preamble to the 2015 Paris Agreement reached between UN members 'to combat climate change and to accelerate and intensify the actions and investments needed for a sustainable low carbon future'.[38] This agreement has been labelled as historical. At this stage, we do not know how, if at all, it will be implemented, namely we do not yet know the impact of *realpolitik*. As Martti Koskenniemi has recently explained, there is no institutional measure or policy that does not appear to be shaped by a particular strategy of a singular actor to respond to a particular context. 'Humanity' does not talk and act; someone has to speak on its behalf. In this regard, he states that the conflict between a developed North and the Global South is the political translation in the present reflecting the implicit bias of any cosmopolitan project (Koskenniemi 2012). However, it is worth noting that this paragraph surprisingly recognises the three levels that mediate interconnectedness – world, globe and planet Earth – that I have aimed at articulating. The paragraph says:

> Noting the importance of ensuring the *integrity of all ecosystems*, including oceans, and the protection of biodiversity, recognised by some *cultures as Mother Earth*, and noting the importance for some of the concept of '*climate justice*', when taking action to address climate change [. . .] (United Nations 2015: 2; my emphasis)

Alas, in this twenty-seven-page document with twenty-nine articles, not a single instance of the word 'democracy' appears. One is tempted to think that the reason why the signatory parties did not refer to democracy in the agreement was because they believed that democracy cannot 'ensure the integrity of all ecosystems' and produce 'climate justice'.[39]

Notes

1. This may appear to be an unqualified statement given that China, representing a significant part of the global population, is not considered a democracy from a Western perspective. Despite the opacity of Chinese politics for a Western-trained mind, I am here interested in the justifications offered to support or

challenge a political regime. In this context, it is important to outline that the first article of the Constitution of the People's Republic of China, adopted in 1982, states that China is a 'socialist state under the people's *democratic* dictatorship'. See *Constitution of the People's Republic of China*, available at <http://english. gov.cn/archive/laws_regulations/2014/08/23/content_281474982987458.htm> (last accessed 11 January 2017).

2. See Benhabib (2004) for a contemporary effort to make them compatible.
3. Therefore, what makes a human being 'human' is the outcome of a particular representation of biological and evolutionary sciences.
4. Raimon Panikkar has called this fusion of horizons 'diatopical hermeneutics'. It 'stands for the thematic consideration of understanding the other *without assuming that the other has the same basic self-understanding*. The ultimate human horizon, and not only differing contexts, is at stake here' (1979: 49; original emphasis).
5. Arendt identified this fact as evidence of a human desire to escape from the human condition.
6. Other pictures were taken before, but not in colour and showing the complete spherical surface of the planet.
7. The environment, in contrast to space, refers to nature as modified by humans.
8. It is important to specify that I am referring to the concept of civilisation from the perspective of the history of world formation, not the other way around. No spatio-temporal assumptions should be made when associating collectivities with particular civilisations. As Arjomand and Tiryakian point out, 'civilizations are not fixed in time and space' (2004: 4).
9. In the history of Western philosophy, this is the core tension that separates Kant from idealism and created two opposing interpretations of epistemic modernity. Hegel aims at overcoming the limits that Kant established in relation to the possibility of 'knowing' the world, namely the need to assume the idea of the absolutely unconditioned in order to know actual phenomena, which confronts the logical and metaphysical impossibility of knowing the unconditioned by means of knowing the totality of phenomena. Hegel starts the other way round: he ontogenetically postulates the unconditioned, Reason, and he derives the totality of phenomena from it.
10. 'As soon as the world becomes picture, the position of man is conceived as a world view' (Heidegger 1977: 134).
11. This is the theoretical assumption that makes the idea of a world-history possible.
12. The following lines are based on the understanding of modernity elaborated by Johann Arnason, Shmuel Eisenstadt and Peter Wagner. The three of them base their conceptual approach, on different levels, on the work of Cornelius Castoriadis.
13. See Duchesne (2011) for an updated defence of this position, combining conceptual and empirical arguments, against all the revisionist historiography that questions any normative superiority of the Western world for explaining its global supremacy in the last two centuries.
14. See Wagner (2016a) for a nuanced version of this argument.
15. In my view, the main problem with the *Nomos of the Earth* is that it connects a historical occurrence, the 'discovery of the New World', which had huge implications for the construction of a world order and the formation of global empires,

with a normative view on the political, namely with the idea that it allowed the bracketing of war among European powers because they could wage war in unoccupied territories where only the law of the stronger applied. I agree with many elements of Schmitt's analysis of the impact of the 'discovery of the New World', but not his normative interpretation, which is based on a particular political philosophy and on a biased narrative on the history of Europe (Rosich 2018).

16. See Rosich (2018) for an extended version of this argument.

17. Raewyn Connell, talking about spatial divisions of the globe, states that '[a]ll these expressions refer to the long-lasting pattern of inequality in power, wealth and cultural influence that grew historically out of European and North American imperialism' (2007: 2012).

18. The distinction, very widely used in the Francophone scholarship, made between mundialisation – making a human world common to all, though there are different ways of doing it – and globalisation, has the same result, namely the idea that universalism has to be understood in spatial and totalising terms and as it is defined in set theory: either as a shared world of which every single human being is a part, or as the whole extension of the globe's surface where human beings reside. See Derrida and Rottenberg (2002: 371, 386); Nancy (2007). I have suggested elsewhere that this is only possible if we consider the individual as the primary political and social actor.

19. Among them: Kenneth Pomeranz (2000), Jürgen Osterhammel (2014), Jack Goldstone (2009), Christopher Bayly (2004), John Darwin and David Armitage (Armitage and Subrahmanyam 2009).

20. Another strategy would be to contend that in order to justify European domination, elites had to produce a particular ideology to legitimise it. However, this explanation is too simplistic regarding the relation between ideas and experience.

21. This dualism, as the Axial Age hypothesis has aimed to show, was constituted simultaneously in different civilisations during the first millennium BCE (Arnason et al. 2005). The particular understanding of the relation between both worlds and the respective historical trajectory is what, supposedly, makes Europe unique (Eisenstadt 2003: I, 349).

22. I have discussed the main methodological problems in Rosich (2018). They are related to diffusionism, reductionism, positivism, path dependency, *overgeneralising* and inference methods.

23. Historical evidence in this context means those empirical elements that allow for the interpretation of 'social imaginary significations'.

24. I think it is worth quoting Chakrabarty at length: 'On one side is the indispensable and universal narrative of capital— History 1, as I have called it. This narrative both gives us a critique of capitalist imperialism and affords elusive but necessarily energising glimpses of the Enlightenment promise of an abstract, universal but never-to-be-realised humanity. Without such elusive glimpses, as I have said before, there is no political modernity. On the other side is thought about diverse ways of being human, the infinite incommensurabilities through which we struggle—perennially, precariously, but unavoidably—to "world the earth" in order to live within our different senses of ontic belonging. These are the struggles that become—when in contact with capital—the History 2s that in practice always modify and interrupt the totalizing thrusts of History 1' (2000: 254).

25. Capitalism is a particular understanding of 'life'; it corresponds to a concrete social imaginary signification and in other settings their dynamic is not interpreted as conflictive but as complementary.

26. Crossing the 'planetary boundaries' – a set of thresholds that should not be overcome if the Earth is to be a 'safe operating space' for humanity – is the consequence of mastering nature. For the scientific concept of planetary boundaries, see Rockström et al. (2009).

27. I can only discuss here the 'who' question. The interdependent issues related to how and when cannot be addressed here in detail. They refer to what has been the global human driver of this epochal transformation – capitalism, imperialism, emancipation from domination, freedom – and what dimension of the human condition – cultural, genetic, evolutionary, economic, political, epistemic, and so on – is implied in this new sort of agency called 'geological force'.

28. For instance, the philosophy of history of Immanuel Kant, one of the most influential thinkers of modernity, is based on the idea that 'the means which Nature employs to bring about the development of innate capacities is that of antagonism within society, in so far as this antagonism becomes in the long run the cause of a law-governed social order' (Kant [1784] 1989: 44). I see no way of disconnecting nature from society in such a statement. Indeed, I believe that Kant's works are the first attempt to read, as Dipesh Chakrabarty suggests we have to do, both histories as interdependent.

29. Christophe Bonneuil and Jean Fressoz (2016) offer a summary with examples of these different intellectual critiques.

30. To respond that it is natural selection and historical contingency that have endowed humans with the required 'natural force' to transform the Earth may blur the distinction between self-made and non-self-made history, but it just displaces the discussion onto other sorts of oppositions concerning, for instance, whether mathematical laws govern nature or not.

31. In relation to this invented collective subject, Timothy Clark quotes a telling paragraph of Michel Serres, one of the first thinkers to talk about the Anthropocene without using the word: 'Seen from above, from this new high place, Earth contains all our ancestors, indistinguishably mingled: the universal tomb of universal history. What funeral service do all these vapour plumes herald? And since, from up here, no-one perceives borders, which are abstract in any case, we can speak for the first time of Adam and Eve, our first common parents, and thus of brotherhood. One humanity at last' (2015: 4).

32. The reference to the concept of 'force' in these texts is puzzling. Their aim is to equate human performance with natural events having the capacity to alter the shape of the Earth, 'the forces of nature' like volcanoes, earthquakes or orbital changes. This may suggest that when the outcome of human performance is 'intended', we are fully responsible agents, and when it is negative, it is unintended and is determined by natural laws that we did not know of.

33. As long as this is anthropologically true, and this is not evident at all. For instance, Freud identified two different, contradictory anthropological instincts. He called them 'Eros' and 'Thanatos'. One is directed towards life and the other towards destruction.

34. Political theory has theorised democracy from the internal perspective as if the external one was a consequence of its workings. In historical and conceptual

terms, this is not justifiable. Even Claude Lefort, the inspiration from which my reflection starts, seems to assign ontogenetic priority to the inner workings of the democratic polity. The reappearance of the democratic imaginary in historical terms, the so-called Age of Revolutions, is a phenomenon that has to be investigated from its beginnings as a response to global developments. The dialectics between empire and claims to independence are of paramount importance for that purpose. See Rosich (2018).

35. See Rosich (2016) for an analysis from the perspective of historical injustice.
36. To determine is to establish a limit. Without determination, there is nothing.
37. The philosophical trend known as biopolitics stems from this tradition. See Fuster (2014) for a critique on the same grounds of the 'left oriented' politics of vulnerability based on the idea of precarious life, best represented by the current work of Judith Butler.
38. See the United Nations website on climate change, available at <http://unfccc.int/paris_agreement/items/9485.php> (last accessed 11 January 2017).
39. Indeed, this is what past communist countries claimed during the 'Cold War'. Now it is a justification offered as well by some voices in China. See Purdy (2015: 256).

References

Arendt, H. [1958] (1998), *The Human Condition*, Chicago: University of Chicago Press.

Arjomand, S. and E. A. Tiryakian (2004), 'Introduction', in *Rethinking Civilization Analysis*, London: Sage, pp. 1–13.

Armitage, D. and S. Subrahmanyam (2009), *The Age of Revolutions, c.1760–1840 – Global Causation, Connection, and Comparison*, New York: Palgrave Macmillan.

Arnason, J. (1991), 'Modernity as project and as field of tensions', in A. Honneth and H. Joas (eds), *Communicative Action: Essays on Jürgen Habermas's The Theory of Communicative Action*, Cambridge, MA: MIT Press, pp. 181–213.

Arnason, J. (2003), *Civilizations in Dispute: Historical Questions and Theoretical Traditions*, Leiden: Brill.

Arnason, J. (2006), 'Understanding intercivilizational encounters', *Thesis Eleven*, 86: 1, 39–53.

Arnason, J. (2014), 'Merleau-Ponty and the meaning of civilizations', in K. Novotný, P. Rodrigo, J. Slatman and S. Stoller (eds), *Corporeity and Affectivity: Dedicated to Maurice Merleau-Ponty*, Leiden: Brill, pp. 293–312.

Arnason, J., S. Eisenstadt and B. Wittrock (2005), 'General introduction', in *Axial Civilizations and World History*, Leiden: Brill, pp. 1–18.

Assmann, J. (2008), *Gods and Men: Egypt, Israel, and the Rise of Monotheism*, Madison: University of Wisconsin Press.

Bayly, C. A. (2004), *The Birth of the Modern World, 1780–1914: Global Connections and Comparisons*, Malden, MA: Blackwell.

Benhabib, S. (2004), *The Rights of Others: Aliens, Residents, and Citizens*, Cambridge: Cambridge University Press.

Bonneuil, C. (2015), 'The geological turn: narratives of the Anthropocene', in C. Bonneuil, C. Hamilton and F. Gemenne (eds), *The Anthropocene and the Global Environmental Crisis: Rethinking Modernity in a New Epoch*, London: Routledge, pp. 17–31.

Bonneuil, C. and J. Fressoz (2016), *The Shock of the Anthropocene*, New York: Verso.

Brotton, J. (2013), *A History of the World in 12 Maps*, London: Penguin.

Castoriadis, C. (1997), *The Imaginary Institution of Society*, Cambridge, MA: MIT Press.

Chakrabarty, D. (2000), *Provincializing Europe: Postcolonial Thought and Historical Difference*, Princeton: Princeton University Press.

Chakrabarty, D. (2009), 'The climate of history: four theses', *Critical Inquiry*, 35: 2, 197–222.

Chakrabarty, D. (2014), 'Climate and capital: on conjoined histories', *Critical Inquiry*, 41: 1, 1–23.

Cheah, P. (2016), *What Is a World? On Postcolonial Literature as World Literature*, Durham, NC: Duke University Press.

Clark, T. (2015), *Ecocriticism on the Edge: The Anthropocene as a Threshold Concept*, London: Bloomsbury.

Connell, R. (2007), *Southern Theory: The Global Dynamics of Knowledge in Social Science*, London: Polity.

Connell, R. (2011), 'Sociology for the whole world', *International Sociology*, 26: 3, 288–91.

Cosgrove, D. (2001), *Apollo's Eye: A Cartographic Genealogy of the Earth in the Western Imagination*, Baltimore: Johns Hopkins University Press.

Delanty, G. and A. Mota (2017), 'Governing the Anthropocene: agency, history, knowledge', *European Journal of Social Theory*, 20: 1.

Derrida, J. and E. Rottenberg (2002), 'Globalization, peace, and cosmopolitanism', in *Negotiations: Interventions and Interviews, 1971–2001*, Stanford: Stanford University Press, pp. 371–86.

Duchesne, R. (2011), *The Uniqueness of Western Civilization*, Leiden: Brill.

Dussel, E. (2007), *Política de la Liberación: Historia Mundial y Crítica*, Madrid: Trotta.

Eisenstadt, S. (2003), *Comparative Civilizations and Multiple Modernities*, 2 vols, Leiden: Brill.

Fuster, À. L. (2014), 'More than vulnerable: rethinking community', in J. Sabadell-Nieto and M. Segarra (eds), *Differences in Common: Gender, Vulnerability and Community*, Amsterdam and New York: Rodopi, pp. 121–41.

Fuster, À. L. and G. Rosich (2015), 'The limits of recognition: history, otherness and autonomy', in P. Wagner (ed.), *African, American and European Trajectories of Modernity: Past Oppression, Future Justice?*, Edinburgh: Edinburgh University Press, pp. 42–63.

Goldstone, J. (2009), *Why Europe? The Rise of the West in World History, 1500–1850*, New York: McGraw-Hill.

Heidegger, M. (1977), *The Question Concerning Technology*, New York: Harper & Row.

Herod, A. (2009), *Geographies of Globalization: A Critical Introduction*, Oxford: Blackwell.

Husserl, E. [1913] (2014), *Ideas for a Pure Phenomenology and Phenomenological Philosophy*, vol. 1, Cambridge: Hackett.

Kant, I. [1784] (1989), 'Idea for a universal history with a cosmopolitan purpose', in *Political Writings*, Cambridge: Cambridge University Press, pp. 41–53.

Koskenniemi, M. (2012), 'The subjective dangers of projects of world community', in

A. Cassese (ed.), *Realizing Utopia: The Future of International Law*, Oxford: Oxford University Press, pp. 3–13.

Latour, B. (2014), 'Agency at the time of the Anthropocene', *New Literary History*, 45: 1, 1–18.

Mignolo, W. (2012), *Local Histories/Global Designs: Coloniality, Subaltern Knowledges, and Border Thinking*, Princeton: Princeton University Press.

Nancy, J.-L. (2007), *The Creation of the World or Globalization*, Albany: State University of New York Press.

Osterhammel, J. (2014), *The Transformation of the World: A Global History of the Nineteenth Century*, Princeton: Princeton University Press.

Osterhammel, J. and N. P. Petersson (2005), *Globalization: A Short History*, Princeton: Princeton University Press.

Panikkar, R. (1979), *Myth, Faith, and Hermeneutics*, Mahwah, NJ: Paulist Press.

Pomeranz, K. (2000), *The Great Divergence: China, Europe, and the Making of the Modern World Economy*, Princeton: Princeton University Press.

Purdy, J. (2015), *After Nature: A Politics for the Anthropocene*, Cambridge, MA: Harvard University Press.

Rockström, J. et al. (2009), 'Planetary boundaries: exploring the safe operating space for humanity', *Ecology and Society*, 14: 2.

Rosich, G. (2016), 'Autonomy in and between polities: democracy and the need for collective political selves', in G. Rosich and P. Wagner (eds), *The Trouble with Democracy: Political Modernity in the 21st Century*, Edinburgh: Edinburgh University Press.

Rosich, G. (2018), *The Contested History of Autonomy: Interpreting European Modernity*, London: Bloomsbury Academic.

Rosich, G. and P. Wagner (eds) (2016), *The Trouble with Democracy: Political Modernity in the 21st Century*, Edinburgh: Edinburgh University Press.

Ryan, M. T. (1981), 'Assimilating new worlds in the sixteenth and seventeenth centuries', *Comparative Studies in Society and History*, 23: 4, 519–38.

Schmitt, C. [1951] (2006), *The Nomos of the Earth in the International Law of the Jus Publicum Europaeum*, New York: Telos.

Steffen, W., J. Grinevald, P. Crutzen and J. McNeill (2011), 'Anthropocene: conceptual and historical perspectives', *Philosophical Transactions of The Royal Society*, 369: 1938, 842–67.

Stråth, B. and P. Wagner (2017), *European Modernity: A Global Approach*, London: Bloomsbury.

Therborn, G. (2014), 'From civilizations to modernity: divisions and connections of the world, and their legacy—a historical social geology', in S. A. Arjomand (ed.), *Social Theory and Regional Studies in the Global Age*, Albany: State University of New York Press, pp. 267–90.

United Nations (2015), *The Paris Agreement to the Convention on Climate Change*, <http://unfccc.int/files/essential_background/convention/application/pdf/english_paris_agreement.pdf> (last accessed 11 January 2017).

Wagner, P. (2008), *Modernity as Experience and Interpretation: A New Sociology of Modernity*, Cambridge: Polity.

Wagner, P. (2012), *Modernity: Understanding the Present*, Cambridge: Polity.

Wagner, P. (2016a), *Progress: A Reconstruction*, London: Polity.

Wagner, P. (2016b), 'World-sociology: an outline', *Social Imaginaries*, 2: 2, 87–104.

Waters, C. N. et al. (2016) 'The Anthropocene is functionally and stratigraphically distinct from the Holocene', *Science*, 351: 6269, 137–47.

Wendt, A. (2003), 'Why a world state is inevitable', *European Journal of International Relations*, 9: 4, 491–542.

3

The BRICS Countries: Time and Space in Moral Narratives of Development

Cláudio Costa Pinheiro

Modernity has not only been merely preoccupied with progress and advance,
but also loss and disappearance. Loss is also good to think in regard to what it
means to be Modern.

Sumathi Ramaswamy, *The Lost Land of Lemuria*

IN NOVEMBER 2001, an economist at a London investment bank was
going over lists of international GDP indicators, comparing the
developed countries of the G7 with what he called 'some of the largest
emerging market economies'. He concluded that Brazil, Russia, China
and India would be the world's leading economies by 2050, surpassing
the six most prosperous countries of the West. Although the statement
was bold, it came within a brief seven-page working paper brightly
titled 'Building Better Global Economic BRICs' (O'Neill 2001). The
very suggestion of a 'better world' right around Christmas time was a
welcome relief after a fiscal year marked by the impact of the September
11 attacks.

Time has passed and Jim O'Neill's argument has gained resonance.
Since 2001, his futurological forecast has attracted its share of fans.
International media brought together market economists and government technocrats for live debates, skyrocketing online sales of self-help
literature on global developmentalism. At the heart of the argument, an
old question persisted: can peripheral countries play leading roles on
the world's political and economic agenda for promoting development
and progress?

In further articles and interviews O'Neill, senior analyst at Goldman
Sachs Bank, insisted that the BRICs would be the new global locomotive,
moving down the target date of the forthcoming future, from 2050 to
2039 and then to 2032 – sustained by the projection of the huge annual
growth rates of those countries between 2001 and 2012, and aspects like

the Brazilian discovery of offshore oil reserves, in 2006. BRICs eventually became the *topos* of discussions that associated emerging countries with a new developmental wave. The BRICs idea turned O'Neill into a celebrity of neo-developmentalism and a bestselling author (O'Neill 2011, 2013). Beyond the author's persona, this concept has also helped reorganise the political agenda of all the peripheries of international capitalism, not just the BRIC countries. Of course, not everyone agreed with O'Neill's exercise in predicting such a future. It has received much criticism and has even been disregarded as fortune telling.

Nevertheless, others have taken this prediction seriously and in 2006, the first summit of the BRIC countries coincided with the UN General Assembly. Shortly after that, the financial crisis of 2007–8 would ratify O'Neill's forecast, paralysing North Atlantic economies and sparing emerging markets. As a result, the importance of the BRICs grew significantly. Later, in 2011, South Africa – part of IBSA, another bloc of emerging countries that included Brazil and India – was incorporated and BRIC became BRICS, though the addition was questioned by several experts, including O'Neill himself, who had suggested Mexico or Turkey instead. In any case, O'Neill's acronym evoked a metaphor of bricks that would rebuild the architecture of the world's economy and politics, and BRICS ultimately became reality. This should not be surprising; after all, as Robert Merton once said, representations are 'self-fulfilling prophecies' (1948).

Recent reaccommodations in world geopolitics and global economics, however, seem to have changed expectations about the capacity of these emerging countries to address development and promote wealth distribution. Some analysis has gone as far as announcing the end of the BRICS bloc. These forecasts emerged in 2013 and gained momentum in 2015, coinciding with the downturn of GDP taxes in the BRIC countries. Actually, the present contribution does not aim to discuss what the future of the BRICS will be – nor even if there will be one. After all, as the famous quote attributed to John Kenneth Galbraith says, 'the only function of economic forecasting is to make astrology look respectable'.

This piece, on the contrary, aims at taking Merton's statement one step further, observing how representations and prophecies are assimilated into an agenda that comprises development theories, narratives of modernity and exercises of place-making.[1] This chapter considers revisiting these three axes, observing how vocabularies of development were largely organised around binary oppositions (identified with the

rhetoric of progress or the absence thereof) and contributed to defining a certain *semantics of inequality*. Furthermore, these vocabularies
referred to modernity as an encompassing *condition* that concurs in
conceiving development indistinguishably in terms of time and space,
associating areas of poverty (or the absence of wealth) with the past,
and a cartographic imagination of futures with expectations of prosperity. In addition, developmental analysis not only helped to consolidate
readings of progress in terms of *cartographies of time* and *chronologies
of space* – ultimately illustrated through concepts like Third World,
Global South or Developed Countries – but also conceptualised time
and space as variables provided with moral attributes, a dimension
emphasised by some authors (Sack 1997; Smith 2000; Lee and Smith
2004). With that in mind, this chapter then turns to the relevance
of BRICS for social sciences, analysing how the acronym describes
geographies (of prosperity and lack thereof) and revisits some artifices
of place-making operative in sociological debate from the end of the
Second World War onwards – addressed through approaches like 'area
studies' and 'cultural areas'.

Modernity, time and spaces of uneven development

Although the process of place-imagining predates modernity – Plato
described Atlantis in 360 BC – tales of fantastic lands became a
common *topos* during the period. Representations and prophecies
about prosperous and impoverished lands mesmerised Europeans
since the Middle Ages, but the fascination with this sort of literature
and accounts grew significantly in modern times. A considerable
number of the first European voyages of exploration were inspired by
myths of fantastic worlds filled with extraordinary treasures. During
this period, Europeans sailed off to the Americas, Africa and Asia
in search of promised lands described in a plethora of myths and
narratives (Johnson 1998; Manguel and Guadalupi 2000). These narratives included the mythical City of the Caesars (rumoured to exist
in Patagonia, Argentina), the island of Hy-Brazil spotted by Saint
Brendon, and the mythological continent of Lemuria (which was
somewhere between Africa and India, according to nineteenth-century
Indian theory), brilliantly analysed by Sumathi Ramaswamy (2001) and
many others.

Modernity did much more than systematically connect parts of
the globe, as a consequence of colonialism, trade, the expansion of

Christian missions and of an enormous apparatus of technologies produced to satisfy Western *curiosity* concerning the *other* (Stagl 1995). It also supposed exercises of imagination and of invention of geographies as indistinguishable attributes of a topology of power. As Edward Said (1978) has argued, modernity has made imagination a privilege of power (of colonisers over colonised). This strengthens the difference between centre(s), which have the power to imagine, and periphery(ies) as the product or subject of the imagination (in political, economic, social and cultural terms). In this regard, Said analyses Orientalism as a technology and as a Western repertoire of power that associates imagination with the production of representations, ultimately referring back to a structure of domination in the service of colonialism.

It would be interesting to provoke a dialogue between Said and Ramaswamy. After all, reflecting on both progress and its absence is a condition of modernity; one that evokes the gap between centre – a place of prosperity and the crafter of the imagination – and peripheries – *loci* of the absence of prosperity and an adjective of metropolitan poetics and policies of representation. Although Said does not use the argument of a moral economy of development that separates 'us' from the 'other', he evokes this tension between contradictory structures that characterise modernity. This historical-culturalist interpretation of macro-narratives on the invention of *otherness* has also influenced the debate on economic theory.

From the eighteenth century onwards, various theoretical models tried to explain diversity (of peoples, languages, lands, and so on) in terms of evolutionary hierarchies around concepts of progress. Adam Smith's classic *An Inquiry into the Nature and Causes of the Wealth of Nations* (1776) – most probably one of the first works to discuss the political economy of progress – divided the world into 'prosperous' and 'savage' nations. His essay provides an economic and moral explanation of the 'different progress of opulence in different nations', towards 'wealth and improvement'.

Smith's concepts of *wealth* and *progress* evoke a semantic constellation of arguments ultimately related to moral concepts of evolution, which he associated with categories such as *improvement, progress, wealth, civilisation*, and so on. In this regard, 'wealthy nations' (civilised and prosperous) stood in stark contrast to 'savage and barbarous nations' (wild and poor). For Smith, *difference* and *diversity* in historical, economic and social terms are inevitably bound to ideas of advancement and progress and to narratives of its absence. *Progress* would become the ultimate goal of humanity but access to its benefits would be limited to certain people and territories. This assumption nourished binary oppositions – *antinomies of modernity* – that have organised the understanding of otherness since post-Enlightenment times. In addition to consolidating a structure of antinomies in economic thought, Smith's essay established a set of categories that would persist until the Second World War (Arndt 1981; Rist 2009). The idea of 'material progress' as a synonym for 'economic development' became central to economic debate between the late nineteenth and mid-twentieth centuries.

Economists utilised the concept of economic development, especially when debating economic theories and theories of empire in the late nineteenth century. The concept was mainly identified with ideas such as industrialisation, modernisation and Westernisation (see, among others, Marshall 1890; Schumpeter [1911] 1934). The promotion of economic development was associated with colonialism and its mandate became more apparent in the late nineteenth century, under the notion of *trusteeship*. *Trusteeship* (Arndt 1981: 463) referred to a legal and political concept based on the idea that progress should be attained under the *tutelage* of the colonial metropolises. The concept would be very popular until the Second World War, after which it gained new wind and was reframed in a new vocabulary. During this period, it basically reproduced the binary divisions between development and lack thereof, reframing the idea of development, which became 'development-promoting policies', 'assisted development' and similar terms. Later, in the 1940s to 1950s, concepts like 'backward areas', 'poor countries' and 'underdeveloped areas' began to replace the 'savage nations' of Adam Smith.

Harry Truman's 1949 inaugural address is a key part in this movement insofar as it has the effect of consolidating not just a new vocabulary, but a wholly new ontology of *otherness* based on economic rationality. 'We must embark on a bold new program for making the benefits of our scientific advances and industrial progress available for *the improvement and growth of underdeveloped areas*' (Truman 1949; my emphasis). That speech immediately made two billion people across the world underdeveloped. While the lexicon varied, it still remained organised through pairs of binary opposition consolidating views of progress and development through a *semantics of inequality*. In turn, the *antinomies of modernity* based on this semantics (Kaiwar

55

and Mazumdar 2003) lent support to the idea that the international geopolitics of development tends to create a global division between the countries that accumulate wealth and those unable to develop. This lengthy process summarises Ramaswamy's argument by presenting modernity through experiences of development and its absence. The post-war period was very fertile in terms of fashioning narratives of global development, narratives that presented new mythologies and a new lexicon while expressing concern over the fair distribution of wealth.

Jim O'Neill's exercise of imagining the BRICS as the hope for a new developmentalism is not the first case of a situation analysis, with ambitions of futurological forecasting aspects of global geopolitics, eventually becoming a self-fulfilling prophecy. Others have attempted to introduce a new lexicon and new arrangements of international geo-politics by defining alterity in terms of moral aspects of development and progress.

In August 1952, the French magazine *L'Observateur* published one of the most important articles of the twentieth century: *Trois mondes, une planète*. This half-page essay became internationally known for coining the concept of the *Third World*. The author, the French geographer and demographer Alfred Sauvy (1898–1990), described a world divided into binary poles of opposing powers: 'East and West', 'capitalism and communism'. It was also a world inhabited by a residual bloc of under-developed regions, that is, the former and existing European colonies in Africa, Asia and the Americas, leaving other countries little option but to choose between one of the other two worlds, that is, the Soviet Union or the United States.

The article and the term gained immense popularity and helped consolidate the political semantics of the Cold War; it became a man-datory reference in almost all debates concerning the international system at that time. Sauvy became famous and earned a prominent place on the global development agenda, joining the *Conseil d'Études Économiques* of the *Secrétaire d'État à l'Économie Nationale et aux Finances*, and becoming chairman of the Commission on Population and Development at the United Nations Economic and Social Council. He also joined the Collège de France (1962) and held posts at several academic institutions.[2]

That article in *L'Observateur* set off an avalanche of academic texts, development programmes, media debates on global economy, and so on. Several of these relied on the idea that the concept of a Third World could encapsulate a global division between states and regions, hierarchically organised between those who won and those who lost the race for development, with the winners achieving prosperity and wealth, and subsequently reaching modernity. As a concept, then, *Third World* was converted into an epistemic reality with an almost ontological density, shared by the mainstream media, in academic debates, and by the institutions of global governance aimed at promoting development and addressing inequality.

Starting in the 1950s, a series of initiatives culminated in new vocabularies intended to describe and rewrite the global political structure of the post-war period. The foundation of the Arab League (1945), the Bandung Conference (1955), the Cuban Revolution (1959), the meetings of the Non-Aligned Movement (1961 onwards), the Organization of African Unity (1963), the oil crisis and participation of Organization of the Petroleum Exporting Countries (OPEC) (1970s), the Brandt Commission (1980), the South Commission (1986–7) and many others marked a search for new models of development, but also disputes over the semantic classifications that characterised global geopolitics. It was the beginning of decolonisation in Asia and Africa and the concept *Third World* seemed to identify these new countries emerging from the dusk of colonialism. But Sauvy's idea of a Third World hid striking distinctions between contexts of the periphery of capitalism, where the countries in Latin America had little in common with regions of Asia and Africa whose daily struggle against colonialism continued.

Roughly speaking, at that time Latin America oscillated between what was considered as the successful experiences of progress and modernisation of the First World and the search for new pathways for regional development, as evident in Economic Commission for Latin America and the Caribbean (ECLAC) debates on structuralism or dependency theory. At the other side of this underdeveloped world, African and Asian countries sought out new models that could break with the neo-colonial hegemony of the West. Some parts of the Third World believed in Sauvy's prophecies and drifted towards one of the dominant poles, while others sought out new inspirations. Divergence in terms of beliefs and pathways of development were expressed in a vocabulary and semantics of inequality ascribed to the lack of development in peripheral contexts.

Correspondingly, the Bandung Conference vocalised demands for a new development agenda in order to devise a new international architecture of power out of the framework of colonialism (Chatterjee

2005). Similar demands for stronger political participation in the global arena were presented by the members of the Non-Aligned Movement (which held its first meeting in September 1961) or by OPEC (captaining concerns of other commodity-producing countries), following the oil crisis of the 1970s.

Third World was not a concept universally adopted; only certain intellectuals and politicians in Latin America, Asia and Africa used it in reference to the development agenda that would identify countries in the region. In some places, the term has consolidated notions of otherness and difference based on economic indicators, when material progress was viewed as a necessary condition for overcoming poverty. In other contexts, the enemy was the phantom of colonialism, 'neo-colonialism', a term coined by Sukarno, President of Indonesia in 1955 and instilled by Jean-Paul Sartre, Kwame N'Krumah, Frantz Fanon and others.

In the late 1960s, new research on inequality helped renew debate about the semantics of inequality, proposing another lexicon for development. The concept of the South emerged from discussions on global inequality, that is, the capitalist system's failure to secure global well-being (Gregory 1994). In this context, the South shared the semantics of other binary divisions that had organised nations in terms of antinomies of modernity – synonymous with terms like the Third World, peripheral, semi-peripheral or underdeveloped countries. In these discussions, the North–South divide was identified with an extension of 'material inequalities' that separated 'affluent nations' (North America, Western Europe and Japan) from the 'poor countries' (in Asia, Africa and Latin America) struggling for a new international economic order that could rework the unsustainable balance. At that time, the South was economically and geographically identified with 'poor developing nations in the Southern Hemisphere' (Amuzegar 1976: 547). This approach made the *South* almost undistinguishable from Sauvy's idea of the Third World, and initiatives such as the Brandt Commission (1977–8) and the South Commission (1987) again set global geography in antinomian terms. Common issues surrounding both concepts included the fight against poverty, commodity prices on the global market, corruption, militarism and especially industrialisation. However, the South became a much more polyphonic category, considering it was used in many different contexts, addressing different meanings.

In the early 1970s, the concept of the South became a tool of political articulation, given the success of OPEC initiatives to raise the global prices of oil and to change, albeit temporarily, the global balance of power. In their successful push to increase prices, oil-producing countries tried to inspire a political movement for the recovery of international commodity values and to give the peripheral countries a more prominent role in global politics. In this context, the concept of the South represented a place of political enunciation, rather than a mere geography of absence or a lack of material progress. The concept has evolved into a far more complex amalgamation of actors, ideas, and theories of political and economic connections, distancing itself from euphemisms of poverty to highlight a new outline of power structures in a multi-polar world.

All these attempts at new lexicons capable of describing the global structure of power ended up in one way or another reinforcing the same antinomian divisions described by Adam Smith in the eighteenth century and views on modernity not far from Ramaswamy's own. In all the discussions, two aspects were made relevant to the sociological debate, recapturing the idea of how the BRICS could impact on the agenda of social sciences. First, the range of these vocabularies also suggests disputes about how to classify these *semantics of difference* as geographies imagined by the centre (the case of terms like Third World) versus those imagined on the peripheries (as Non-Aligned Countries and the South). This dispute alludes to a discussion over the 'place of utterance' (Bhabha 1994), a question of who defines geographies of development and of how they are defined. In Edward Said's terms, we must ask how the periphery builds agency based on its own definition of itself – a definition, it should be noted, considered an attribute of power.

Furthermore, an important aspect in imagining these geographies within both economics and the social sciences is that these elements allow for comparisons between contexts (countries, territories, and so on).

What forged identity among the countries and regions of the Third World? They shared non-development and a commitment to promoting material progress in a context where periphery was identified with poverty, non-democratic governments and inequality (economic and social). Basically, the Third World meant exclusion from the benefits of economic development and global politics. What created identity among movements like Bandung and the Non-Aligned Movement? The need to respond to colonialism (and neo-colonialism) in order to reorganise the political and economic agendas that characterise the relationship between centre (metropolis) and periphery (colonies). And what creates identity among the participants of the Global South? A desire to address political utterance in a global context where peripheries are associated with specific forms of politic-economic participation (as in the case of the OPEC countries).

Elements of a *bricology*?[3]

But what was so relevant and unique about the emergence of the so-called BRICS? Initially, the same condition that animated the peripheries of capitalism since the end of the Second World War: an expectation of change for the future. There was a belief that the traditional hierarchical structures of the global economy that had characterised the entire twentieth century – the US–USSR bipolarity, addressing development; and the Third Word, illustrating underdevelopment – could then be overcome.

There was also trust that this bloc of emerging countries could vocalise the demands of a periphery that was about much more than economic and political exclusion. As the world saw international geopolitics become increasingly multi-polar, this became particularly relevant. The BRICS recognised that they were what centres imagined as periphery, thus deprived of the epistemic devices for creating self-representations.

In spite of these positive expectations, critics continued to insist that BRICS was an inadequate term for a coalition or political configuration, insisting on the supposed 'lack of identity' among these countries. This argument gave rise to economic and sociological arguments, both with points in common. According to these arguments, the BRICS initiative offers a remarkable opportunity to assess how sociological theory can explain global capitalism in a dialogue with economic theory by reviving experiences such as ECLAC, dependency theory or world-systems theory, rehabilitating the relevance of social sciences on the agenda of development theories.

The idea of BRICS helps to revisit the historical debate on development theories (Rist 2009) and the insistence on antinomies as a way to understand modernity (Kaiwar and Mazumdar 2003). It has also encouraged a review of global geopolitical divisions vis-à-vis the development debate. It other words, it establishes the relationship between concepts like 'centre and periphery' and 'development and underdevelopment' in a context of changes to financial flows, population and the political importance of certain regions. The economic analysis has focused on whether the new acronym represents a new grammar of developmentalism, with economically peripheral countries capturing a much bigger portion of wealth while the old core nations experience a severe economic crisis. As the renowned Brazilian economist Maria da Conceição Tavares has suggested, the centre–periphery division had been overtaken by the idea of 'intermediate developing countries' (Conceição Tavares 2010) – an argument that evokes Giovanni Arrighi's thesis on the reconceptualisation of semi-peripheries of capitalism (Arrighi 1990).

But the BRICS do not precisely fit into the rhetoric that separates imagined geographies in terms of progress or lack thereof. Instead, BRICS is a way to reflect on the historical belief about geographies of prosperity and future utopias. Thus, BRICS evokes another aspect of modernity that Ramaswamy did not consider: modernity is not only preoccupied with explaining the past and the present (i.e. interested in *progress* and its *loss*) but also with making predictions, with *future expectations*. O'Neill's acronym does not refer to the present, but to idyllic expectations for the future. Or, to borrow Reinhart Koselleck's ([1979] 2006) category *Erwartungshorizont*, a *horizon of expectations*, a hope for the future. V. Y. Mudimbe (1988: 17–19) has reached a similar conclusion, viewing Africa as an intermediate space of 'marginality' divided between 'the so-called African tradition and the projected modernity of colonialism' – or, in the terms I employ, squeezed between past and future.

Economics, especially political economy, has traditionally been taken as the science of predicting or narrating the future (Johnson and Kenyon 1993), as can be seen in the term used for predicting scenarios of development, 'economic forecasting'. The BRICS are not the only recent example of economic theory imagining the future potential of geographies and prosperity to come. A similar projection into the future characterised the development models of Singapore, Hong Kong, Taiwan and South Korea – the so-called Asian Tigers or Dragons – in the 1990s (Vogel 1991).

Situational analyses of the global economy like O'Neill's (frequently presented as 'economic theories') help us to understand how this field structures its discursive arguments concerning prosperity on two different levels. First, such arguments can be seen as teleologies and prophecies of development (that is, they provide an organised look at the past and prospects for the future), and a narrative of its absence (that is, poverty, underdevelopment, dependence). At another level, (imagined) geographies are necessarily embedded in the representations of an expected prosperity in the future. This consideration allows us to examine how current economic theory is related to a long tradition of mythologies concerning development, progress and prosperity, produced by exercises in imagination and place-making.

Imagining future expectations for places suffering from shortcomings in the present could represent a major challenge to sociological theory. Accordingly, it seems natural to contrast this view with the criticism of theories of modernity as an expression of a European experience conceived of as *universal*[4] and the imposition of models of *Western development*[5] as the single and inexorable path for world progress. In addition, the sociological theory approach to analysing the future could prove useful once again, since the *rhetoric of emergence* has characterised much of the analysis of peripheral societies, not only in terms of its economic bias, but also in politics or studies on social structure, morphology, and so on.

Futurology and forecasting may sound like unusual reflections in present-day sociology, but they have been popular in our field and have also been a very common demand on social scientists more generally. In the 1980s, the American Anthropological Association sponsored a 'commission on futurology' to consider forecasting scenarios with regard to population flows and the impacts of development in local contexts (Burman 1982, 1985). On the other hand, sociology itself has a long tradition of dealing with methods of forecasting, with a supposedly scientific field – *social forecasting* – that determined regularities and predicted social behaviour (individual, institutional or collective); this can be found in some of Robert Merton's writing (Henschel 1982; Horowitz 1974–5).

The relationship between *geographical imagination* and *future expectations* helps us to summarise a final point in this chapter: the importance of spatiality for development debates and their consequences for the social sciences.

One recurring critique regards the heuristic value and the presumed relevance of the concept of BRICS to the social sciences. Some analysts suggest a certain 'artificiality' of this alliance based on the 'lack of identity'. According to these critiques, Brazil, Russia, China, India and South Africa lack *commonalities*, cultural aspects such as history, language, culture and a shared social identity that would be required to create synergy among them. The critics thus argue that it is unfeasible for BRICS to form an economic bloc – or even serve as the basis for a comparative sociological analysis. This assumption is based on a large degree of naivety. First of all, it is clear that the critics ignore the connections between these countries (that is, the commonalities) while also assuming that cultural identity translates into economic commitment and solidarity.

In addition to the attempts to define the 'other' of Western development (the 'savage', 'wild' and 'barbarous nations' of Adam Smith, the Third World, the Global South, and so on), reflecting on the lack of identity among BRICS leads to another important question in the social sciences and economics: how the social sciences are used to pigeonhole geographical and cultural contexts in order to justify comparisons.

Soon after the Second World War, the world began to be divided into cultural areas, configuring the 'area studies' approach. Although the intention was to overcome the colonial outline of non-European societies, it generally reproduced this same divide. The impetus for 'area studies' came from US and European academia (neither of which were considered 'areas') and ultimately maintained the same imperial borders, such as those conceived after the Berlin Conference (van Schendel 2002: 647–8). This definition of *area studies* led to the study of purportedly homogeneous, self-contained units detached from social realities. The process of developing 'area studies' as a form of compartmentalizing knowledge about societies other than North Atlantic ones had something in common with the 'scramble for Africa' a few decades earlier. This had consequences not only for how this pigeonholed world was approached but also for who studied and who financed the research on this new map of global subdivisions (Parmar 2012). Area studies helped consolidate specialised and spatialised academic communities that existed as self-contained dominions. In the case of US academia, area studies brought competition for renown and research funding, and raised intellectual borders based on a geographical regionalisation of the world. This process contributed to a lack of communication between different specialists in area studies and to the creation of borders, rituals and native categories (the researchers) used to define these subdivisions, which came to form academic fiefdoms.[6]

Generally speaking, it was assumed that an area would represent a cultural region, a geographical entity identified by cultural and historical aspects of identification. People (ethnicities, groups, communities, and so on) were associated through cultural commonalities (historical and linguistic connections, and so on) in a territory assigned to an area. It is true that area studies was not the only framework available for defining cultural geographies. Furthermore, area studies was associated with other culturalist understandings and scientific priorities for geographies of development. Area studies emerges as a relevant concept for the humanities in the post-war period, where it vied for hegemony with concepts such as 'culture-area' (Wissler 1927; Newman 1971) or 'socio-cultural area' (Mintz 1971), both very popular in the social sciences and linguistics, and 'emerging economies' (van Agtmael 2007), as a representation of otherness in the discourse on development in economics. It is relatively apparent that the critiques of a lack of shared identity between the BRICS countries are also based on expectations that 'culture' should produce connections. In addition, although area studies did not reify political borders, not even the nation state, it assumed that an area presupposed territorial contiguity. That is, although area studies recognises the nation state as a modern fable and although culturalist borders established no connections with political boundaries, the culturalist approach created new physical boundaries based on shared elements of 'culture' and on expectations of territorial and cultural contiguity. The BRICS countries are dispersed across the map and, moreover, disconnected from the culturalist perspective; it would thus be highly unlikely for sociology to consider them a sociologically relevant unit and, correspondingly, to adopt them as a configuration under the terms of area studies.

The approach of area studies has been revised and criticised in recent years (van Schendel 2002; Slocum and Thomas 2003; Miyoshi and Harootuniam 2002). Since the turn of the century, the social sciences have reconsidered the importance of spatiality in response to studies on globalisation (Appadurai 2000; van Schendel 2002; Slocum and Thomas 2003) and sought to rekindle the relationship between local–transnational–global spheres. Here social scientists have begun focusing on the interconnections, flows and articulations between centre and periphery (Appadurai 1996; Clifford 1997; Hannerz 1989), in the search for a global system that structures many local processes and brings them into being (Friedman 2000, 2001) while considering the importance of networks and local meanings within a global domain (Ong 1999; Tsing 2000). Appadurai went so far as to suggest the idea of *processual geographies* (2000), investing in analytical models that surpass fixed areas. This movement arose from a crisis of explanatory models that linked the place-imagining of contexts and geographies with the elements that identified these contexts as units that could be compared with one another.

Then again, the question that concerns us here is how to deal with the BRICS from the point of view of sociological theory. By seeking cultural elements in common, we are also at risk of inventing some sort of *bricology* – ironic contemporary versions of colonial views like those of Brazilianists, Sinologists or Indologists – with their jargon, borders and idiosyncrasies. Although this search would be legitimate, it would create a path towards the type of specialisation that has already been so intensely criticised in recent years.

Yet within the supposed fragility and insignificance of the BRICS, there is an argument about the relevance of sociology to economic theory. The economic concept of 'emerging' (markets, economies and countries) breaks with expectations within area studies of territorial continuity as an attribute of cultural identity. The analysis of the 'economic miracle' of the 1990s, which pointed to the Asian Tigers as a model to be followed to promote global development, was also characterised by disparities, as Singapore, Hong Kong, Taiwan and South Korea existed outside a single area within area studies and were not geographically contiguous. The economic and sociological argument of that *bricolage* was based on how those economies fostered a new reading of the international capitalist system. In an emulation of the Weberian argument, the 'Tigers' shared a 'Confucian ethics of capitalism' (Hayhoe 1992; Lew et al. 2011).

In a sense, we can consider that Third World and Global South have arisen from the logics of area studies, given the rhetoric of absence and incompleteness (that is, the *conditions of otherness* of development: poverty, lack of development, unfinished modernity) as the element of identity between the countries and regions that made up those blocs. But in terms of the BRICS, what factors would help us establish a sociological approach towards this geopolitical configuration?

Concluding remarks

From games of bricolage to theories of bricology?

The historical construction of theories of development has been largely associated with place-imagining and place-making, two inextricable exercises that helped to structure modernity around antinomies. This démarche also played a role in the semantics of inequality that organised global geopolitics and conceived of development as perpetual motion. Here the world was divided between contexts (countries, territories, regions and areas) that had attained modernity and those that had not. Analysing the emergence of new models of development also involves tackling expectations to reflect on the decline of other forms of development and on the disappearance of certain sites of prosperity.

It might prove useful to analyse the BRICS within this framework, as this configuration challenges the social sciences to think about which elements could be relevant for the purposes of comparison in sociological analysis: the importance of spatiality as a variable or expectations for the future. Accordingly, we can approach the BRICS as a discursive event (real or imaginary, the distinction is irrelevant here) that provides access to a debate where modernity is associated with the imagination of geographies of development *connectedly*, in following the methodology proposed by Sanjay Subrahmanyam (1997, 2005). This author also criticises area studies for impertinently grouping distinct social and political experiences, pigeonholed into the culturalist approaches ultimately referred to within the notion of 'area'. What he proposes, then, is that we should connect the contexts to particular analytical elements, though this does not necessarily entail shared stories or cultures as a condition for sociological analysis.

We could finally highlight two debates surprisingly neglected in discussions about the BRICS to date: its approximations to the literature on empires, and on civilisational analysis. First, all BRICS members arose as postcolonial states largely based on the experiences of empires. All five of these countries share a history of configuring or integrating trans-regional empires faced with the task of classifying diversities (of people and territories) and of ruling difference, which ultimately transformed into inequality. This type of long-term political experience has provided these states with the know-how associated with institutions and political categories for governing difference. Therefore, it is important to recognise that these countries constructed knowledge traditions for the colonial rule of difference (Souza Lima 2002), which interpreted diversity (ethnic, political, religious, gender, and so on) in terms of inequality (Therborn 2011: 20). Brazil, Russia, China, India and South Africa all have a long history of dealing with native populations, for example, grouping them under imperial ruling categories and later incorporating them into national states (institutions and populations), which were ultimately reconfigured by other post-independence political structures.

These circumstances affected the national traditions of sociological thinking (in political science, sociology, anthropology and history – since economics is a separate case here). Although these traditions drew on the idiosyncratic political experiences of each country and determinedly reflected on the historical constitution of categories of diversity (again: ethnic, political, religious, gender, and so on), the dialogue between sociological agendas of peripheral countries has never existed in any systematic way. Thus, although rural studies occupy a prominent place in Brazilian sociology and are also a backbone of Indian sociology, the dialogue between these two nationally based sociological traditions is virtually non-existent.

Similarly, another debate curiously absent from observations on the BRICS is civilisational analysis. Civilisational analysis has grown out of a well-established sociological debate, particularly relevant to comparative approaches between large structures – where civilisation constitutes 'the largest comprehensible unit of sociocultural study' (Kavolis 1995: 19) – and particularly to the entire discussion on modernity. It has not been drawn upon to approach sociological comparisons of the BRICS countries, although this literature is not at all incompatible with historical approaches to Indian, Russian, Chinese and Brazilian social sciences, where historical experience and cultural identity have frequently been understood through the framework of civilisation.

Much of the story of the concept of BRICS and its further development finds echoes in other emerging peripheries of the Global South. During the 1990s, and especially the 2000s, unexpected political configurations began to appear along the peripheries of the Global South – like MERCOSUR (the Southern Common Market, from 1994), IBSA (the India–Brazil–South Africa Agreement, 2003), ASPA (the Summit of South American–Arab Countries, 2005), ASA (the Africa–South America Summit, 2006) and others, and that is only considering initiatives in South America. Those responsible for these initiatives consciously attempted to avoid the bipolarities that characterised global geopolitics during the Cold War, investing in alternative multi-polar orders and helping to address agency in peripheral countries as part of alternative geographies of development.

BRICS might be much more resourceful to social sciences as a methodological approach and viewpoint for dealing with large and complex units of analysis where historical experiences of political configuration – as empires – and theoretical approaches to the analytical unit – as civilisation – can play a role in guiding the research. It would also help to move the centre of the analysis away from its current association with forecasting economics and towards a cultural approach to 'civilization analysis as a sociology of culture' (Kavolis 1995), where the debate on decentring modernity can be readdressed. As such, the BRICS might offer an interesting challenge to sociological theory. It could be used to produce 'connections' between political experiences and the sociological agendas of those countries – traditionally confined to arguments about the incomparability of their national or regional arenas. This may help keep BRICS from being transformed into another area of studies, preventing a new field of *bricology* in the studies of peripheral countries. Finally, it could contribute to the development of a different approach to comparative studies in economics and the social sciences, whereby it would make sense to connect and compare geographic configurations like Latin America and the Arab world.

Notes

1. Place-imagining and place-making refer to a trend in international academia that associates social sciences and geography. See Agnew and Duncan (1989); Gregory (1994); Miyoshi and Harootuniam (2002).
2. In two recent interviews, the famous French anthropologist Georges Balandier has claimed he gave Sauvy the idea for the phrase and Sauvy later used it without acknowledging him (Balandier et al. 2010; Balandier et al. forthcoming 2017).
3. I am adapting the French term *bricolage* as it allows the word-play with the BRICS. Thanks to Lena Lavinas for the suggestion of this term in the debates of the ANPOCS-BRICS forum.
4. European modernity is presented as the success of a particular epistemic approach that 'should be' applied globally, as previously criticised by Chatterjee (1997); Eisenstadt (2000); Chakrabarty (2000); Randeria (2002).
5. Western development is sometimes taken as a synonym for prosperity and *material progress* (Smith [1776] 1904), and is at other time synonymous with *economic development* (Schumpeter [1911] 1934), *economic progress* (Clark 1940), or even *industrialisation* (Marshall 1890; Arrighi 1990).
6. 'The scramble for the area led to an institutional anchoring of academic communities worldwide, which trained separately, became engaged in area-specific discourses and debates, formed well-established reference circles, and developed similar mechanisms and rituals for patrolling their intellectual borders' (van Schendel 2002: 648).

References

Agnew, John A. and James S. Duncan (eds) (1989), *The Power of Place: Bringing Together Geographical and Sociological Imaginations*, Boston: Unwin Hyman.
Amuzegar, Jahangir (1976), 'The North–South dialogue: from conflict to compromise', *Foreign Affairs*, April, 547–62.

Appadurai, Arjun (1996), *Modernity at Large*, Minneapolis: University of Minnesota Press.

Appadurai, Arjun (2000), *Globalization and Area Studies: The Future of a False Opposition*, Amsterdam: Centre for Asian Studies Amsterdam.

Arndt, Heinz W. (1981), 'Economic development: a semantic history', *Economic Development and Cultural Change*, 29: 3, 457–66.

Arrighi, Giovanni (1990), 'The developmentalist illusion: a reconceptualization of the semiperiphery', in William G. Martin (ed.), *Semiperipheral States in the World-Economy*, Westport, CT: Greenwood Press, pp. 11–42.

Balandier, Georges, George Steinmetz and Gisèle Sapiro (2010), 'Tout parcours scientifique comporte des moments autobiographiques', *Actes de la recherche en sciences sociales*, 5: 185, 44–61.

Balandier, Georges, Cláudio Costa Pinheiro, Afranio Garcia and François Bonvin (forthcoming 2017), 'Entrevista com Georges Balandier', *Mana*.

Bhabha, Homi K. (1994), *The Location of Culture*, London: Routledge.

Burman, B. K. Roy (1982), 'Commission on futurology', *Current Anthropology*, 23: 4, 469–70.

Burman, B. K. Roy (1985), 'Commission on futurology', *Current Anthropology*, 26: 2, 301–2.

Chakrabarty, Dipesh (2000), *Provincializing Europe: Postcolonial Thought and Historical Difference*, Delhi: Oxford University Press.

Chatterjee, Partha (1997), *Our Modernity*, Amsterdam: Sephis.

Chatterjee, Partha (2005), 'Empire and nation revisited: 50 years after Bandung', *Inter-Asia Cultural Studies*, 6: 4, 487–96.

Clark, Colin (1940), *The Conditions of Economic Progress*, London: Macmillan.

Clifford, James (1997), *Routes*, Cambridge, MA: Harvard University Press.

Conceição Tavares, Maria da (2010), 'Não tem mais centro e periferia', Interview, *Folha de São Paulo*, 12 September, <http://www1.folha.uol.com.br/fsp/mercado/me1209201010.htm> (last accessed 11 January 2017).

Eisenstadt, Shmuel N. (2000), 'Multiple modernities', *Daedalus*, 129, 1–29.

Friedman, Jonathan (2000), 'Globalization, class and culture in global systems', *Journal of World-Systems Research*, 6: 3, 636–56.

Friedman, Jonathan (2001), 'Globalization, dis-integration, reorganization, the transformations of violence', in *Globalization, the State, and Violence*, Lanham, MD: AltaMira Press, pp. 1–34.

Gregory, Derek (1994), *Geographical Imaginations*, Oxford: Blackwell.

Hannerz, Ulf (1989), 'Notes on the global ecumene', *Public Culture*, 1: 2, 66–75.

Hayhoe, Ruth (1992), 'The Confucian ethic and the spirit of capitalism (Reviewed Work: The Confucian Continuum: Educational Modernization in Taiwan by Douglas Smith)', *Curriculum Inquiry*, 22: 4, 425–31.

Henschel, Richard L. (1982), 'Sociology and social forecasting', *Annual Review of Sociology*, 8, 57–79.

Horowitz, Irving L. (1974–5), 'Sociology and futurology: the contemporary pursuit of the millennium', *Berkeley Journal of Sociology*, 19, 37–53.

Johnson, David and Peter Kenyon (1993), 'Forecasting and futurology', *Australian Economic Review*, 26: 2, 4–18.

Johnson, Donald S. (1998), *Phantom Islands of the Atlantic: The Legends of Seven Lands that Never Were*, New York: Avon Books.

Kaiwar, Vasant and Sucheta Mazumdar (2003), *Antinomies of Modernity: Essays on Race, Orient, Nation*, Durham, NC: Duke University Press.

Kavolis, Vytautas (1995), *Civilization Analysis as a Sociology of Culture*, Lewiston, NY: Edwin Mellen.

Koselleck, Reinhart [1979] (2006), 'Espaço de experiência e horizonte de expectativas', in *Futuro passado - contribuição à semântica dos tempos históricos*, Rio de Janeiro: Contraponto, pp. 311–37.

Lee, Roger and David M. Smith (eds) (2004), *Geographies and Moralities: International Perspectives on Development, Justice, and Place*, Malden, MA: Blackwell.

Lew, Seok-Choon, Woo-Young Choi, and Hye Suk Wang (2011), 'Confucian ethics and the spirit of capitalism in Korea: the significance of filial piety', *Journal of East Asian Studies*, 11: 2, 171–95.

Manguel, Alberto and Gianni Guadalupi (2000), *The Dictionary of Imaginary Places*, New York: Mariner Books.

Marshall, Alfred (1890), 'The growth of free industry and entreprise', in *Principles of Economics*, London: Macmillan.

Merton, Robert K. (1948), 'The self-fulfilling prophecy', *The Antioch Review*, 8: 2, 193–210.

Mintz, Sidney (1971), 'The Caribbean as a socio-cultural area', in Michael M. Horowitz (ed.), *People and Cultures of the Caribbean: An Anthropological Reader*, Garden City, NY: Natural History Press, pp. 17–46.

Miyoshi, Masao and Harry D. Harootuniam (2002), *Learning Places: The Afterlives of Area Studies*, Durham, NC: Duke University Press.

Mudimbe, V. Y. (1988), *The Invention of Africa*, Indiana: Bloomington.

Newman, Arthur (1971) 'Sociologists' concepts of culture: some inadequacies', *Educational Theory*, 21: 3, 288–96.

O'Neill, Jim (2001), *Building Better Global Economic BRICs*, Global Economics Paper No: 66, London: Goldman Sachs.

O'Neill, Jim (2011), *The Growth Map: Economic Opportunity in the BRICs and Beyond*, New York: Portfolio/Penguin.

O'Neill, Jim (2013), *The BRIC Road to Growth*, London: London Publishing Partnership.

Ong, Aihwa (1999), *Flexible Citizenship: The Cultural Logics of Transnationality*, Durham, NC: Duke University Press.

Parmar, Inderjet (2012), *Foundations of the American Century*, New York: Columbia University Press.

Ramaswamy, Sumathi (2001), *The Lost Land of Lemuria: Fabulous Geographies, Catastrophic Histories*, Berkeley: University of California Press.

Randeria, Shalini (2002), 'Entangled histories of uneven modernities: civil society, caste solidarities and legal pluralism in post-colonial India', in Yehuda Elkana, Ivan Krastev, Elisio Macamo and Shalini Randeria (eds), *Unraveling Ties: From Social Cohesion to New Practices of Connectedness*, Frankfurt am Main: Campus, pp. 284–311.

Rist, Gilbert (2009), *The History of Development: From Western Origins to Global Faith*, London: Zed Books.

Sack, Robert D. (1997), *Homo Geographicus: A Framework for Action, Awareness, and Moral Concern*, Baltimore and London: Johns Hopkins University Press.

Said, Edward (1978), *Orientalism*, London: Penguin.

Schumpeter, Joseph A. [1911] (1934), *Theory of Economic Development*, trans. Redvers

Opie, *Harvard Economic Studies*, 46, Cambridge, MA: Harvard University Press.

Slocum, Karla and Deborah A. Thomas (2003), 'Rethinking global and area studies: insights from Caribbeanist anthropology', *American Anthropologist*, 105: 3, 553–65.

Smith, Adam [1776] (1904), *An Inquiry into the Nature and Causes of the Wealth of Nations*, 5th edn, London: Methuen, <http://www.econlib.org/library/Smith/smWN.html> (last accessed 11 January 2017).

Smith, David M. (2000) *Moral Geographies: Ethics in a World of Difference*, Edinburgh: Edinburgh University Press.

Souza Lima, Antonio Carlos (2002), 'Tradições de conhecimento na gestão colonial da desigualdade: reflexões a partir da administração indigenista no Brasil', in Cristina Bastos, Miguel Vale de Almeida, and Bela Feldman-Bianco (eds), *Trânsitos Coloniais: Diálogos Críticos Luso-Brasileiros*, Lisbon: Imprensa de Ciências Sociais (da Universidade de Lisboa), pp. 151–72.

Stagl, Justin (1995), *A History of Curiosity: The Theory of Travel 1550–1800*, Chur: Harwood.

Subrahmanyam, Sanjay (1997), 'Connected histories: notes towards a reconfiguration of Early Modern Eurasia', *Modern Asian Studies*, 31: 3, 735–62.

Subrahmanyam, Sanjay (2005), *Explorations in Connected Histories*, Delhi: Oxford University Press.

Therborn, Göran (2011), 'Inequalities and Latin America: from the Enlightenment to the 21st century', Working Paper 1, *desiguALdades.net Working Paper Series*, <http://www.desigualdades.net/Working_Papers/Search-Working-Papers/Working-Paper-1-_Inequalities-and-Latin-America_/index.html> (last accessed 11 January 2017).

Truman, Henry (1949), 'Truman's inaugural address, January 20, 1949', *Harry S. Truman Library and Museum*, <https://www.trumanlibrary.org/whistlestop/50yr_archive/inagural20jan1949.htm> (last accessed 8 February 2017).

Tsing, Anna (2000), 'The global situation', *Cultural Anthropology*, 15: 3, 327–60.

van Agtmael, Antoine (2007), *The Emerging Markets Century: How a New Breed of World-Class Companies Is Overtaking the World*, New York: Free Press.

van Schendel, Willem (2002), 'Geographies of knowing, geographies of ignorance: jumping scale in Southeast Asia', *Environment and Planning D: Society and Space*, 20: 6, 647–68.

Vogel, Ezra (1991), *The Four Little Dragons: The Spread of Industrialization in East Asia*, Cambridge, MA: Harvard University Press.

Wissler, Clark (1927), 'The culture-area concept in social anthropology', *American Journal of Sociology*, 32: 6, 881–91.

4

Russia between East, West and North: Comments on the History of Moral Mapping

Maxim Khomyakov

Introduction

THE IDEAS OF Global South and Global North today seem to have substituted the previous geopolitical notion of an East–West divide as well as the concepts of the First, Second and Third Worlds. It is probably too obvious that this new divide is as biased and as loaded with ideological constructs and unavoidable contradictions as both previous ones. If we pay closer attention to the details, we find the difficulties, which blur the picture. How, for example, did Australia turn out to be in the Global North or Russia, the former leader of the 'Eastern' or 'Second' World, drift towards the Global South together with its polar regions and Arctic ambitions? It is not really clear how one can unite culturally, geographically, economically and politically different countries into a single unit as wide as a Global North or Global South. If North is neatly defined as European and North American societies (with the possible inclusion of Australia and New Zealand), one can only wonder whether we do not face here the good old Eurocentric world-outlook in just slightly changed clothes. This really becomes obvious when a relatively homogenous 'North' is opposed to a 'South' containing countries as different as India, Brazil, China, Russia and South Africa. Political will and overlapping interests can probably bring these countries closer within the frameworks of the BRICS countries club; but they cannot change the background of very different histories, the background from the depths of which they ask and answer questions concerning their being in the modern world.

The interesting question, thus, is not why this or that country is included in (or excluded from) the putative or real Global South, but how a particular culture positions itself in a world understood in terms of various geographical, geopolitical and geocultural divides. Essentially the same question is about the ways in which a particular culture maps the globe. Of course, this mapping or positioning is a historical phenomenon and does change with the passing of time. Like large tectonic plates, cultures can also drift to the West or East, float to the South or North and cause violent eruptions when they collide. Thus, countries, which several decades ago were defined as Eastern, now seem to belong to the West or North. Sometimes this drift, accelerated by politics, can be as radical and fast-moving as the widening gap between Russia and Ukraine is. Thus, the most interesting question is not so much about the current cultural positioning, but rather the history of the mapping.

This mapping, being geographical, is, however, also political, economic, cultural, moral, religious, and so on. This means that it is based upon the answers to questions about political allies, economic collaborators, cultural relatives, moral connections or religious communities. These answers define 'our' cultural identity – not only in the sense of understanding who 'we' really are, but also in the sense of who 'we' were or who 'we' want to be. In this process of self-positioning the tenses are interconnected, so that not only does past history define future actions, but also the changing answers we give to the question of who we want to be in the future make us revisit and reinterpret our past. This constant process of autonomous reinterpretation of our position in the world influences our real world experience. Taken together, these experiences and interpretations define the particular form of modernity a particular society takes (Wagner 2008).

Here we are going to generally outline the history of Russian world-mapping over the last two or three centuries. We start with a very brief description of the eighteenth-century understanding and pay the closest attention to the nineteenth century, which arguably defines in many ways the position of Russian culture until the present. After another very short consideration of twentieth-century Russia, we will draw some general conclusions. Of course, this account will necessarily be very sketchy and incomplete. Detailed discussion of the nineteenth-century interpretation of the relations between Russia and Europe or the West alone would require thousands of pages, since all great Russian writers and intellectuals of that time answered the question about these relations in their own ways. Their understanding of Russia's relation to Asia and the East is another equally long story. We believe, however, that this account, even if incomplete and imperfect, remains very useful, since it helps us to better understand the nature of the Russian quest to make its own way in modernity.

It must be said here from the very beginning that the idea of Russia somehow belonging to any kind of Global South has never been present in Russian culture. The South, as we will see, has always been an alien 'other' of Russia, which itself oscillated between North, East and West, between Europe and Asia, between the Slavic world and the Central Asian nomadic empires. These concepts, along with the idea of Eastern (Orthodox) Christianity, form the landscape in which Russia keeps defining its place in the modern world.

Russia as the European North

Sixteenth-century Russia, liberating itself from what later became known as the Tatar yoke, took national pride in its being the only existing Orthodox kingdom. In 1510, in his letters to the Grand Prince of Moscow, Vasili III Ivanovich, the monk Philotheus of Pskov (1465– 1542) argued for a theory of Moscow as the Third Rome, which became the core of the young Russian state's political ideology and geopolitical mapping for at least two centuries. Since, according to Philotheus, 'two Romes have fallen, and the Third stands, and a fourth shall never be' (see Toumanoff 1954–5: 438; Duncan 2000: 11–12), the fall of Moscow would necessarily have eschatological consequences. That is why, when in the troubled seventeenth century some people decided that both tsar and clergy had fallen into heresy, they saw in it clearly apocalyptic signs of the approaching Doomsday. The result was the complex eschatology of the Old Believers, a conservative religious movement in many aspects similar to some denominations of Western European Protestantism. The idea of the Third Rome, however, made Russia the messianic centre, culturally isolated from the rest of the world, and did not really promote thinking about its relation to the other parts of the globe. At the same time it was the sixteenth century that witnessed a great expansion of the Moscow Kingdom, one of the most impressive acts of which was the beginning of the colonisation of Siberia.

The contacts with the external world were intensified in the second half of the seventeenth century, when Russia started attracting foreigners (especially Germans and Dutch) to live and work in Moscow. The crucial breakthrough in this respect was, however, made by Peter the Great (1672–1725), who, with the founding of St Petersburg, according to the famous saying of Pushkin's (actually taken from Italian writer Francesco Algarotti), 'cut the window through on Europe' (Pushkin 1960: 285). In addition to moving the capital from Moscow to this newly founded *northern capital*, he established (in 1721) the Russian Empire and reformed Russian life according to Western European standards, using for this purpose the most cruel means. He defeated the Swedish troops of Charles XII, made Russia an important European sea power and started to actively interfere in European affairs. Russia as a young European power developed really fast and already Catherine the Great (1729–96), who was in correspondence with both Diderot and Voltaire, came to be widely praised as a European enlightened ruler. In her *Nakaz* (*Instructions*), a statement of legal principles, she defined Russia as a 'European Power' of 'European People' (Ekaterina II 1849: 4).

Throughout the eighteenth century, thus, Russia positioned itself as an essentially European, or Northern European, country not only according to its physical geography, but also in accordance with its interests, values, actions, and so on. Thus, the first independent modern Russian scientist, the founder of Moscow University, Michael Lomonosov, praised the daughter of Peter the Great, Elisabeth I, for her giving 'calm to the whole Europe' (Lomonosov 1803a: 282) and 'subduing military noise in the whole Europe' (Lomonosov 1803b: 284). Welcoming the teenage Peter III, he calls him 'future possessor of the North' (Lomonosov 1959a: 62), but in his ode to Elisabeth II of the same 1742 he mentions the 'cold North', 'sultry steppes', 'American waves from the Eastern countries' and 'Baltic shores', that is, all four cardinal points, as loyal to the Russian Empress (Lomonosov 1959b: 284–90). In dedication to Peter III, prefacing Lomonosov's *Compendium of Eloquence*, he again speaks of the Russian Emperor as called to the 'adornment and defence of the whole North' (Lomonosov 1952: 92). It is just very natural, then, that Lomonosov paid such close attention to the Russian North and Siberia, urging the exploration of the Northern Sea Route to the eastern parts of the Russian Empire. And his main conclusion is not surprising either: 'Russian might will grow with Siberia and the Northern Ocean and will reach the main European settlements in Asia and America' (Lomonosov 1950: 630).

The Great French Revolution frightened both enlightened Catherine the Great and Russian noble society. One of the results of this shock and fear was the idea of an opposition between a stable European North and revolutionary South of Europe. Russia was now increasingly viewed as a potential rescuer of Europe and a successor of the fallen France as far as the Enlightenment was concerned. Talented poet and gifted statesman of the first half of the nineteenth century, a close friend of Pushkin and the first head of the Imperial Russian Historical Society, Prince Peter Vyazemskiy clearly expresses this idea in his poem 'Petersburg'. He specifically insists on the fact that Russia is glorious not only with its military victories, but also with the arts and sciences. The beginning of this glory was the 'stately spirit of Peter and intellect of Catherine'. Thus, 'the day was dimming in the South when dawn we had'. In the South rebellion and prejudices 'threatened to reduce to ashes the sanctuary of Enlightenment', but 'the North became its asylum'. So, when in Europe the old world was ignited with revolt and sedition, a 'creative spirit hovered over young Russia and called it to its feat . . .' (Vyazemskiy 1880: 158–9). That is why all arts and sciences, which used to inhabit the South, are now Russian natives (Vyazemskiy 1880: 159). The Messianic idea of Russia as the rescuer of Europe became archetypical for Russian culture and in various forms has been repeated throughout the nineteenth, twentieth and even twenty-first centuries whatever real or perceived dangers threatened Europe. It still very much defines the complex relation of Russian society towards its European alter ego.

The beginning of the nineteenth century witnessed a national rise and great Russian success in Europe. Having defeated Napoleon, Russia established itself as a mighty European power. Since this time Russia has been actively interfering in European affairs and thus has become an integral part and (some would also think – a guarantor) of the European system of international security. The national rise has naturally been accompanied by blooming culture. Defeat of the Decembrist revolt in 1825 delayed development and started a long period of conservative reaction but did not shatter this understanding of Russia as a fast-developing European country. Thus already in 1844 one of the early Slavophiles, a brilliant writer and a follower of Schelling and Hoffman, Prince Vladimir Odoyevskiy, did not hesitate to announce in the midst of the dark times of the reaction of the reign of Nicolas I: 'The nineteenth century belongs to Russia' (Odoyevskiy 1913: 423). Interestingly, it was written some eight years before the Crimean War, which, together with the revolutions of 1848–9, significantly changed Russian feelings towards Western Europe.

Russia as the Christian East: Russia and Slavdom

It was not, however, Prince Odoyevskiy who initiated the discussion of so-called *Slavophiles* and *Westernisers* on the identity of Russia.

Russian visitors to Europe started making comparisons already in the eighteenth century. The comparisons were always ambiguous: on the one hand, Russia seemed to be a backward country in need of urgent modernisation, while on the other hand, Russian noble travellers abhorred what they perceived as the petty bourgeois lifestyle of Western Europe. Thus, already Denis Fonvisin, a writer and memoirist of the eighteenth century, during his European travel complained: 'money is the first God of this land. Moral corruption has reached the degree that mean acts are not punished even by contempt . . .' (Fonvisin 1959: 461). Nikolay Gogol, with his aesthetic mindset, thought that only comparatively backward Italy managed to preserve the creative spirit, which long ago used to penetrate Western Europe: 'All Europe is only to look at, and Italy is to live in' (Zenkovskiy 1926: 50).

One should also remember the fact that the Russian nobility of this time often did not read Russian at all and spoke it only as a second language. Their first language was French, and English and German were also widely spoken. Peter the Great's reforms created a Russian European nobility, who lived in Russia as if in a foreign colony. This unfortunate divide persisted throughout the nineteenth century. The noble 'European' stratum was gradually widening and in the 1860s it started to include lower classes, mostly sons of the clergy, to form a peculiar social phenomenon: a rationalistic intelligentsia. Although they started to talk and to write Russian, their rationalistic mindset differed greatly from the Orthodox mysticism of their own fathers and of the majority of the peasant population. This 'intelligentsia–people' divide, so characteristic of Russian culture of the nineteenth century was, so to speak, the internal dimension of a growing awareness of the difference between Russia and Western Europe. It is at this time that Russia started to understand itself as East in contrast to the West of European culture.

In different times the basic cleavage of Russian society has been conceptualised differently: as the East–West contradiction, as the Orthodoxy–rational science divide, and so on, but it is the 'intelligentsia–people (*narod*)' opposition that became the idée fixe for all Russian literature. Thus, the famous Russian Husserlian philosopher, Gustav Shpet (1879–1937), described this problem of Russia as the main problem of Russian philosophy:

the 'people', and the 'intelligentsia' as the creative spokesman of the people, are related to one another both philosophically and culturally. Russian philosophy approaches its problem of *Russia* as the problem of the relations of the above-mentioned terms, sometimes from the side of 'the people', sometimes from the side of the 'intelligentsia', but always solves the only problem, the problem of the relation itself. The difference and even opposition of the answers – *sub specie* of the people and *sub specie* of the intelligentsia – defines the peculiar dialectics of Russian philosophy . . . (Shpet 2008: 76)

Internal and external divides reinforced each other: those critical of Western Europe also wanted to correct the excesses of Russian enlightenment and to find a specific Russian way in modern civilisation; those who thought of the West as the best implementation of modern civilisation naturally wanted to finish what Peter the Great had only started and to 'Westernise' the whole country. The split itself, however, has always been understood as a symptom of a deadly disease of Russian culture. *Westernisers* of the early nineteenth century saw the nature of this illness in the ignorance and backwardness of the people, while *Slavophiles* of the time interpreted the divide as a deadly split between borrowed enlightenment and original Russian life. One of the fathers of Slavophilism, Alexey Khomyakov, in his article of 1845 called this borrowed science 'colonial' (Khomyakov 1900: 24) and vehemently condemned its discord with the life that had created great Russia 'before foreign science came to gild its tops' (Khomyakov 1900: 22). Being a follower of Schelling and a lover of Britain, Khomyakov, however, thought that scholarship (especially in the social sciences and humanities) must correspond to the life of the nation, must be of the same roots, so to speak. The absence of such correspondence led to a situation in which 'there was knowledge in the upper classes, but this knowledge was absolutely remote from life; there was life in the lower classes, but this life never rose to consciousness' (Khomyakov 1900: 22). This split was the primary object of analysis for Russian philosophy and sociology and arguably also became one of the reasons for the Russian Revolution.

The Westernisers were the first to start this discussion. It was a brilliant noble officer, a participant in the war against Napoleon, mystical philosopher, younger friend of the great Russian historian, Karamzin, and older associate of the great Russian poet, Pushkin, Peter Chaadayev, who in 1829–31 in his 'Philosophical Letters' (written, by the way, in French) vehemently criticised Russia as a country that had deviated from the ways of humankind:

One of the saddest features of our peculiar civilisation is that we are only discovering the truths that have already become truisms in other places and even among the peoples lagging far behind us. This is because we were never united with other peoples; we do not belong to any great families of humankind; we belong neither to the West nor to the East, and we do not have the traditions of either of them. As if standing out of time, we were not touched by the world-wide education of humankind. (Chaadayev 1914b: 110)

Russian spiritual life, according to Chaadayev, is very underdeveloped. However:

standing between two main parts of the world, East and West, resting with one elbow against China and with the other against Germany, we should have linked in us both principles of the spirit, imagination and reason, and should have combined in our civilisation the history of the whole globe. This, however, was not the destiny designated for us by Providence. (Chaadayev 1914b: 116)

Being an ardent preacher of the Catholic unity of Europe and of the beneficial influence of Catholicism upon the formation of European civilisation, he naturally saw the first cause of this unfortunate deviation of Russia in that it had borrowed its Christianity from the 'miserable Byzantine, deeply despised by (European) peoples' (Chaadayev 1914b: 118). Separated from the rest of Europe, Russia became a victim of the Tatar yoke, and, after liberation from it, a victim of the yoke of its own state power, which succeeded the Tatars in its despotism (Chaadayev 1914b: 111). This characterisation was partly a result of what Chaadayev saw in Russia after he came back from his foreign trip. This was a new Russia of the conservative reaction of Nicholas I, when all Chaadayev's Decembrist friends were either in prison or in Siberia (see Gershenzon 1908: 63–4). *Philosophical Letters*, in spite of all their 'social mysticism' (Gershenzon 1908: 64), became a manifesto for the later Westernisers.

Chaadayev, of course, was very far from unbelieving in Russia. At the beginning of the 1830s he even wrote to Nicolas I and rather naively offered his services as a counsellor to the government. After the publication of his first 'Philosophical Letter', Chaadayev, however, was pronounced insane and was subjected to humiliating daily medical examinations. In his *Apology of the Insane*, written in 1837, he made the turn, which became so distinctive for almost all Russian Westernisers –

from Chaadayev to Herzen and for all Russian socialists – from Herzen to Lenin. For Chaadayev, Russia was so weak and backward because Providence had saved it for a much greater mission (Gershenzon 1908: 150–1). This mission resided in 'solving most of the problems of the social order, fulfilling the majority of the ideas generated by the older societies, and answering the most important questions that humankind faces' (Chaadayev 1914a: 227). To do this, however, Russia would have to reject all old prejudices and truly become European, would have to fulfil what had been started by Peter the Great.

'Peter the Great', emphasises Chaadayev, 'found at home only a blank sheet of paper and wrote with his own strong hand the words *Europe* and *West*; and we belong to Europe and the West ever since' (Chaadayev 1914a: 220). East and West for him are two main parts of the world, corresponding to two principles, two ideas. The principle of the East is deep contemplation of the mind, which leaves the whole Earth to the arbitrariness of the social authorities. The idea of the West is a notion of action inspired by reason. East was the first to be prominent in the history of humankind, while modernity is rather the time of the West. Now:

> we live in the East of Europe . . . however we never belonged to the East. The East has its own history which has nothing to do with ours. . . . We are simply northern people, both in terms of our climate and in terms of our ideas . . . It is true that some of our regions border on the states of the East, but our centres, our life are elsewhere; our life will not be there until . . . a new geological cataclysm throws southern organisms into the polar ices. (Chaadayev 1914a: 224)

This was not, however, a mere repetition of the idea of the Northern European Russia of the eighteenth century. For Chaadayev, his great Russia is still in the future, and this future depends on the fulfilment of the Westernising vision of Peter the Great.

The leader of the first Slavophiles, Alexey Khomyakov, did not really disagree with this last conclusion. His idea was also to find Russia's own place in the modern world, but he thought that this should be done by addressing history across a longer duration than the history of Imperial Russia, which started with Peter the Great. His main disagreement with Chaadayev is exactly about the exaggeration that Peter the Great found in Russia only a blank sheet of paper. In 1836, answering Chaadayev, he exclaims:

Do not we ourselves break the unity with impressions of our past? Why are our tops being separated from the bottom? Why do they live in the motherland as if they were guests; why do they not only speak and write, but also think in the foreign ways? (Khomyakov 1994a: 452)

Khomyakov sees the distinctiveness of Russia in its Slavic character. For him the Slavic world, which has not disgraced itself with the crimes of other Europeans, 'safeguards for humankind, if not an embryo, then the possibility of renewal' (Khomyakov 1994b: 493). Khomyakov, being one of the most educated people of his time, elaborated a complex and detailed philosophy of history, based upon findings of comparative and historical linguistics, history of religion, geography and ethnography. Elements of this philosophy were incorporated in his *Semiramis* – an impressive historical, linguistic and philosophical treatise (written in the 1840s).

According to Khomyakov, geography and history can be organised according to tribes, according to faiths and according to states. And it was only the history of the third type that had been satisfactorily developed by modern scholarship. That is why Khomyakov himself focused upon the histories of faiths and tribes with a clear purpose in mind – to give Slavic peoples the place in world history that they, according to him, deserved.

The whole history of humankind in this philosophy is defined by the struggle of the Global North and South in the form of *Iranian* and *Kushite* principles. These principles, being the principles of religion, define also the main features of the *enlightenment* of the particular peoples and, thus, penetrate the whole culture of the nations and tribes (Khomyakov 1994c: 442).

The Iranian, Northern principle is a principle of the freedom of creative spirit, and produced spiritual, ethical religions of the Absolute. The Kushite, Southern (actually Ethiopian, African) principle is a principle of material necessity, and produced religions worshipping natural life and its laws (Khomyakov 1994c: 190–1). The symbol of life in Kushism is a snake and ophiolatry is a distinctive feature of its religion. Hostility to the snake, which can be found in many religions and mythologies (from Judaism to the Hercules myths) is, then, a characteristic feature of the Iranian beliefs (Khomyakov 1994c: 190). Kushism is naturally inclined to pantheism and emanatism, while Iranism is disposed to monotheism and creationism (Khomyakov 1994c: 199, 203). Iran's invention is poetry and philosophy, while the main art of Kush is architecture: 'colossi of poetry and thought were rising in the North against the stone colossi of the South' (Khomyakov 1994c: 324).

Khomyakov interprets all cultures as formed by the struggle of the two principles. Sometimes they mix, sometimes they form fighting religions and denominations, but it is almost always possible to identify the primary source. Thus, although ancient Greek religion is a combination of Iranism and Kushism, in Hercules' fight with the Hydra Khomyakov sees the story of the Iranian fight with the Southern snake and thus identifies this myth as a Northern one. In the religion of Maya, however, he discerns Kushism:

> the same mass of the temples and buildings, the same insanity of the stonemasons . . . the same frenzy of the debauchery, the same worshipping-producing force of the matter, and especially the same holiness of the snake, which so sharply separates the Egyptian and Phoenician world from the Iranian one. (Khomyakov 1994c: 236)

In India both principles coexist in purely Iranian Brahmanism with Northern Vishnuism on the one hand and in almost absolutely Kushite Shivaism with its Buddhist alter ego on the other hand (Khomyakov 1994c: 176).

The struggle of Global North and South is, thus, the main content of world history. It is obvious for Khomyakov that even if Kushite materialism so easily spoils Iranian spirituality, a final victory is on the side of the Northern principle:

> An inexplicable law, giving everywhere victory to the North over the South, has been fulfilled in Greece as it has been fulfilled in the struggle of Persia with Egypt, of Rome with Carthage, of the Turk with the Arabian, of the Teuton with the Roman. The animal skin, club and sword of the Iranian superseded the Kushite's armour and arrow. (Khomyakov 1994c: 210)

The spiritual North always supersedes the material South.

Of all Iranian languages, the Slavic ones along with Sanskrit are, according to Khomyakov, the closest to the original proto-language. Khomyakov discovered a stunning parallelism between the Russian and Sanskrit languages and even published an impressive *Comparison of Russian and Sanskrit Words* (Khomyakov 1904). According to him, both the Slavic tribes and the Brahmans of India originated in eastern and north-eastern Iran, while all other Iranian European ethnic groups (including Celtic, Hellenic and Teutonic ones) belonged to western and south-western Iran (Khomyakov 1994c: 380). Kushism influenced the Iranian south so that ancient German or Teutonic tribes moved away from the pure and peaceful Iranian spirituality.

Khomyakov thinks that Slavic groups *colonised* Europe before in their turn they were *conquered* by the Germanic tribes (Khomyakov 1994c: 363). The conquerors were aristocratic and militant nomads, while the Slavic tribes represented peaceful democratic farmers, whose character-istic features were tolerance and an aspiration for universal values. As one piece of evidence of the historical enslavement of the Slavs by the Teutons, Khomyakov refers to the etymology of 'slave' (Latin *Sclavus*) from Slav (Khomyakov 1994c: 90). Interestingly, he also links the spreading of the three branches of Christianity with this opposition of the German and Slavic tribes. Catholicism, the product of Rome, spread in the western part of the Roman Empire, which had been conquered by the Teutonic tribes. This is a branch of Christianity that combines Roman logical formalism with the Hellenic worship of beauty. The Byzantine Empire, according to Khomyakov, was over-populated by Slavs, who influenced its Christianity greatly, bringing to the Orthodoxy symbols and images that the Eastern branch of Christianity treated, however, freely. The German Reformation was also, for Khomyakov, the result of the Slavic influence (through occupied Slavic territories in Prussia and such Slavic pre-reformers as Jan Hus), due to which Christianity abandoned Roman formalism, but was left shapeless.

In this way three Christian teachings were formed in Europe . . .: a German, shapeless one; Eastern or Greek and Slavic, dressed in symbols, but free from these symbols; Western or Roman, logical in its form like the civic law of Rome and bending its knees before the beauty of the symbol like Hellenic antiquity. (Khomyakov 1994c: 306)

Thus, for Khomyakov and other Slavophiles, Russia as a leader of Slavdom is a deeply European country, even if this *Europeanness* is dif-ferent (and sometimes really opposite) to the Roman and German civi-lisation of Western Europe. With the discussion between *Slavophiles* and *Westernisers*, the old understanding of Russia as a Northern country, however, started to transform into the idea of Russia as a

European East, Orthodox and Slavic world. The differences between the parties in this discussion, however, in reality were not too great, which enabled another great political philosopher of the Westernisers' camp, Alexander Herzen, to say in his memoirs some ten to fifteen years later: 'The struggle between us is over long ago and we have extended hands to each other' (Herzen 1946: 284).

Although the Slavophiles' philosophy seemed to be quite close to the official ideology of the reactionary government of Nicolas I, expressed in the famous triad *Orthodoxy, Autocracy and Nationality*, in reality sometimes it was almost as critical of the conservative government as the ideology of socialist Westernisers was. It is wrong to try to describe the parts in its discussion along the traditional political lines of a left–right or reactionary–progressivist divide. The main question in this discussion was about the historical identity of Russia and of its place in the modern world.

Let us recall here again that the question was not only (and even not so much) about how Russia relates to Europe, but how it should be reformed (or rather, how it should be modernised): according to Western European patterns or in its own peculiarly Russian way. The question also concerned the internal Russian division between the people and the intelligentsia, between Orthodoxy and rational thinking; in short, between the internal West and East of Russian culture. In the final analysis both Slavophiles and Westernisers arrived at the same conclusion on the peculiarity of the Russian way of being modern. Two disillusionments, however, still had to happen: with the European revolutions in 1848–9 and with the Crimean War in 1853–6.

European revolutions (and especially the French Revolution of 1848) witnessed by Russian socialist *Westernisers* had a catastrophic influence on their perception of Europe as a land of the Great French Revolution. Instead of the leader of progress they now found the land of petty bourgeois shopkeepers. The Second (this time socialist) Rome of Europe had again (and archetypically) fallen, ceding its place to the Third Rome of Russia. On an international scale, through its contribution to the defeat of European revolution, the conservative Russia of Nicolas I gained the status of the 'European gendarme', which led to a strengthening of its power and to its interference in all European and Middle Eastern affairs. In its turn, it contributed to the European fear of a powerful, aggressive Russia and to the rise of anti-Russian propaganda, which reached its culmination during the Crimean War. The events of 1848–56, thus, contributed to the widening of the gap between

Russia and Western Europe, and, in its turn, to new attempts at repositioning Russia as an independent Eastern European civilisation.

Disappointment in Europe during and before the revolutionary events of 1848 in France led socialist and Hegelian philosopher Herzen to a negation of progress and of the goal of history as such. Already at the end of 1847 he wrote: 'the goal of each generation is the generation itself. Nature never makes generations the means for the achievement of the future; it does not care about the future . . . it has a heart of the bayadere and Bacchante' (Herzen 1948: 31). 'In history everything is improvisation, everything – will, everything – *ex tempore*, there are no limits and itineraries ahead; there are conditions, holy anxiety, the fire of life . . .' (Herzen 1948: 33). This theoretical rebellion against a Hegelian logic of history together with disappointment in European societies, penetrated with the spirit of shopkeepers, led Herzen to the greatest crisis of his life. 'I am not dead, but I became old', wrote Herzen in Paris immediately after the events of June 1848 (Herzen 1948: 38).

In the 'betrayal of shopkeepers' he saw evidence of the imminent death of Europe:

Everything becomes petty and withers on the exhausted soil: there are no talents, there is no creativity, there is no power of thought, there is no power of will; this world has outlived the times of its fame . . . the brilliant epoch of industry is passing away . . . the lifestyle is getting less and less elegant and less graceful, everybody is huddling up, is afraid, everybody lives like a shopkeeper; the manners of the petty bourgeoisie have become common . . . everything is temporary, is rented, is shaky. (Herzen 1948: 53)

This world is dying and its death is similar to the collapse of Rome, with inevitable dark ages to come:

Don't you see the new Christians going to build, new barbarians going to destroy? They are ready; they are like lava stirring heavily under the earth, inside the mountains. When their hour comes, Herculaneum and Pompeii will disappear, both good and bad, both right and wrong die together. This will be no judgment, no punishment, but cataclysm, overturn. (Herzen 1948: 54)

Socialism in modernity corresponds to Christianity of the time of the fall of Rome. Like Christianity it is unrealisable. Like any ideology it is not going to build Paradise on Earth. Like any ideology it is temporary:

> Socialism will develop ... up to its extreme consequences, up to absurdity. Then again the cry of denial will be extorted from the titanic chest of the revolutionary minority ... socialism will take the place of the today's conservatism and will be overcome by the coming revolution unknown to us. (Herzen 1948: 103)

Herzen's advice to intellectuals is Nietzschean (before Nietzsche) and stoic – to preach death and to enjoy private life:

> Preach the message of death, point to the people each new wound in the chest of the old world, each success of destruction; point out the sickliness of its intentions, the pettiness of its pursuits ... preach *death* as a good message of the coming expiation. (Herzen 1948: 71)

> Do you remember the Roman philosophers of the first ages of Christianity? Their position had many similarities with ours: present and future slipped away from them, they were hostile to the past ... One good which remained for these foreigners of their time was a clear conscience, a consolatory awareness that they were not afraid of the truth ... they also had another good: personal relations ... some sun, sea or mountains in the distance, noisy greens, a warm climate ... (Herzen 1948: 99)

Herzen could not stop here, and his disappointment with the fallen Rome of modern Europe led him to almost religious faith in the Third Rome of Russia. 'Belief in Russia saved me on the edge of moral death', he wrote in 1858 (Herzen 1955: 14). Here we see this almost illogical move, which we have already noticed as archetypical for Russian thought of the nineteenth century. The future belongs to Russia exactly because this country is so weak and backward. In Europe liberals betrayed revolution out of fear, while Russia has nothing to fear: 'Liberals are afraid to lose their freedom – we do not have freedom ... they are afraid of losing personal rights – we still must obtain them ... Europe is sinking because it cannot abandon its cargo, which contains a lot of jewels ...' (Herzen 1955: 13). Of course, these all are negative benefits, but Herzen also finds a positive one: the peasant community as a genuinely Russian form of 'spontaneous communism'. In Russia of the nineteenth century land was used and owned by communities of peasants. This backward (traditional Slavic) institution gave to the Russian socialists hope that Russia would be able to avoid the extremes of the coming catastrophe and to be the first to enter the new world: 'Do not be afraid, be calm, our field has a lightning-rod – communal ownership of the land!' (Herzen 1955: 13).

Thus, in Herzen, and later – in *narodniki* – Slavophiles meet with Westernisers, and Russia is understood as a peculiar civilisation, different from Western Europe. Both camps, however, hoped that it had something to say to Western Europe and probably even possessed the capacity to save it from the extremes of the coming thunderstorm. In Russia they saw *the hope of Western Europe* – the messianic idea, which became so prominent in Soviet times. A very powerful idea of the *distinctiveness* of the Russian way in modernity was present in both camps. Neither of them, by the way, was counter-modern or counter-European, in spite of being critical both of modernity and of Europe. England, for Khomyakov, was 'a country of holy miracles' and the philosopher himself contributed to these technological miracles through patenting his several inventions in London, one of which was a powerful steam engine. Herzen's Nietzschean rejection of Europe was based upon its inability to live up to its own principles. For both the Russian way was alternatively European and alternatively modern.

The gap between Western Europe and Russia was, however, gradually widening. Since the mid-1840s anti-Russian propaganda in Western Europe had been increasing and it reached its culmination during the Crimean War, which had been widely understood both in Russia and in Europe as a war of the West against a strengthening Russia. Lord Palmerston had famously planned the partition of the Russian Empire and presented the Crimean War as a war of civilisation against barbarism. In his speech in the House of Commons on 31 March 1854, Lord Palmerston declared

> But what I want the Government to say is, that by the help of God, and relying on the stout hearts and strong arms of England, we shall do our utmost to carry this war to such an issue as will prevent Russia hereafter from returning to her aggressions, and from threatening the independence, freedom, and civilisation of Europe—that we shall take care to reduce her within limits beyond which she will not hereafter be able to go. (Palmerston 1854)

Some political activists in today's Russia, by the way, do find quick and easy comparisons with the anti-Russian propaganda in today's Crimean and Ukrainian crisis. In spite of such similarities, of course, the post-Cold War relations between Russia and Western Europe are totally different from what they were in the colonial and imperial world of the nineteenth century.

In the nineteenth century the anti-Russian sentiments of European societies were perceived in Russia as a mean betrayal by the West. While in Russia the war was presented as a defence of Orthodox peoples and Slavs, oppressed by the Ottoman Empire, in the West it was perceived as an aggressive attempt to gain control of the Bosporus and possess Constantinople. If in the Napoleonic Wars Russian society did not see enmity on behalf of Western Europe as such, but only menace on the part of Napoleon, in the Crimean War

> Russian society felt with extreme pain that in fact the West 'took up the arms' against Russia to hit it and to weaken its influence among Slavs. For the first time in this war Slavic self-consciousness ha[d] been thunderstruck by the West's deep hatred of Slavdom. (Zenkovskiy 1926: 123)

The great Russian poet, diplomat and rather conservative political thinker, Fedor Tutchev, wrote during the war: 'It could be foreseen long ago that this rabid hate ... which was increasingly stirred up year by year, would eventually break loose. This moment came' (see Aksakov 1886: 250). '[T]he whole West came to demonstrate its denial of Russia and to block up its road to the future' (Tutchev 2005: 175). The *misunderstanding* between the West and Russia was mutual; it has been recurrently present since this time and, unfortunately, does dominate their interrelations today. Western Europe still (and sometimes fairly) sees Russia as a threat to the international domination of modern liberal democracy, while Russia charges it (equally not without the foundation) with double standards and a strange suspicion towards a fellow European nation.

If both the *Slavism* of early Slavophiles and the *peasant communism* of early socialists and *narodniks* were not in any sense anti-Western, perceiving Russia rather as *the other* of Europe, a kind of alter ego, after the 1850s their successors defended Russia's radical otherness, which was too often directed *against* Western Europe. Interestingly, this time also witnessed the birth of organic and civilisational approaches in

Russian sociology, which further underpinned the idea of the peculiar young Russian world poised to substitute a dying European civilisation. Nikolay Danilevskiy and Konstantin Leontiev are probably two the most interesting authors in this respect.

Although the main sociological book *Russia and Europe* by the natural scientist Danilevskiy was published in 1869, it starts with a detailed description of the injustices that led to the Crimean War (Danilevskiy 2016: 13–39). The main starting questions he asks are 'Why is Europe hostile to Russia?' (Danilevskiy 2016: 39–86), 'Is Russia Europe?' (Danilevskiy 2016: 87–109) and 'Is European civilisation identical with universal civilisation?' (Danilevskiy 2016: 111–37). Danilevskiy emphasises the fact that:

> Europe does not recognise us as her kin. She sees in Russia and in Slavs in general something alien to her, but at the same time something that cannot be for her the raw material . . . Therefore Europe sees in Russia and in Slavdom not only an alien, but also an inimical, principle. (Danilevskiy 2016: 76)

Russia is not Europe at all. Danilevskiy describes it almost in Chaadayev's words:

> [Russia] was not nourished from any of the roots with which Europe absorbed both salutary and harmful juices immediately from the soil of the ancient world destroyed by her; was not nourished with those roots also, which draw nourishment from the depth of the German spirit. (Danilevskiy 2016: 94)

Fighting Eurocentrism and speaking highly of China, Danilevskiy rethinks the notion of progress and makes it relative to particular civilisations. Each civilisation has its own principle, its own idea, the development of which is the progress of this particular civilisation: 'Progress . . . is not an exclusive Western or European privilege, and stagnation is not an exclusive Eastern or Asian stigma; both are only characteristic signs of the age of the people . . .' (Danilevskiy 2016: 117). If this is so, there are no universal things in history and 'progress does not consist in going in one direction, but in walking in different directions all over the field of human historical activity . . .' (Danilevskiy 2016: 132).

The main unit of history is not humankind, then, but some 'cultural-historical types'. These units are similar to living organisms and go through their own stages of long primary growth (the 'ethnographic period'), short blooming (the 'civilisation stage') and senile apathy (Danilevskiy 2016: 160). Thus, the idea of 'infinite development or infinite progress' should be 'counted among the most extreme absurdities' (Danilevskiy 2016: 163). Danilevskiy's theory of 'cultural-historical types' is rather elaborate and detailed and cannot be discussed here. Let us mention only that he counts ten developed types (Chaldean, Hebrew, Arab, Indian, Persian, Greek, Roman or ancient Italian, Germanic, Egyptian and Chinese) and looks forward to the blooming of the Slavic one (Danilevskiy 2016: 134). One of the main laws is that the cultural-historical types can fully develop only when they enjoy political independence and form a state or a system of states. Another one is that the principles of civilisation cannot be transferred from one cultural-historical type to another.

Politically it means that all Slavic peoples must gain independence and together form a political system of states. This is a *conditio sine qua non* of their development:

> for each Slav: Russian, Czech, Serb, Croatian . . . the idea of Slavdom must be the highest idea, higher than science, higher than liberty, higher than enlightenment . . . simply because none of them is reachable without its implementation, without spiritually, nationally and politically distinctive, independent Slavdom . . . (Danilevskiy 2016: 189)

Danilevskiy's political pan-Slavism was, thus, a natural result of his theory.

Importantly, Europe, according to Danilevskiy, was drooping. The blooming epoch of Europe was the sixteenth and seventeenth centuries, when 'Rafael, Michelangelo and Correggio painted, Shakespeare wrote his dramas, Kepler, Galileo, Bacon and Descartes laid the foundations of the new thinking . . .' (Danilevskiy 2016: 249). This blooming time was over for Europe; even if it had not yet rotted, it was getting old. Slavdom, however, was only advancing onto the stage of history. It still had everything ahead, while for Europe the best time was over. Western Europe's hatred of Slavdom was partly explained by this fact. Interestingly, Oswald Spengler, thirty-nine years later in his *Decline of the West*, repeated this conclusion (Spengler 1926), although it is not clear if he was really acquainted with Danilevskiy's theory.

According to Danilevskiy, there are four main activities, through participating in which different cultural-historical types fulfil their destiny. These activities are: (1) religious activity, through which humans relate to God; (2) cultural activity, through which human society interacts with the external world: science, art and industry; (3) political activity, in which human beings directly relate to each other; and (4) social and economic activity, in which humans relate to each other, not directly, but through the conditions created by the use of external things (Danilevskiy 2016: 677). The first cultural-historical types were syncretic and did not focus on any particular activity. The Jewish talent, however, was religion; the Hellenic type focused upon the arts and aesthetics; Roman civilisation reached perfection in politics.

The European cultural-historical type was much more complex and achieved prominence both in politics and in culture. Moreover, the cultural activity of the Europeans was great in all three spheres of science, art and industry. Only in art Europe 'should yield the pass to the Greeks in the degree of the perfection of the results achieved'. The Europeans, however, widened the sphere of art and found their own 'new ways' in it (Danilevskiy 2016: 687).

As far as the young Slavic type is concerned, it is too early to mention its achievements, but Danilevskiy finds promising signs in all four main human activities, thus hoping that 'the Slavic type will be the first full four-foundational cultural-historical type. The most original of its features will be the first satisfactory solution of the social-economic problem' (Danilevskiy 2016: 722). Again as it was for both Westernisers and Slavophiles, so too for Danilevskiy communal land-ownership is the main evidence of Russia's ability to produce a 'just social-economic organisation' (Danilevskiy 2016: 728). This hope later became the main driver of the Russian Revolution and of the grandiose communist experiment of the twentieth century. The system of communal land-ownership in some forms existed up to the Soviet collectivisation of 1928–37, but started to deteriorate already by the beginning of the twentieth century.

Politically and intellectually Danilevskiy is really ambiguous. On the one hand, his pan-Slavism and Russian nationalism can be seen as an underpinning of nascent fascist, or in any case extreme right, political sentiments. They have been shared by many great philosophers and writers, including, for example, Dostoyevskiy, who called Danilevskiy's book the 'future handbook of all Russians for a long time' and praised its conclusions as miraculously coinciding with his own 'conclusions and persuasions' (Dostoyevskiy 1986: 30). On the other hand, both early

Slavophiles and Danilevskiy contributed greatly to the establishment of civilisational theory in Russia, to a criticism of the excesses of colonial Eurocentrism of the time, and in the final analysis, to an understanding of Russia as a peculiar, distinct civilisation existing alongside the great European world. The Slavophiles were predecessors of the theories of multiple modernities on the Russian soil of the nineteenth century.

The idea of Russia as a European, Christian East has also been shared by a follower of both Danilevskiy and Herzen, a very original Russian conservative thinker and diplomat, Konstantin Leontiev, who, however, was in doubt about the putative benefits of communal land-ownership and did not aspire to pan-Slavic unity at all. If for Danilevskiy a 'cultural-historical type' is a linguistic unity, for Leontiev neither language nor 'tribe' are really important. For him civilisations are defined by the state power, by culture and by religion. Tribal Slavdom is too diverse or weak in these respects and cannot provide a stable ground for distinctive development.

Leontiev focused on the Byzantine roots of Russian culture instead. For him 'to love a tribe for its being the tribe is a strain and a falsehood'; what matters are religious and state ideas (Leontiev 1996: 108). These Byzantine ideas that formed the great Russian culture were, according to Leontiev, autocracy (*Samoderzhavie*) and orthodoxy (*Pravoslaviye*). 'It was Byzantism that gave us all our power in our struggle with Poland, Sweden, France and Turkey. Under its banner we will be able to withstand the onset of an international Europe as a whole . . .' (Leontiev 1996: 104).

In a short book published in 1875 under the name *Byzantism and Slavdom* Leontiev endeavoured to provide a theoretical underpinning for his conservatism, which older Slavophiles had famously charged with preaching a 'lascivious cult of the truncheon' (Ivan Aksakov, quoted in Solovyev 1914a: 507). Any development, according to Leontiev, is an 'ascent from the simplest to the most complex, gradual individualisation and separation from the external world on the one hand and from . . . all similar and related phenomena' (Leontiev 1996: 125). The culmination of development is 'the highest degree of complexity, united by some internal despotic unity' (Leontiev 1996: 126). This is true for any phenomenon of an organic nature. Everything in the developed organism is subjected to the form of this organism, to the 'despotism of the internal idea' (Leontiev 1996: 129). In decrepit and dying organisms, at the same time, forms are dissolving, fading and the unity of the organism is gradually destroyed.

Cultures are similar to organisms in their development; they all go through the three stages of '(1) primary simplicity, (2) blooming complexity, and (3) secondary mixing simplification' (Leontiev 1996: 129). Blooming cultures are characterised by complex differences, which are so characteristic of aristocratism, and by a despotic and autocratic unity of the state, which holds together different parts of the whole. That is why Leontiev thinks that egalitarianism and liberalism, equality and liberty, are both phenomena of a dying culture. They both are ruinous for the culture: 'culture is nothing else but distinctiveness; and distinctiveness today almost everywhere is dying primarily because of political freedom. Individualism is killing the individuality of people, regions and nations' (Leontiev 1996: 108). That is why for him the Chinese and the Turk are 'of course more cultural than the Belgian and the Swiss' (Leontiev 1996: 108).

Egalitarian and liberal progress 'struggling with every despotism . . . is nothing else but the process of decay, the process of . . . secondary simplification of the whole and of the mixing of the components . . .'. It is similar in character to any destructive process in nature, such as burning, the melting of ice or any deadly illness, which transforms blooming organisms into equal skeletons and free atoms (Leontiev 1996: 130). Conservatism is the only responsible political philosophy in a time of decay, while every progressivist is right at the very beginning of cultural development.

The problem with Europe and Russia was that for both of them the blooming period was over. In the history of humankind no state had lived for more than twelve centuries, and the majority of them had existed for a much shorter period of time (Leontiev 1996: 138). Europe was a bit older than Russia, but Russia was not really young either. Leontiev was rather ruthless in his verdict on Russia: 'millennial poverty of the creative spirit is still no guarantee of a rich harvest to come' (Leontiev 1996: 154). But the most dangerous thing Russia could do at the time would be to follow the European path.

The problem was that, unlike ancient civilisations, Europe consciously destroyed itself and took senile illness for the ideal:

To tear her ancient chest to pieces Europe believed in democratic progress not as in . . . a step towards a new inequality, a new organisation, a new saving despotism of the form . . . she believed in democratisation, in mixing, in equalisation as the ideal of the state itself. (Leontiev 1996: 147)

The majority of European Slavs shared this pernicious belief and therefore could not be of help to Russia. Only the strong Byzantine principles of deep, Orthodox religious faith and despotic Eastern autocracy could save Russia from an untimely death caused by egalitarian and democratic progress.

Leontiev, however, would not have been Russian if he had not tried to outline a peculiar Russian mission for Europe. Russia must be powerful, for if the West fell and anarchy prevailed, she would be able to save what was still worth saving. If, however, the West took the opportunity to return to its former disciplined state, then Russia still should be powerful in order to be equal to the Western countries (Leontiev 1996: 152).

Leontiev is certainly one of the most peculiar Russian philosophers, in whom extreme conservatism and a fascist aspiration towards a totality of despotic unity are accompanied by a deep melancholy at the decay of the times and by an aesthetic horror of the artist confronting the future domination of mediocrity. Interestingly one of his most respected sources was the left socialist philosophy of Herzen, whose aestheticism led him to a similar melancholy and criticism of modernity. In this sense both Herzen and Leontiev are similar to Nietzsche. There is, by the way, some evidence that Nietzsche knew Herzen's works through his close friend, writer Malwida von Meysenbug, who was also a teacher of Herzen's children. The striking similarity between Herzen's *From Another Shore* and Nietzschean philosophy can be explained only by a direct influence. Leontiev's Nietzscheism is also explained by the direct influence of Herzen. In any case, his political views are on the extreme right end of the political spectrum. This extreme conservatism in both Leontiev and Danilevskiy is also underpinned by their naturalism: the idea of a similarity of civilisations to living organisms inevitably led them to the notion of civilisation passing through periods of birth, development, blooming and decay. In the second half of the twentieth century a similar naturalism led the famous ethnographer Lev Gumilev to similar (although more moderate) political sentiments.

In sum, we can see here that in the majority of the nineteenth-century debates Russia was discussed as a distinct Eastern European or Eastern Christian country. Byzantine, Slavdom as well as the Russian peasant community with its communal land-ownership were the main reference points of these debates. Importantly, the discussions were not simply concerned with the geopolitical issues of where Russia belongs, but also with the ways of modernising Russian internal life and with the problem of the internal Russian divide of the European intelligentsia and Eastern Christian people. That is why the questions of the East and West, of Europe and Slavdom, of Christianity and rational science, are still so important for the Russian identity.

Russia as an Asian power

In this quest for identity the fact that the main territory of Russia is in the Asian part of the country has been rather overshadowed by the discussions of European, Slavic or Byzantine heritage. Feodor Dostoyevskiy in his *Writer's Diary* complained that 'all our Russian Asia, including Siberia, is for Russia still like an appendage, which our European Russia doesn't want to take an interest in. We are, they say, Europe; what should we do in Asia?' (Dostoyevskiy 1984: 32). He himself, however, thought that there should be a new 'turn to the East', since the vital interests of Russia were there. He followed Danilevskiy, who thought that it was in Russia's interests not to free Europe from Napoleon, but to make an agreement with him, which Napoleon himself reportedly sought to advance (Danilevskiy 2016: 64–6). If, however, for Danilevskiy pursuing Russian interests in coming to an agreement with Napoleon would have meant the liberation of the Slavs from Austrian and Turkish rule, Dostoyevskiy thought that Russia in this case would have been able to advance in the East, leaving Europe to Napoleon (Dostoyevskiy 1984: 34).

Russia's mission was in Asia. Although she should not 'leave Europe for good' since:

> Europe is also mother to us . . . our second mother . . . [her] civilising mission in Asia . . . will elevate our spirit. . . . In Europe we were dependents and slaves; we will come to Asia as the masters. In Europe we were Tatars; in Asia we are Europeans. Our mission, our civilising mission in Asia will attract our spirit . . . Just build two railroads . . . one to Siberia, another to Central Asia . . . (Dostoyevskiy 1984: 36–7)

Interestingly, this understanding of Russia as a civilising European power in Central Asia had been widespread in nineteenth-century Europe, even if sometimes the interests of Russia there clashed with those of the British. Danilevskiy complained that the European powers sought to limit the potentially global reach of Russia to the narrow task of civilising Central Asia, ironically observing that:

> to be built during a thousand years, to create a state of eighty million people . . . only in order to treat five or six million vagabonds of Kokand, Bukhara and Khiva, possibly together with two to three million Mongolian nomads, to European civilisation . . . This is the great destiny, the world-historical role, which lies ahead of Russia as a bearer of the European Enlightenment . . . (Danilevskiy 2016: 98)

Evidently, Danilevskiy had a right to complain, since this understanding of Russia's global role seems to have been shared by many in Europe. Friedrich Engels, for example, wrote in 1851 to Marx: 'Russia, on the other hand, is truly progressive by comparison with the East. Russian rule, for all its infamy, all its Slavic dirtiness, is civilising for the Black and Caspian Seas and Central Asia, for the Bashkirs and Tatars' (Engels 2010a: 363). A bit more favourably, he predicted in 1888 that after the overthrow of tsarism, 'the noble nation of Great Russia . . . will be free to carry out its true civilising mission in Asia and to develop its vast intellectual resources in exchanges with the West' (Engels 2010b: 134). This prediction has been realised, since 'liberation' of Central Asia from 'the remains of feudalism' became one of the main directions of the eastern politics of the Soviet Union.

Of course, all these discussions of Russian civilising power happened in the context of European colonialism. It was not until the beginning of the twentieth century that this colonial discourse about Central Asia started to shatter. Soviet (contradictorily both colonial and anti-colonial) power contributed to this process domestically, while so-called *Eurasianism* influenced the discussions from abroad. In the late nineteenth century, however, Asia had been perceived either as a threat or as an object of civilising interference.

One of the greatest Russian philosophers of this time, Vladimir Solovyev, in one of his early works, the article 'Three Forces' written in 1877, spoke of Russia and the Slavs in more or less traditional words. Distinguishing the force of totalising unity, which he saw as active in the East, from the force of equally totalising individuation active in Europe, he praised Russia as a bearer of the third force, which would give harmony to an otherwise split humanity. This third force is 'revelation of the Highest Divine World and . . . the people through whom this force will work must be only a mediator between humankind and this world . . .' (Solovyev 1911: 237). If the first force in religion means worshipping a dehumanised God, and the second a godless humanity, the task of the third force is to bring God and humankind closer to each other, to create, according to the title of one of his later works, the condition of God-manhood (Solovyev 1912). The first two forces had already brought their peoples to the point of decay, and thus it was high time for the third force to become active. Russia and Slavdom were, thus, not East or West, but East-and-West, the third force, correcting the excesses of the first two forces and fulfilling the historical mission of humankind. Naturally and again archetypically:

> [the] external image of the slave . . . [and] the miserable position of Russia in economics and other respects not only cannot be an objection against her vocation, but rather confirm it. Since the highest force that the Russian people must bring to the humankind is not of this world . . . (Solovyev 1911: 239)

Later Solovyev started to doubt, and in one of his poems of 1890 (*Ex oriente lux*) he states that 'the light, which came from the East / reconciled East with the West', and he asks: 'Oh Russia! . . . / Which is the East you desire to be: / the East of Xerxes or of Christ?' (Solovyev 1974: 81). During the 1890s Solovyev's increasingly eschatological expectations were accompanied by the premonition of the 'enemy from the East' (Mochulskiy 1995: 183–4, 202–12). In 1894 he wrote the poem *Panmongolism*, the very title of which obviously positions it in contrast to the ideas of pan-Slavism. Here he describes the 'last times', when Russia (and after it all Christian Europe) is conquered by a new Mongolian invasion:

> Innumerable as locusts
> and similarly insatiable
> guarded by the unearthly power
> the tribes go to the North.

> Oh, Russia! Forget your glory:
> The two-headed Eagle is destroyed
> and yellow children for amusement
> the shreds of your flags are given.

. . .

Thus the Third Rome is lying in the dust
and a fourth shall never be. (Solovyev 1974: 104)

The same theme was present in the eschatological 'Three Conversations', where Solovyev describes the conquest of Europe by Asia, the establishment of the kingdom of the Antichrist and the unification of Christian churches as a prelude to the Doomsday and resurrection of the dead (Solovyev 1914b).

After the real Doomsday of the Russian Revolution of 1917, the symbolist poet and Solovyev's follower, Alexander Blok, had already counted Russians among the Asian tribes:

Millions are you – and hosts, yea hosts, are we
And we shall fight if war you want, take heed
Yes, we are Scythians – leafs of the Asian tree,
Our slanted eyes are bright aglow with greed. (Blok 1961: 24)

He describes the historical role of Russia as raising 'the shield up . . . / to shelter you, the European race / from the Mongolians' savage raid and sieges' (Blok 1961: 24). European hostility towards Russia (this time already Soviet) threatened to destroy the shield. This would lead, according to Blok, to the Apocalypses described by Solovyev:

we shall just watch the mortal strife
with our slanting eyes so cold and narrow.

Unmoved shall we remain when Hunnish forces
The corpses' pockets rake for plunder,
set town afire, to altars tie their horses,
burn our white brothers' bodies torn asunder. (Blok 1961: 25)

The only chance for Europe to survive is to ally with the semi-Asiatic, Scythian Russia: 'To the old world goes out our last appeal: / to work and peace invite our warming fires. / Come to our hearth, join our festive meal. / Called by the strings of our Barbarian lyres' (Blok 1961: 25).

After the Revolution the communists were looking forward to the international world revolution, and the positioning of Russia in terms of the cardinal points lost its importance. Internationalism and the global outlook of communism became the official ideology. With this orientation to the East in mind, the Soviet civilising mission in Asia became prominent in the politics of Soviet Russia. During the Cold War the struggle between the Eastern and Western blocs as the Second and the First Worlds defined the content of global politics. However, with all its internationalism and ambitions to assume the leadership of the new world, domestic Soviet politics was a kind of multiculturalism with special attention paid to the eastern republics. This attention to the East even led to the formation of a peculiar genre in Soviet cinematography – 'Easterns' (analogous with American 'Westerns'). The plot of all 'Easterns' focused upon struggles against militant gangs in Central Asia or the Caucasus during the Civil War. The most famous film of this genre, *White Sun of the Desert* (1970), combines it with the theme of the liberation of oriental women. The struggle against the 'remnants of feudalism' for the liberation of women in the Caucasus was also the focal point of another extremely popular film, the comedy *Kidnapping, Caucasian Style* (1967). This discourse of civilisation, applied to the Muslim East of the Soviet Union, was really prominent in twentieth-century Russia.

The focus on the East, although in a different form, has also been shared by some Russian exiles, who through this common interest even developed some sympathy with Soviet Russia. They represented the so-called *Eurasianism* movement (*Evraziystvo*), the ideology of which is still quite popular in some post-Soviet countries, including Russia and Kazakhstan. *Eurasianism* is thought to have been born in Sofia in 1921, when the first Eurasianists published their first volume of collected papers. However, in 1914 the famous Russian and (later) American historian Georgiy Vernadskiy (1887–1973) wrote a paper on the Russian colonisation of Siberia, which already expressed some of the Eurasianist ideas (Vernadskiy 1914). The group of the first Eurasianists included linguist Nikolai Trubetskoy, geographer Petr Savitskiy, religious philosopher Gyorgy Florovsky and writer Petr Suvchinsky. During the next several years a number of other famous intellectuals joined Eurasianism in the main centres of Russian emigration: Berlin, Prague, Warsaw, Paris, and so on. The movement split in 1928 due to disagreements about how to interpret Soviet power. If the majority of the older Eurasianists had never really been sympathising Soviets, the group of younger writers gathered in French Clamart tried 'to link Eurasianism's historical conception of Russia with an awakening Marxist political conscience' (Laruelle 2008: 20). We can also add to this mixture Nikolay Fedorov's peculiar teaching on the transformation of the nature, whose follower Nikolay Ustryalov (1890–1937) combined it with both Eurasianism and his own national-Bolshevism.

As for the Eurasianists, 'in the great mass of the lands of the Old World, where past geography discerned two continents – "Europe" and "Asia" – they started to discern a third, middle continent – Eurasia . . .' (Savitskiy 1997: 76). This continent represents a more or less 'natural' field for political, cultural and similar forms of unity. Being the 'third', it also presupposes a specific 'third' developmental trajectory – neither capitalism nor communism, neither liberalism nor dictatorship:

> In the Eurasionists' interpretation, the 'third way' was no longer the solution for a Europe stuck between the expansion of communism and the purported failure of the liberal Western model, but rather a statement of Russia's cultural irreducibility to the West. (Laruelle 2008: 26)

In the very first of their publications the Eurasianists separated themselves from the old Slavophiles because 'the concept of the "Slavdom" ha[d] not justified the hopes' of its exponents: 'We address our nationalism . . . not only to the "Slavs", but to the whole circle of peoples of the "Eurasian" world, between whom the Russian people takes a middle position' (Predchuvstviya 2002: 106). If, however, Russia existed in the midst of the Asians, it would of necessity be greatly influenced by them.

Another famous representative of the movement, Nikolai Trubetskoy, understood the Eurasian state of Russia as a central part of the former Mongolian Empire created by Genghis Khan (Trubetskoy 1995: 213). The great khan is understood by Trubetskoy as 'a bearer of the large and positive idea, and in his life the aspiration for creation of the organisation prevailed over the aspiration for destruction' (Trubetskoy 1995: 222). Being an integral part of the Mongolian Empire, Russia adopted an Asian understanding of state power. When the Russian people, however, freed themselves from the yoke, they united this idea of the state with Byzantine Orthodoxy. In this way the Mongolian idea become Russian, and 'the ideas of Genghis Khan were brought back to life, but in an absolutely new, unrecognisable form' (Trubetskoy 1995: 227). The reforms of Peter the Great were, for Trubetskoy, anti-Asian and, therefore, anti-national (Trubetskoy 1995: 243), thus leading to the 'defacement of Russia' (Trubetskoy 1995: 246). This anti-national character of the Empire made the Russian Revolution inevitable. Although the USSR partly continued with the anti-national European politics of the Empire, it for the first time 'spoke with Asians as with equals, as with fellow-sufferers' (Trubetskoy 1995: 253). The main historical aim of Russia in his day, then, was 'to realise its true nature and to return to the performance of its own historical tasks' (Trubetskoy 1995: 260). The most important feature of this historical task was attention to the East without European imperial colonialism which, according to Trubetskoy, was very alien to Russia.

Eurasianism is very much alive today. First of all, we should mention Lev Gumilev (1912–92), the son of the poets Nikolai Gumilev and Anna Akhmatova, one of the most interesting, even if highly controversial, ethnologists and ethnographers, who openly called himself 'the last Eurasianist'. In his introduction to the new edition of Trubetskoy's works, he emphasises the absence of any 'Tatar yoke' and prefers to speak rather of the 'political and military union' of Russia with the Tatars (Gumilev 1995: 41). Unfortunately, we cannot go here into the details of his fascinating theory of ethnogenesis and his interesting, rather poetical description of the history of various nomadic people around and inside Russia. It was Gumilev who revived *Eurasianism* in the new post-Soviet Russia. This movement, however, is still as ridden with contradictions as it used to be in the 1920s. Being conservative in its essence, it sometimes degenerates into an ideology of the extreme right (especially when it is politicised) and sometimes it is reduced to a generally elusive framework of loose ideas and principles. In this last vague form it is proposed by Kazakhstan's President Nazarbayev as a national idea of Kazakhstan (Nazarbayev 2015). Apart from naming one of the main Kazakh higher education schools L. N. Gumilev National Eurasian University, this 'Eurasian' idea has not provided Kazakhstan with any viable political ideology. The extreme right form of Eurasianism in contemporary Russia has found its institutional expression in the political party 'Eurasia' of Alexander Dugin (Dugin 2002).

Eurasianism in various forms seems to dominate contemporary Russian geopolitical thinking. Being inclined to geographical naturalism and primordialism, it is also prone to *Blut und Boden* types of ideology. On the other hand, since it considers Eurasia as a multicultural habitat, it is free from narrow nationalism and has a distinct anticolonial character. Being contradictory in political terms, it can be very decent academically (e.g. in Nikolai Trubetskoy, Georgiy Vernadskiy or Lev Gumilev), but also sometimes serves very conservative (and even neo-imperial) ideologies of the extreme right political parties (in

Alexander Dugin). Some versions of Eurasianism still represent a really peculiar mixture of naturalism, Marxism, Orthodoxy and Russian cosmism. This kind of mixture, however, is called for in contemporary Russia, which still cannot fully recover from the shock and stupor of the collapse of 1991.

Conclusion

For several centuries moral mapping has provided Russia not only with the basis for self-identification, but also with the frameworks for redefining its future and for solving pressing problems of the times. Russian intellectuals, writers, politicians and activists proposed solutions to policy issues on the basis of this moral mapping. That is why interpretations of Europe and Asia, of North, West and East, have always been very important in the Russian context. Close attention to Asia almost invariably meant political tensions with Europe and vice versa. Moreover, it has always been possible to identify the political standing of almost any politician or public intellectual judging from his or her interpretation of the West and East.

At the same time, Russia has never been linked to the real South: only to the South of the Asian Turkic nomads. Not too much has really been changed in this respect today. In the current political and intellectual landscape the split between Western and Eastern parties, between a European and a distinctive 'Russian' orientation, is as huge as it has ever really been in the twentieth century. The current Ukrainian and Crimean crises, the revival of the concept of a 'Russian World' (*Russkiy Mir*), the sudden return to Cold War rhetoric, and the political emphasis on the notions of sovereignty and independence in the epoch of global capital and transnational corporations all demonstrate the importance these categories still have for the Russian experience and interpretation of modernity.

In these quests for self-identification it is possible to identify some basic archetypical ideas, invariably present in the discourse. The first is a peculiar *love-and-hate* obsession with Europe. The understanding of Russia as 'the shield' of Europe against nomadic Asian tribes is archetypal. Interestingly, this understanding is mirrored today in the attempt by Ukrainian powers to position themselves as 'the shield' of Europe against an aggressive Russian Empire. Ukraine itself, with all its inescapable schisms, represents a tragic implementation of this obsession with Europe as the alter ego of Russia.

Second and relatedly, Russia is always between West and East, the intelligentsia and the people, Orthodoxy and science. It is always seeking its *middle way* in modernity: a really formidable task for any society. The split was incorporated in the internal *modernisation* divide of Russian society of the nineteenth century and in the external post-Crimean War break-up with Europe. Archetypically this idea is being repeated today in the discussions by political parties of the choice between a peculiar Russian way in modernity and the transfer of Western political institutions onto Russian soil. This vision also dominates discussions of the prospects of European or Asian partnerships.

What is important is that these discussions, this permanent choosing, this oscillation between West and East, between Europe and Asia, are absolutely unavoidable since they themselves constitute *a peculiarity* of Russian modernity. I believe that in order to understand the complexities of contemporary Russia's political behaviour, including its behaviour in the international arena, it is absolutely necessary to bear this peculiarity of Russian self-identification in mind.

It is just too natural, then, that civilisational approaches are as popular in Russia today as they were in the 1880s. After the collapse of the Soviet Union and the fall of the Marxist 'formation' approach, civilisational theories became really widespread. One university manual, published in 1994, describes civilisation as 'the main typological unit of history' (Semennikova 1994: 35) and Russia as a 'civilisationally heterogeneous society', as a 'peculiar ... conglomeration of peoples of different development types, united by a powerful, centralised state with the Great Russian nation as its nucleus' (Semennikova 1994: 109).

Both as a distinct civilisation and as a 'conglomeration of peoples', Russia has its main interests in the East and North, in the Arctic, Siberian and Far Eastern regions. The main resources and the main potential for the future development of the country are here. Famous dissident (and a conservative writer) Aleksandr Solzhenitsyn, in his letter to the leaders of the Soviet Union, called on them to develop Siberia and the Russian North, and to abandon communist ideology to China (Solzhenitsyn 1974). From the time of Lomonosov the idea that Siberia and the Northern Ocean were integral to the growth of Russian might has occupied the minds of the Russian people.

Current developments in international relations, however, do make the pursuit of new global allies necessary. The emerging Global South seems to be a natural ally for the deeply northern and semi-Asian Russia, simply because both are seeking alternatives to the neo-liberal global order established after the fall of the Berlin Wall. One of such possible alternatives to neo-liberal world governance structures is seen today in the institutions of the BRICS organisation. The viability of this alternative will, however, very much depend on the quality of the seemingly strange alliance of the Global North with the Global South.

References

Aksakov, I. (1886), *Biographiya Fedora Ivanovicha Tutcheva*, Moscow.

Blok, A. (1961), 'The Scythians', *International Socialism*, 6, 24–5.

Chaadayev, P. (1914a), 'Apologiya sumasshedshego', in *Sochineniya I pisma*, vol. 2, Moscow, pp. 215–81.

Chaadayev, P. (1914b), 'Philosophicheskiye pisma', in *Sochineniya I pisma*, vol. 2, Moscow, pp. 106–75.

Danilevskiy, N. (2016), *Rossiya i Europa*, Moscow: De'Libri.

Dostoyevskiy, F. (1984), 'Dnevnik pisatelya za 1881 god', in *Polnoye sobraniye sochineniy*, vol. 27, Leningrad: Nauka, pp. 5–40.

Dostoyevskiy, F. (1986), 'Pismo N. N. Strakhovu ot 18 marta 1869', in *Polnoye sobraniye sochineniy*, vol. 29, book1, Leningrad: Nauka, pp. 29–33.

Dugin, A. (2002), 'Evraziya prevyshe vsego', in *Osnovy evraziystva*, Moscow: Arktogeya Tsentr, pp. 5–15.

Duncan, P. (2000), *Russian Messianism: Third Rome, Revolution, Communism and After*, London and New York: Routledge.

Ekaterina II (1849), 'Nakaz comissii o sostavlenii projecta novogo ulozheniya', in *Sochineniya*, vol. 1, St Petersburg, pp. 3–117.

Engels, F. (2010a), 'Letter to Marx, 23 May 1851', in *Collected Works*, vol. 38, Lawrence & Wishart, ebook, pp. 361–65.

Engels, F. (2010b), 'Letter to Ion Nadejde, 4 January 1888', in *Collected Works*, vol. 48, Lawrence & Wishart, ebook, pp. 132–5.

Fonvisin, D. (1959), 'Pismo k Paninu ot 15/26 yanvarya 177', in *Sobraniye sochuneniy v dvukh tomakh*, Moscow and Leningrad: Gosudarstvennoye Izdatelstvo Khudozhestvennoy Literatury, pp. 460–3.

Gershenzon, M. (1908), *P. Y. Chaadayev. Zhizn I myshleniye*, St Petersburg.

Gumilev, L. (1995), 'Istoriko-philophskiye sochineniya knyazya N. S. Trubetskogo', in N. Trubetskoy, *Istoriya, Cultura, Yazyk*, Moscow: Progress, pp. 31–54.

Herzen, A. (1946), *Byloye i dumy*, Leningrad: OGIZ.

Herzen, A. (1948), 'S togo berega', in *Izbranniye philosophskiye proizvedeniya*, vol. 2, Leningrad: OGIZ, pp. 5–133.

Herzen, A. (1955), 'Pisma iz Frantsii i Italii 1847–1852', in *Sobraniye sochineniy v tridtsati tomakh*, Moscow: Izdatelstvo Akademii Nauk SSSR.

Khomyakov, A. (1900), 'Mneniye inostrantsev ob Rossii', in *Polnoye Sobraniye Sochineniy*, vol. 1, Moscow, pp. 3–30.

Khomyakov, A. (1904), 'Sravneniye russkikh slov s sanskritskimi', in *Polnoye Sobraniye Sochineniy*, vol. 5, Moscow, pp. 537–87.

Khomyakov, A. (1994a), 'Neskolko slov o philosophicheskom pisme', in *Sochineniya*, vol. 1, Moscow: Moskovskiy philosophskiy fond. Izdatelstvo 'Medium', pp. 449–55.

Khomyakov, A. (1994b), 'Vmesto Vvedenia k Sborniku Istoricheskikh I Statisticheskikh

Svedeniy . . .', in *Sochineniya*, vol. 1, Moscow: Moskovskiy philosophskiy fond. Izdatelstvo 'Medium', pp. 486–93.

Khomyakov, A. (1994c), 'Semiramis: investigation of the truth of the historical ideas', in *Sochineniya*, vol. 1, Moscow: Moskovskiy philosophskiy fond. Izdatelstvo 'Medium', pp. 15–448.

Kidnapping, Caucasian Style, film, directed by Leonid Gayday. USSR: Tvorcheskoye Obyeduneniniye 'Luch', 1967.

Laruelle, M. (2008), *Russian Eurasianism: An Ideology of Empire*, Washington DC: Woodrow Wilson Center Press.

Leontiev, K. (1996), 'Visantism i slavyanstvo', in *Vostok, Rossiya i slavyanstvo*, Moscow: Respublica, pp. 94–155.

Lomonosov, M. (1803a), 'Nadpis 20', in *Polnoye Sobraniye Sochineniy*, vol. 1, St Petersburg: Imperatorskaya Akademiya Nauk, pp. 281–2.

Lomonosov, M. (1803b), 'Nadpis 21', in *Polnoye Sobraniye Sochineniy*, vol. 1, St Petersburg: Imperatorskaya Akademiya Nauk, pp. 282–3.

Lomonosov, M. (1950), 'Kratkoye opisaniye raznyh puteshestviy po severnym moryam I pokazaniye vozmozhnogo prohodu Sibirskim Okeanom v Vostochnuyu Indiyu', in *Izbranniye philosophckiye proizvedenia*, Moscow: Gospolitizdat, pp. 624–30.

Lomonosov, M. (1952), 'Kratkoye rukovodstvo k krasnorechiyu', in *Polnoye Sobraniye Sochineniy*, vol. 7, Moscow and Leningrad: Izdatelstvo Akademii Nauk SSSR, pp. 89–378.

Lomonosov, M. (1959a), 'Oda na pribytiye iz Golstinii I na den rozhdeniya tgo imperatorskogo vysochestva gosudarya velikogo knyazya Petra Theodorovicha 1742 goda fevralya 10 dnya', in *Polnoye Sobraniye Sochineniy*, vol. 8, Moscow and Leningrad, pp. 59–68.

Lomonosov, M. (1959b), 'Oda na pribytiye eya velichestva velikiya gosudaryni imperatritsy Elisavety Petrovny iz Moskvy v Sanct-Peterburg 1742 goda po koronatsii', in *Polnoye Sobraniye Sochineniy*, vol. 8, Moscow and Leningrad, pp. 82–102.

Mochulskiy, K. (1995), 'Vladimir Soloviev: Zhisn i ucheniye', in *Gogol, Soloviev, Dostoyevskiy*, Moscow: Respublica, pp. 63–218.

Nazarbayev, N. (2015), <http://newskaz.ru/politics/20150311/7705167.html> (last accessed 12 January 2017).

Odoyevskiy, V. (1913), *Russkiye Nochi*, Moscow: Put.

Palmerston, H. J. T. (1854), 'War with Russia – the Queen's message', transcription of Commons sitting, 31 March 1854, <http://hansard.millbanksystems.com/commons/1854/mar/31/war-with-russia-the-queens-message#S3V0132P0_18540331_HOC_12> (last accessed 12 January 2017).

Predchuvstviya i sversheniya (predisloviye k sborniku *Put k Vostoku*) (2002), in *Osnovy evraziystva*, Moscow: Arktogeya Tsentr, pp. 103–6.

Pushkin, A. (1960), 'Medniy Vsadnik', in *Sobraniye Sochineniy*, vol. 3, Moscow: Gosudarstvennoye Izdatelstvo Khudozhestvennoy Literatury, pp. 285–99.

Savitskiy, P. (1997), 'Evraziystvo', in *Russkiy uzel evraziystva*, Moscow: Belovodie, pp. 76–94.

Semennikova, L. (1994), *Rossiya v mirovom soobshestve tsivilizatsiy*, Moscow: Interprax.

Shpet, G. (2008), *Ocherk razvitiya russkoi philosophii*, Moscow: ROSSPEN.

Solovyev, V. (1911), 'Tri sily', in *Sobraniye sochineniy*, vol. 1, St Petersburg: Prosvesheniye, pp. 227–39.

Solovyev, V. (1912), 'Chteniya o bogochelovechestve', in *Sobraniye sochineniy*, vol. 3, St Petersburg: Prosvesheniye, pp. 3–185.

Solovyev, V. (1914a), 'Leontiev', in *Sobraniye sochineniy*, vol. 10, St Petersburg: Prosvesheniye, pp. 506–9.

Solovyev, V. (1914b), 'Tri razgovora', in *Sobraniye sochineniy*, vol. 10, St Petersburg: Prosvesheniye, pp. 81–221.

Solovyev, V. (1974), *Stikhotvoreniya i shutochniye piesy*, Leningrad: Sovetskiy pisatel.

Solzhenitsyn, A. (1974), *Letter to the Soviet Leaders*, London: Index on Censorship.

Spengler, O. (1926), *Decline of the West: Form and Actuality*, New York: A. Knopf.

Toumanoff, C. (1954–5), 'Moscow the third Rome: genesis and significance of a politico-religious idea', *Catholic Historical Review*, 40: 4, 411–47.

Trubetskoy, N. (1995), 'Naslediye Chenghiskhana. Vzglyad na russkuyu istoriyu ne s zapada, a s vostoka', in *Istoriya, Cultura, Yazyk*, Moscow: 'Progress', pp. 211–66.

Tutchev, F. (2005), 'Pismo Ern. F. Tutchevoy', in *Polnoye sobraniye sochineniy i pisma v shesti tomakh*, Moscow: Classika, pp. 169–75.

Vernadskiy, G. (1914), 'Protiv Solntsa: rasprostraneniye russkogo gosudarstva k vostoku', *Russkaya mysl*, 1, 56–79.

Vyazemskiy, P. (1880), 'Peterburg. Otryvok', in *Polnoye Sobraniye Sochineniy*, vol. 3, St Petersburg, pp. 157–60.

Wagner, P. (2008), *Modernity as Experience and Interpretation: A New Sociology of Modernity*, Cambridge: Polity Press.

White Sun of the Desert, film, directed by Vladimir Motyl. USSR: Lenfilm Studio, 1970.

Zenkovskiy, V. (1926), *Russkiye mysliteli i Europa*, Paris: YMCA Press.

5

Digging for Class: Thoughts on the Writing of a Global History of Social Distinction

Jacob Dlamini

In February 1930, Leo Frobenius, the German archaeologist and ethnologist, announced to the world that he had identified the 'source of the civilization which created Zimbabwe and many hundreds of ruins' ('The Zimbabwe Riddley', *Cape Times*, 1 February 1930) scattered around southern Africa.[1] Zimbabwe, a ruined stone city, is a Late Iron Age archaeological site in the south of the country that today also goes by the name Zimbabwe. The city was once the capital of a pre-colonial kingdom that existed between the tenth century and the fifteenth century. The kingdom thrived on a gold and ivory trade that linked it to a commercial network that involved the east African coast, parts of the Middle East, India and China. The Indian Ocean was the centre of this network and the heart of one of the world's most dominant trade systems at least until the fifteenth century. The city had first come to the knowledge of Europeans through Portuguese explorers in the sixteenth century but controversy over its origins had raged among Europeans almost from their first contact with its ruins. Many Europeans believed that Zimbabwe, with its sophisticated architecture, including curved and five-metre-high walls built without mortar, could not have been the work of Africans. The site was believed to be too complex to have been produced by Africans. Enter Frobenius to settle the matter.

When he made his announcement, Frobenius was in Cape Town, en route back to Germany after a research trip to India. Speaking to the *Cape Times*, a top English-medium newspaper in the Union of South Africa, Frobenius said the archaeological sites that dotted southern Africa were more than just ruins. Ruined cities such as Zimbabwe, local rock paintings and decayed mines were all related to a 'culture of the highest order'. And this culture was not African – Frobenius said. How had he arrived at his conclusion? 'Logically, he had piled one deduction upon the other', the *Cape Times* reported. Frobenius said:

The people who made Zimbabwe had knowledge of geology we had lost. The extent and distribution of their mines proved it. Nor were their paintings primitive. There was also evidence of a highly developed science of metallurgy. The creators of these ruined cities made bronze wire – a craft of the most difficult kind. Nowhere in Africa except in Egypt had native people mastered it. This people, their culture which produced Zimbabwe, came from somewhere else. ('The Zimbabwe Riddley', *Cape Times*, 1 February 1930)

So where did these people and their culture come from? Frobenius said that, having examined similar ruins in India during his recent trip: 'I found [in India] not a father or a mother of Zimbabwe, but a brother' ('The Zimbabwe Riddley', *Cape Times*, 1 February 1930).

So who were the parents? They were, he said, Sumerian and came from 'somewhere near the Caspian Sea'. How did they end up in southern Africa? Well, in 'search of gold, frankincense and myrrh, the creators of [Zimbabwe] spread through Arabia and Mesopotamia, manned their ships and sailed down the west coast of India, the east coast of Africa, and spread industry and culture across southern Africa' ('The Zimbabwe Riddley', *Cape Times*, 1 February 1930). This, in short, was Frobenius's announcement. He was wrong. After more than a century of digging, researchers have established beyond a doubt that the people who built Zimbabwe and associated sites were indeed African. However, to be charitable to Frobenius, we should say that while his conclusion about the origins of Zimbabwe was wrong, his intuition that Zimbabwe was born global and that the site could only be understood in a global context was correct. As the research agenda proposed in this essay would show, Zimbabwe and the hundreds of sites like it, including Mapungubwe (which preceded Great Zimbabwe) were indeed born global, the products of Africans who understood themselves to be part of a world bigger than their worlds.

Digging for class: a global history of social distinction

This schematic and preliminary essay is about the global history of social distinction. It is about the possible terms and outline of a research agenda concerned truly with a global history of social distinction. What might a truly global and interdisciplinary history of social distinction look like? What might Africa offer if used as a conceptual base of operations for such a research project? This essay seeks to offer suggestions about how scholars might use Africa as a conceptual base from which to launch an archaeological, historical and theoretical investigation into the emergence of social hierarchies in human society. How did social distinction emerge as an animating feature of human life? What led to its emergence, and how was it legitimated across space and time? These are, in fact, some of the oldest questions in the humanities and social sciences. But this essay seeks to suggest ways in which these questions can be asked anew, and to gesture towards possible fresh answers through an interdisciplinary approach that involves archaeology, history and social theory. It argues that scholars can come up with fresh answers through a methodology founded on three related innovations. The first innovation would involve making Africa the main, but by no means exclusive, conceptual base of operations. This means, as I will elaborate below, making Africa key to theoretical and intellectual debates about the origins not simply of human evolution but of social and political complexity in human life. The second innovation would entail a recuperation of Africa's history as indeed a global history, one that cannot be understood unless one understands what is going on at the same time in other parts of the globe. The third innovation, arguably *the* most original aspect of this schematic essay, would be the reanimation of some of the oldest intellectual debates about what we would today call global history (see, for example, Conrad 2016) through a retracing – mainly intellectual but also literal in places – of the international journeys undertaken by Frobenius (see Frobenius 2014). By following his intellectual and physical travels through Africa, Asia and Europe, this essay argues, scholars can show how we might go about asking and finding both local and global answers to some of humanity's most pressing problems.

The three innovations mentioned above are designed to suggest possible new ways of approaching African history in particular and global history in general. These new ways would help us challenge assumptions about the timelessness of Africa and the supposed marginality of the continent to the development of complexity in human life. This supposed marginality accounts for Africa's relative absence in ongoing attempts by scholars around the world to theorise, for example, the advent of the modern world. This essay seeks ultimately to offer suggestions about how scholars might make Africa a part of more than simply the history of human evolution. Scholars need to make African history an important reference point in intellectual conversations about the study of phenomena such as the birth of agriculture, the development of social and political complexity, as well as the emergence of states. By looking at what African history has to say about the rise of social distinction in human life, scholars can give new life to debates such as those, for example, between thinkers like Karl Marx, who believed in class struggle as the motor of human history, and Max Weber, who offered an arguably more varied and less politically instrumental notion of social stratification.

The three innovations outlined above would also, it is hoped, make the burgeoning field of global history truly global by making Africa more than a marginal reference point. More than that, this essay seeks to inaugurate an interdisciplinary conversation about the global history of social distinction. The historical scope of the research project outlined here is the period from the ninth century to the twentieth century. This means that our research starts in the Iron Age and goes to the end of the twentieth century. The essay proposes this scope – which goes against the standard periodisation found in many History departments – because it offers the best way to bring the histories of Africa, Asia and the Americas into a productive interdisciplinary conversation with the histories of Europe, and to have that conversation start long 'before European hegemony', to borrow Janet Abu-Lughod's phrase (Abu-Lughod 1989). By employing Frobenius as their interlocutor in a research endeavour such as the one outlined here, proponents of global history can use his work to develop further his intuitions about the global nature of African and Asian history. But, going farther than Frobenius ever went intellectually, proponents of global history would develop these intuitions in ways that raise questions about the emergence of social distinction in the world. What, then, is the state of the art of research on Africa in global history and how does this essay say we can add to it?

Two Germans meet on a hill in Africa . . .

Mapungubwe, the site proposed here as a historical and conceptual reference point, is situated to the south of Frobenius's Great Zimbabwe ruins. Located in present-day South Africa, Mapungubwe sits near the confluence of the Limpopo and Shashe rivers. Founded sometime during the eleventh century, the polity existed until the thirteenth century, when it was replaced by the civilisation that gave us Great Zimbabwe. Mapungubwe is significant for our purposes because it was the first polity in southern Africa to see the development of a

spatial expression of social distinction. At the centre of the polity was
the Mapungubwe hill, atop of which lived the elite. Below them lived
mid-level elites and, further below the mid-level elites, lived commoners. The Mapungubwe hill, essentially a rock outcropping with neither
the soils for agriculture nor the space for a big settlement, was home to
elites whose position in the polity depended on the elites' monopoly of
trade (mainly gold and ivory), as well as their position as sacred leaders
of the polity. In fact, Mapungubwe is considered the first archaeological site in southern Africa to see the development and spatial expression of sacred leadership. In addition, the economic and social life of
Mapungubwe had what archaeologists refer to as a cattle complex,
meaning cattle were at the centre of the polity's economic and ritual
life.

Now let us imagine a global history of social distinction that begins
thus: two Germans meet on a hill in southern Africa ... That might
strike some as the beginning of a tasteless joke. But what if our two
Germans are Karl Marx and Max Weber, and what if the hill they meet
on is Mapungubwe? What began as the making of a bad joke might, in
fact, prove to be the start of a fruitful conversation about the historical
emergence of social distinction in human society. If class struggle is, as
Marx would argue, the motor of human history and class distinction
is, as Weber would say, driven in large part by vocational specialisation, might Mapungubwe not be one of the best archaeological and
historical sites for the testing of those claims? Mapungubwe had it all:
it had sacred leadership, spatial segregation, vocational specialisation,
as well as a division of labour through which commoners, for example,
grew food for elites who did not and could not grow food on the hill
on which they (the elites) lived as an expression of their special status
in the polity. Let us imagine how different the global history of social
distinction would sound if told, not simply as the rise of capitalist
developments in certain corners of Western Europe that were then diffused outwards to other parts of the world, but as a messier process of
global exchanges and encounters.

I am not suggesting that Mapungubwe is the only archaeological site to tell us about the global emergence of social distinction.
However, I do think it would add immensely to our understanding
of global processes of change and connection to make a place like
Mapungubwe part of the story of globalisation before the fact. The
truth is that Mapungubwe attained its status precisely because of its
connections to the outside world. Using their monopoly of trade with

the outside world and sacred leadership within the polity, the elites of Mapungubwe used both their trade monopoly and sacred leadership to justify their position. The question to ask is not how this justification was made but, more importantly, how and why commoners accepted the social distinction that came to define their polity. This is just one of the questions that the research agenda proposed here would raise.

The state of the art

The past twenty years have seen a burgeoning in the field of global history. Scholars such as Lynn Hunt (2014), Jürgen Osterhammel (2014), Enrique Dussel (2011), John Darwin (2008), C. A. Bayly (2004), Dipesh Chakrabarty (2000) and Kenneth Pomeranz (2000) have offered us what we might call, after Dussel, a 'critical world history'. They have produced work bent on 'provincializing Europe', to borrow Chakrabarty's felicitous term, by challenging assumptions about Europe being the birthplace of the modern world. Scholars engaged in this work of decentring Europe from the conceptual and empirical heart of the modern world have joined voices offering various suggestions for how to think about a world without Europe at its centre. Some of these voices talk about 'vernacular modernities' (Robert Dixon and Veronica Kelly 2008); others speak of 'alternative modernities' (Dilip Gaonkar 2001); yet others say 'multiple modernities' (Shmuel Eisenstadt 2000). These scholars have, each in his or her own way, added much-needed complexity to our understanding of the world and its global connections. Yet, for all these intellectual and scholarly advances in our understanding of the world and its interconnectedness, Africa is absent from their considerations. The continent remains hidden behind 'global shadows', to use anthropologist James Ferguson's apt description of Africa's relationship with the rest of the world (Ferguson 2006). Works whose noble ambition is to give us a truly global history of the world have little or nothing to say about Africa in global history. That is, they make general statements about Africa and its alternative, multiple or vernacular modernities without at the same time giving us a real sense of the human element that is the heart of history. Even in the best work on global history (e.g. Osterhammel's and Bayly's books), Africa remains at best marginal.

Part of the explanation for the marginality of Africa in global history is that the continent is seen by many scholars and non-scholars alike as having nothing to offer scholars and researchers interested in the emergence of such complex phenomena as social distinction and state-formation. Even in cases such as Mapungubwe, where the hard work of digging up ancient histories has been done and evidence found that points to the complexity of African life forms, this evidence has not fed into broader intellectual and theoretical debates about phenomena such as class. Africa is generally not considered a place that offers lessons about some of life's most difficult challenges. Why is this so and what does it tell us about the state of the art in the field of comparative global history?

Let me start with the second of these two questions. Despite recent advances in the study of global history, the field remains very much uneven. This is in part a function of the backgrounds of the scholars writing global history. Osterhammel, for example, is a student of Chinese history with an excellent grasp of the archives that define his primary area of research. Bayly, to use another example, was a student of Indian history, with a firm grasp of Britain's imperial archive. These backgrounds do not, as we know from these two scholars' exceptional books on global history, limit what they can say about the world beyond their areas of expertise. But the backgrounds do influence how they relate to areas outside of their expertise. We see this most clearly in their treatment of Africa. It remains at best cursory. It breaks no new ground.

The ghost of Hegel

Now to return to the first question for why this is so, why Africa is generally considered by many scholars to be marginal to intellectual and theoretical debates about the complexity of human life. There is no simple answer to this question. But, for any answer to be comprehensive, it would have to take in the Enlightenment and the race theories espoused by some of the Enlightenment's thinkers; the advent of capitalism around the world, Western imperialism and its enactment of a particular kind of globalised world, the 'Scramble for Africa', colonialism, decolonisation and the emergence of the postcolonial world. These are by no means definitive and they certainly do not go in a straight line, with one following the other. However, one statement that can be made with some certainty for why Africa continues to be marginal to intellectual and theoretical debates about the complexity of human life is that the ghost of Georg Hegel has haunted the writing of global history since the nineteenth century. When Hegel said that

Africa existed outside of History, still involved in the conditions of mere nature, he cast a spell on the study of the continent that has yet to be broken, despite the best intentions of many scholars, African and non-African alike. It was Hegel who made it possible for people like historian Hugh Trevor-Roper to claim, as he did in 1963, that there was no such thing as African history, merely the history of Europeans in Africa. Speaking against the backdrop of the decolonisation in Asia and Africa, Trevor-Roper said there might yet come a time when one could teach African history. In the meantime, scholars had to make do with European history and the history of Europeans in the world.

Trevor-Roper was an anachronism even as he spoke these words in 1963. But his words are worth mentioning because they are important for understanding the state of the art in contemporary studies of Africa in global history. Unless we understand these words, we cannot hope to understand why, despite all the major advances in the writing of a critical global history, Africa remains marginal to the intellectual history of human life. Why is it that Africa's offering to the world of theorising is limited only to stories about human origins? Hegel's prejudice does not help us answer these questions. But remembering his claim about Africans living in conditions of mere nature is helpful. This should not be taken to mean that Hegel and Trevor-Roper have the last word on the study of Africa in global history, or that these two men have set a permanent agenda for the study of Africa. As this essay shows below, there have been valiant challenges to Hegel (and the likes of Trevor-Roper) for at least a century and these challenges have helped bring about a qualitative change in how we today approach the study of Africa. Scholars working across a range of disciplines have helped us develop a much more nuanced understanding of Africa's place in global history. From archaeology to history and zoology, scholars have uncovered African pasts that have qualitatively changed how we understand the origins of complexity in human life. Some of this research, especially in archaeology, has fed into new approaches to the study of the human past. But these approaches have been limited, by and large, to the discipline of archaeology. Despite lay and professional archaeologists from various parts of the world spending more than a hundred years digging at Mapungubwe so we can gain a better understanding of how social distinction emerged, their findings have yet to filter into broader debates in the rest of the humanities and social sciences about social distinction and stratification.

In 1946, W. E. B. Du Bois published *The World and Africa: An*

Inquiry into the Part which Africa Has Played in World History. This was one of the first scholarly monographs to try to write Africa into global history. As Du Bois, the first black American to obtain a PhD from Harvard University, explained in the foreword:

> Since the rise of the sugar empire and the resultant cotton kingdom, there has been consistent effort to rationalise Negro slavery by omitting Africa from world history, so that today it is almost universally assumed that history can be truly written without reference to Negroid peoples. (Du Bois 2003: vii)

Du Bois decried this omission, saying it was 'scientifically unsound and also dangerous for logical social conclusions' (Du Bois 2003: vii). He said:

> Therefore I am seeking in this book to remind readers in this crisis of civilisation, of how critical a part Africa has played in human history, past and present, and how impossible it is to forget this and rightly explain the present plight of mankind. (Du Bois 2003: vii)

This was a year after the formal end of the Second World War and the 'crisis of civilization' mentioned by Du Bois referred to the destruction wrought by that war. Du Bois, a sociologist trained in the US and in Germany, had written about the place of Africa in world history before. Although widely read, these earlier writings had not reversed the omission of Africa from global history:

> I still labor under the difficulty of the persistent lack of interest in Africa so long characteristic of modern history and sociology. The careful, detailed researches into the history of Negroid peoples have only begun, and the need for them is not yet clear to the thinking world. (Du Bois 2003: viii)

But Du Bois said he was determined to charge forward, 'even though that interpretation has here and there but slender historical proof' (Du Bois 2003: viii).

What followed was a masterful survey of global history that began with what Du Bois saw as the collapse of Europe in light of the Second World War, the 'Scramble for Africa', the origins of humans in Africa, the different civilisations that made up Africa, relations between China and Africa, as well as the role of black Americans in the struggles for independence in Africa. Du Bois drew on a number of primary sources and scholars for his work, including Frobenius. Du Bois relied heavily on Frobenius. But he was also critical of Frobenius in places. Du Bois sought to assert the genius of Africans and to highlight the achievements of their civilisations. But as he himself had admitted in the foreword to his book, he had not always firm historical proof. Still, Du Bois's book marked a crucial intervention in intellectual debates about the place of Africa in global history. Because *The World and Africa* was such a pioneering text, it bore the vindicationist impulses of its author. Du Bois wrote the book to vindicate Africa's place in the world. He penned it in order to show that Africa, too, mattered in world history and that, as he said, Africa had played a critical part in human history. When Du Bois wrote his book, he believed that the 'persistent lack of interest in Africa so long characteristic of modern history and sociology' (Du Bois 2003: viii) was due more to ignorance than it was to malice. He believed that he could address this ignorance through his book. He believed that, if he could show that Africa mattered to the world, then the world would take Africa seriously. Alas, that did not come to pass. Africa continued to be haunted by the ghost of Hegel. Africa continued to be seen as a place without civilisation and outside of history. But the failing was not Du Bois's. He tried, using whatever archival and secondary material he had at his disposal. But his book was important for it signalled the possibility of fighting back against the ghost of Hegel. His book showed that Africa, too, could be made a subject of real historical analysis.

Another major pioneer in the study of Africa in global history was Senegalese historian Cheikh Anta Diop. In 1974 he published *The African Origin of Civilization: Myth or Reality*. The book claimed that the Pharaohs of Egypt were of Negroid origin and that the Egyptian civilisation was in fact Negroid. The claim was as controversial then as it is now. More importantly, Diop argued that Africans could not be defined by one phenotype but that they varied greatly. But Diop was more convincing when he argued against European scholars who either ignored or downplayed the originality of African civilisations. An eclectic scholar who had trained in chemistry, history and philosophy, Diop was among the first historians of Africa to draw explicitly from the discipline of archaeology to make his arguments. He used archaeological sources, for example, to support his claim that the Egyptian civilisation was Negroid; he studied Egyptian artefacts and used ancient paintings to draw conclusions that ancient Egyptians were in fact Negroid Africans. Diop also drew from the discipline of linguistics to support his claims about ancient Egypt, arguing in fact that there were linguistic affinities between his native Wolof and the languages spoken by ancient Egyptians (see Diop 1987). This was indeed a bold and ambitious research project and it inspired a body of scholarship defined as Afrocentrism.

Among the major proponents of Afrocentrism are American scholar Molefi Kete Asante. In his most recent book, *African Pyramids of Knowledge* (2015), Asante argues for example that, as he puts it on his personal website, 'Imhotep, the first pyramid builder, and not Homer, should be seen as the first human in antiquity to provide the foundations for subsequent science, art, and mathematics.'[2] Asante's claims have proven popular and his work defines the canon of Afrocentrism. However, the controversial and disputed nature of his claims has limited Asante's appeal outside of Afrocentric circles. Another reason for the limited appeal of Asante's work is that it is driven almost entirely by conjecture. There is little or no primary research to support Afrocentric claims. What scholars like Asante do, instead, is to offer different interpretations of existing evidence and archival material. For example, in his 2014 book *Facing South to Africa: Toward an Afrocentric Critical Orientation*, he argues that Africans can never get away from hegemonic Western epistemes unless they privilege their own stories and histories. But he does not call for a re-engagement with or even development of primary sources. His argument is limited to the interpretation that one brings to bear on extant sources and knowledge systems.

Perhaps the most influential book to come out of the Afrocentric canon is Martin Bernal's *Black Athena: The Afroasiatic Roots of Classical Civilization* (1987). Bernal argues that, in fact, the roots of ancient Greek civilisation are African and that Africans, meaning ancient Egyptians in this case, colonised ancient Greece. Bernal says this colonisation brought civilisation to the Greeks but that this is not acknowledged in histories of ancient Greece and Europe. The claim is controversial and has been subjected to withering criticism. One of the most trenchant criticisms of Bernal's thesis is by Mary Lefkowitz, whose 1996 book *Not Out of Africa: How 'Afrocentrism' Became an Excuse to Teach Myth as History* challenged Afrocentrism's claim that ancient Greeks stole their ideas from ancient Egyptians. Bernal responded to Lefkowitz and other critics with a 2001 book titled *Black Athena Writes*

Back: Martin Bernal Responds to His Critics. But the largely polemical debate between Bernal and Lefkowitz did nothing to break new ground in the study of Africa and global history.

Despite claims by either side to be fighting for history and the historical method, Bernal and Lefkowitz ended up offering nothing more than polemic. But if the polemics presented by Asante, Bernal and Lefkowitz represented one extreme of the historiographical debates about the place of Africa in global history, philosopher V. Y. Mudimbe offered a dense but more complex counterpoint to the polemics cited above. Starting with his 1988 book *The Invention of Africa: Gnosis, Philosophy and the Order of Knowledge*, Mudimbe raised pressing questions about the meaning of Africa and Africans. What was Africa, Mudimbe asked, and what did it mean to be African? Drawing on the work of Foucault, Mudimbe argued that there could be no straightforward answers to these questions. He said Western scholars and missionaries had introduced so many distortions to African systems of knowledge that these distortions had become part of the way in which different Africans thought about themselves, their worlds and their relationship with wider worlds. Mudimbe argued that discourses produced in the colonial encounter between Africans and Europeans had created thought systems within which Africans developed their identities. The implication of this claim was that African identities and the very meaning of the word 'Africa' could not be conceived independently of Europe and the rest of the world. To be African was to be *ipso facto* global. It was to be of the world. To be sure, this was not exclusive to Africa and Africans. Mudimbe's argument could be applied to any part of the world born of the encounter with an imperial and colonial Europe.

Mudimbe followed this book up with *The Idea of Africa* (1994), which argued that even the very name Africa, the very concept of Africa, came from outside of the continent itself. But Mudimbe's books were not without their weaknesses. He claimed, for example, that Europe's discovery of Africa in the fifteenth century 'meant and still means the primary violence signified by the word. The slave trade narrated itself accordingly, and the same movement of reduction progressively guaranteed the gradual invasion of the continent' (Mudimbe 1994: 17). Mudimbe's claim here amounted to a poor interpretation of Africa's global history. By privileging the Atlantic slave trade, Mudimbe ignored the Islamic slave trade centred on the Indian Ocean and which was in fact much older than the Atlantic slave trade. He also ignored the extensive trade relations between Africa, the Middle East and Asia. It was precisely these trade links that allowed the Kingdom of Mapungubwe to flourish. It was through these links that the elites of Mapungubwe were able to develop the monopoly that allowed them to buttress their monopoly on sacred leadership. Mudimbe ignored these crucial connections. Part of the explanation for why he did this was that he was so focused on making Africa a product of European epistemes that he ignored Africa's extensive Arab history. The irony, of course, is that by making such a historiographical move, Mudimbe ended up offering arguments that essentially cut off an important part of Africa's global history. So focused was he on Europe and its philosophers that he seemed to forget, despite his best and stated intentions, that the continent of Africa had a history that predated its complex links with Europe. Mudimbe might have been wrong in his interpretation but his work did represent a valiant effort to inject a degree of sophistication into discussions about Africa and its place in the world. True, Mudimbe's project was not always helped by his resort to jargon and obfuscation. But it at least got scholars of Africa talking, even if a lot of that talk was critical of Mudimbe and his impenetrable writing.

A more recent, philosophically orientated approach to the study of Africa in global history comes from historian and philosopher Achille Mbembe, whose book *On the Postcolony* (2001) examines power and subjectivity in Africa. The book is interested in the pathologies of power in contemporary Africa, which Mbembe places under the concept 'banality of power'. The debt to Hannah Arendt is explicit. Just like Arendt used Europe's imperial adventures in Africa to understand the violence that consumed Europe in the Second World War, Mbembe uses the idea of the 'banality of power' to explore the effect of power on African subjectivity. What sort of African subject is produced by the banal power of the postcolony? Drawing, again from Arendt, on the idea of superfluity, Mbembe looks at the ways in which power in Africa dispenses death and the manner in which African lives are rendered superfluous. While his concern is with political power as it is exercised in contemporary Africa, Mbembe is also interested in the relationship between Africa and European forms of knowledge. He juxtaposes the violence of the postcolony to the violence of European race-thinking. *On the Postcolony* offers little in the way of hope. It challenges one of the most common binaries in African history: resistance versus collaboration. But it is not clear what the book offers as an alternative. It is in that sense a distant cousin to Arendt's 1951 *The Origins of Totalitarianism* (Arendt 1968).

It is a remarkable feature of modern scholarship on the work of Arendt, that so few scholars have seen fit to comment on the fact that Part Two of *The Origins of Totalitarianism*, which deals with European imperialism, is set in southern Africa. Keen to understand how the Nazis could devise a scheme intended to wipe an entire race of people from the face of the Earth and to pursue that scheme even when it interfered with their war aims, Arendt turned to Africa for answers. There she found, especially in the gold mines of South Africa, a seemingly illogical enterprise that sought to make money while also producing superfluous bodies – thousands of African miners whose lives did not seem to interest the mine owners much, beyond the biological. Arendt wanted to understand how an economic system that needed thousands of Africans to function could show such callous disregard for those same Africans. This was a market system without apparent logic. So was the industrial machinery of death produced by the Nazis, Arendt thought. To be sure, some commentators have taken issue with Arendt's argument about the origins of totalitarianism and some have queried her use of secondary sources from the South African case to draw conclusions about Europe. But, for our purposes, Arendt is significant because she is among a few Western thinkers to make the kind of global connections that define this project. At a time when many were saying the outrages of the Second World War were an aberration, out of character with the general thrust of European history, Arendt was making precisely the opposite argument, reminding Europeans of their role in other parts of the world. More importantly, Arendt showed connections between Africa and other parts of the world. However, what she did not show was that these connections predated the Second World War. They went deep into the past. To be fair to Arendt, she was not making an argument about deep history. Hers was an argument driven by a pressing and urgent need to understand the catastrophe that was the Second World War. Still, she and Mbembe, later, offered work that placed Africa in a global context. Their concerns might have been of the moment but they were suggestive of the kinds of connections that help advance global scholarship.

Exorcising the ghost of Hegel

A scholar who has tried to make Africa a part of contemporary intellectual conversations about global history is sociologist Peter Wagner. Working mainly in the subfield of historical sociology, Wagner has written pioneering work about global history. He has done this most explicitly in work that calls into question standard assumptions about the birth of the modern world (see Wagner 2012). Working in conversation with some of the leading lights in global history (Bayly, Chakrabarty, Dussel, Osterhammel and Pomeranz), and arguing with some of the key thinkers in the 'multiple modernities' debate (chiefly Eisenstadt), Wagner has produced work that calls into question some of the foundational myths about the birth of the modern world. In the process, Wagner has raised pointed questions about the assumption that Europe was *sui generis* the birth of the modern world. A sophisti- cated thinker, Wagner is careful not to make it sound like elements of the so-called Industrial Revolution as we understand it were born in a place other than certain parts of Western Europe. But he insists that we be alert to both the contingencies and the global contexts that made said revolution possible. Wagner uses these insights to also initiate debate about what the key assumptions about modernity and its meanings are. He challenges, for example, the idea that the West had long settled elementary questions about organising political life in a given polity; managing life in common, and developing epistemologies suited to the modern world. Wagner draws from Europe's contemporary economic and political crises to show the ways in which what were long thought to be answers have proved to be not fit for purpose. He also shows how, for example, claims about Western Europe's supposedly exemplary record on the environment are predicated on the export of so-called dirty industries to poor parts of the world.

These are important insights with huge implications for how we think about the world and knowledge production. The research agenda proposed by this essay draws inspiration from Wagner's work. But it also seeks to go beyond the scope of that work. By beginning our research in the Iron Age, we can offer a richer and much older account of the kinds of global connections Wagner's work alerts us to. Part of the genius of Wagner's work is that it reminds us of the fundamental fact that humans the world over have to respond to certain basic needs in order to live. In this way, Wagner's work serves to slay the ghost of Hegel. It debunks the idea that entire swathes of the world can exist outside of history. It also makes nonsense of the Hegelian notion that Africa is a place without movement. These are all rich insights and we hope to enrich them even further with the findings of our research. It is clear by now that it will take more than pronouncements that Hegel was wrong – or that his philosophy of history was more prejudice than actual history – and that means more of the kind of interdisciplinary and international research pursued by Wagner, and followed up here. To be sure, I am not suggesting that we replicate Wagner's research agenda. Rather, we should build on Wagner's work but do so in ways that allow us to go backwards and forwards in history. As can be seen from this relatively brief state of the art of research on Africa in global history, the field is uneven. But there have been major advances over the past twenty years. The field of global history is much more established than when Du Bois, for instance, tried to write Africa into global history. As Du Bois himself admitted in his 1946 book, there was little known, especially in the West, about Africa's deep history.

Archaeological debts, or why this project is feasible

We certainly know more than we did when Du Bois, for example, was writing in the 1950s about the world and Africa. But we need to know more. We also need to integrate what we discover into contemporary intellectual conversations about the theory and practice of global history. That is why the research agenda proposed here is so necessary. The agenda is feasible because of the work that archaeologists have been doing over the past twenty years, if not more. Scholars such as Jeffrey B. Fleisher, Thomas N. Huffman, Scott MacEachern, Lynn Meskell and Stephanie Wynne-Jones have conducted some of the most path-breaking work in the field of archaeology. As these scholars (minus Meskell) show in *Theory in Africa, Africa in Theory: Debating Meaning in Archaeology* (Wynne-Jones and Fleisher 2015), archaeologists, historians and social theorists already have the archival material and conceptual tools needed to make Africa a reference point for more than simply the story of human evolution. We have the material needed to start the kinds of interdisciplinary conversations about global phenomena such as social distinction. As MacEachern argues, Africa, too, has a story to tell about the advent of agriculture, socio-political complexity, as well as state-formation. This story can enrich our understanding of human life. But the story is not being heard. Through no fault of their own, archaeologists are not reaching beyond the confines of their discipline. That must change. I suggest that we do away with this neglect by drawing on the pioneering work that archaeologists have done to initiate the kind of crosscutting and interdisciplinary conversation work envisaged here.

An archaeologist who has done a lot to encourage interdisciplinary scholarship on so-called non-Western regions is Lynn Meskell. She pioneered a field called social archaeology. As Meskell and Robert W. Preucel explain in their introduction to *A Companion to Social Archaeology*,

> Archaeology has been defined as the discipline that uniquely provides a world history extending humanity back into prerecorded time. It gives primary evidence for the three 'rites of passage' in the human career, namely the emergence of anatomically modern humans, the origins of agriculture/first settled villages, and the rise of civilizations. (Meskell and Preucel 2004: 3)

But there is also social archaeology, they say, and this 'refers to the ways in which we express ourselves through the things that we make and use, collect and discard, value or take for granted, and seek to be remembered by' (Meskell and Preucel 2004: 3). This observation is particularly relevant to this project. The elite of Mapungubwe used a hill to separate themselves from the rest of their society. In the process, they gave spatial expression to their social distinction. But they also used gold and ivory to trade with other parts of the world. They obtained through that trade goods such as Chinese porcelain which they also used to give meaning to their social distinction. These are important insights that we owe to the excellent work archaeologists have done. It is also thanks to them that we have heard suggestions about how we might engender debate about theory in Africa and Africa in theory. But, as I hope is clear from this extended synopsis, the discipline of archaeology on its own has not succeeded in fostering the kind of interdisciplinary conversation we need to make Africa more than an incidental part of global history. We need history and social theory. We need history to help us connect the work of archaeology with critical historical interpretations of changes over time with regard to the notion of social distinction. We need social theory to help us map out the significance of those changes.

Why Frobenius?

I have chosen Frobenius with care. He is not simply a random guide intended to help scholars get around. As can be seen from this essay's research objectives and the questions posed, the challenge is to find new answers to old questions about the emergence of social distinction. Frobenius offers us a useful frame of reference for developing the answers we seek. Even though Frobenius represents a hegemonic and stubborn strain of Eurocentric thought that presents real obstacles to this project, he asked useful questions about the connectedness of human phenomena across space and time. Some of his answers (on Great Zimbabwe, for example) were wrong but his questions were right. We need those questions. That is why we need Frobenius as our guide. We need him to help us frame the questions we intend to ask. Re-examining his questions would help scholars contribute to the reinvigoration of global history. They would help scholars show how and to explain why Africa is more than a marginal reference point in global history. There is more to Africa than the story of human origins. While the story of human origins is indeed important, it is not the only story. By sparking an interdisciplinary debate about the place of Africa in global history, scholars who take up the research agenda proposed here would show that Africa, too, is an important site for the study of agricultural development, the advent of settled societies, and the formation of states. Mapungubwe and its successor, Great Zimbabwe, were proto-states. That is, they represented some of the earliest attempts at state-formation in southern Africa. The question should not be whether they succeeded or failed. The question should be, rather, about the conditions of possibility behind such a phenomenon. For students of African history, the immediate impact of the research agenda set out here would be to give them the archival and conceptual material that would, it is hoped, allow them to tell a more complete history of Africa and to do so in an interdisciplinary fashion. If done well, the research proposed here would lead to the production of research material that would show students and scholars how and why Africa matters to global history.

By building on the substantial work of archaeology and using that to bring about an intellectual conversation across disciplines, scholars would inspire inter-disciplinarity in the study of global history. It is often the case that scholars of global history who have little or nothing to say about Africa lament the 'lack' of archival material such as written documents. For far too long the lack of written sources in Africa has been taken as a sign of the continent's lack of civilisation. This is wrong. By challenging practitioners of global history to reckon with archives other than written sources and to work with primary sources other than what they are used to working with, scholars would profit from venturing beyond their comfort zones. Global history will not improve its fraught relations with Africa so long as the default lament is that

Africa has no sources. Africa has sources. We just need to know how to look for them, where to look for them and, having found them, how to read them. That is why Frobenius is such an important guide. He tried to work with archives other than written sources. He worked with architectural ruins and rock art. He believed that he could use these sources to great profit. He believed that, through them, he could understand how humans and their civilisations circulated around the world. He was wrong in his conclusions about Great Zimbabwe. That is not what matters. What matters for this project is that he was able to see that he could not make sense of these artefacts without placing them in a global context. By re-posing the questions he asked and making the connections he did, the research project laid out here would have a positive impact on contemporary scholarship about the connectedness of the world. As the use of Frobenius planned here shows, we do not read past thinkers because they are right, necessarily. We read them because they help us see the intellectual blind spots of those who came before us. By inserting Africa into intellectual conversations about human complexity, this study would have a major impact on how we think about the globe, its past and its future. It would have a transformational impact on the study and teaching of global history.

Notes

1. See Dlamini (2010) for my discussion of the *Cape Times* interview with Leo Frobenius.
2. See Asante's personal website, available at <http://www.asante.net> (last accessed 13 January 2017).

References

Abu-Lughod, Janet (1989), *Before European Hegemony*, Oxford: Oxford University Press.

Arendt, Hannah (1968), *The Origins of Totalitarianism*, New York: Harcourt.

Asante, Molefi K. (2014), *Facing South to Africa: Toward an Afrocentric Critical Orientation*, Lanham, MD: Lexington Books.

Asante, Molefi K. (2015), *African Pyramids of Knowledge*, New York: Universal Write Publications.

Bayly, C. A. (2004), *The Birth of the Modern World*, Oxford: Blackwell.

Bernal, Martin (1987), *Black Athena: The Afroasiatic Roots of Classical Civilization*, New Brunswick, NJ: Rutgers University Press.

Bernal, Martin (2001), *Black Athena Writes Back: Martin Bernal Responds to His Critics*, ed. David Chioni Moore, Durham, NC: Duke University Press.

Chakrabarty, Dipesh (2000), *Provincializing Europe*, Princeton: Princeton University Press.

Conrad, Sebastian (2016), *What Is Global History?*, Princeton: Princeton University Press.

Darwin, John (2008), *After Tamerlane*, New York: Bloomsbury Press.

Diop, Cheikh Anta (1974), *The African Origin of Civilization: Myth or Reality*, New York: L. Hill.

Diop, Cheikh Anta (1987), *Precolonial Black Africa*, trans. Harold Salemson, New York: Lawrence Hill Books.

Dixon, Robert and Veronica Kelly (eds) (2008), *Impact of the Modern*, Sydney: Sydney University Press.

Dlamini, Jacob (2010), 'Ancient African culture could not be our own', *Business Day*, 28 October.

Du Bois, W. E. B. (2003), *The World and Africa: An Inquiry into the Part which Africa Has Played in World History*, New York: International Publishers.

Dussel, Enrique (2011), *Politics of Liberation*, Norwich: Hymns Ancient and Modern.

Eisenstadt, Shmuel N. (2000), 'Multiple modernities', *Daedalus*, 129: 1–29.

Ferguson, James (2006), *Global Shadows*, Durham, NC: Duke University Press.

Frobenius, Leo (2014), *Leo Frobenius on African History, Art, and Culture: An Anthology*, ed. Eike Haberland, Princeton: Princeton University Press.

Gaonkar, Dilip (ed.) (2001), *Alternative Modernities*, Durham, NC: Duke University Press.

Hunt, Lynn (2014), *Writing History in the Global Era*, New York: W. W. Norton.

Lefkowitz, Mary (1996), *Not Out of Africa: How 'Afrocentrism' Became an Excuse to Teach Myth as History*, New York: Basic Books.

Mbembe, Achille (2001), *On the Postcolony*, Berkeley: University of California Press.

Meskell, Lynn and Robert W. Preucel (eds) (2004), *A Companion to Social Archaeology*, Oxford: Blackwell.

Mudimbe, V. Y. (1988), *The Invention of Africa: Gnosis, Philosophy and the Order of Knowledge*, London: James Currey.

Mudimbe, V. Y. (1994), *The Idea of Africa*, London: James Currey.

Osterhammel, Jürgen (2014), *The Transformation of the World*, Princeton: Princeton University Press.

Pomeranz, Kenneth (2000), *The Great Divergence*, Princeton: Princeton University Press.

Wagner, Peter (2012), *Modernity: Understanding the Present*, Cambridge: Polity.

Wynne-Jones, Stephanie and Jeffrey B. Fleisher (eds) (2015), *Theory in Africa, Africa in Theory: Debating Meaning in Archaeology*, Abingdon: Routledge.

6

North–South and the Question of Recognition: A Constellation Saturated with Tensions

À. Lorena Fuster

IN RECENT TIMES we have witnessed what appears to be the return of a certain expectation in terms of the emancipatory and transformative potential of the South, at an economic level, but also politically and socially (Gray and Gills 2016). The awakening of this interest is due to the trustworthiness demonstrated by cooperation amongst so-called Southern countries, and stems from the new visibility that this has attained within representational frameworks. The re-emergence of a Southern layout based on the controversial Global South category, the SSC acronym (South-South Cooperation) and especially that of BRICS (Brazil, Russia, India, China, South Africa), have built upon a historic promise. This promise was made in the second half of last century, specifically from the 1960s and 1970s onwards, drawing on novel economic and cultural theories. It was aimed at creating innovations that could rearrange the world and was formulated for the first time in the African and Asian Non-Aligned Countries' Conference in Bandung in 1955, whose principles were the SSC's foundational motto (equality, mutual benefit, respect for sovereignty, non-interference and non-aggression).

In the following decade the history of colonialism that had its origin in the distant sixteenth century was about to end: the process of anti-colonial struggles had – almost entirely – been accomplished in the form of national liberation or by means of the decolonisation process that was achieving its final goals in Africa. 'Recognising that the peoples of the world ardently desire the end of colonialism in all its manifestations' was stated – at last – in the United Nations' *Declaration on the Granting of Independence to Colonial Countries and Peoples* (UN General Assembly 1960).[1]

Along with the apparent heterogeneity of liberated Southern countries, the factors that were common amongst them were their past of subjugation, an economically dependent present and a future already marked in advance by the challenges of reducing their own developmental differences, as well as those of countries without a colonial past and that had experienced significant economic growth during the 1950s and 1960s. Only thereafter could the geographical contrast start to evolve into something patently geopolitical: thus, the debate about economic development entered the global political agenda and was laid out as the North–South divide (for a complete account of the meaning of this binary opposition, see Pinheiro in this volume). At last, the South could join this symbolic–geographic dialectic on its own initiative as the precondition for starting a peer-to-peer dialogue, political autonomy, had been fulfilled. It could then be the subject of a promise with which to stand up for the capability of Southern Hemisphere countries to emancipate themselves in the sense of securing their own economic, political and cultural autonomy, creating alternatives to the liberal policies of the North.

This chapter does not aim to give an account of the history of the North–South debate, but rather to provide an outline, from the perspective of the South's emancipatory promise, in order to situate its logic in a broader context: that of contemporary struggles aimed at recognition. Nevertheless, this is just the first move; the proposal of the chapter is to rethink this North–South dialectic not as being a case amongst others, but as the paradigmatic instance of the theoretico-practical frame that underpins contemporary theories of recognition. From the moment we consider it as paradigmatic, in the double meaning of exemplar and paradigm-founder, we are able to retrieve flashes of some historical and conceptual fragments of what could be called a forgotten history of the concept of recognition. The fragments are: (1) the imaginary evoked by the representation of the Southern Cross in the first atlas of stars, done in the seventeenth century, during the time in which the encounters between the seafarers guided by this constellation with the native Americans were not yet mediated and subsumed by categories that would later be shaped in the philosophy of history; (2) the moment in which Hegel in the summit of the philosophy of history structured the concept of the struggle for recognition, transforming Fichte's account of recognition and departing from key events of his present; (3) the politico-legal uses of the concept of recognition from Hegel onwards, until the fall of the British Empire; (4) the re-emergence of the concept of recognition during the last decades of the twentieth century in relation to the rise of new social movements.

'We must leave the North behind', claimed José Martí in *Our*

America (1891), actually writing it when he was in the North. De Sousa Santos recalled him at the beginning of the century, in the heady days of social movements in both hemispheres. If we follow his theory of translation to understand the 'new constellation of political and emancipatory cultural meanings in an unequally globalised world' (de Sousa Santos 2014: 234), we could state that the possibility of leaving a certain North behind would be a transversal concern valid for all the current struggles against domination and for recognition.

The challenge for the countries of the South was in general to make their own singularities and projects recognised, and in concrete to transform the structures responsible for an unfair global economic order (especially those relating to extractive capitalism), which – as analysed in the 1970s – had been born as a Eurocentric and colonial form of capitalism (Quijano 1972, 2000; Wallerstein 1974–89).

Economically rooted dependency theories – with their post-Marxist reprocessing of Gramsci's concept of hegemony (Prebisch [1948] 1998) – contributed to the creation of an alter-hegemonic and counter-hegemonic imaginary notion that, despite its internal differences, coincided in its attempt to build an anti-colonial project that was also respectful of national sovereignty, inclusive and (to some extent) anti-capitalist, as well as being based on mutual solidarity and cooperation. The different configurations (New International Economic Order or NIEO; the India, Brazil, South Africa Dialogue Forum or IBSA; SSC; BRICS) all pointed towards a horizon of collective self-reliance, trying to generate a South-South collective development paradigm, a horizontal transnationalism based on economic cooperation and able to establish peer-to-peer relations with the North (OECD 2011: 17; UNDP 2013: 1–3).

At the same time – and especially since the 1970s – cultural and philosophical theories have been formulated that have influenced the issue of dependency from various angles and through different vocabularies and categories: liberation theology, cultural studies, subaltern theory and anti-colonial, postcolonial and decolonial theory, to name the most important ones. Although emphasis was initially placed on the need for liberation from these dependencies – at multiple levels (Dussel 1973) – progress was made during that decade and the next in terms of the research and analysis of how the coloniser–colonised dependency developed, as well as what kind of subjectivities and social, political, symbolic and epistemic institutions and practices had been generated as a result in different contexts.

The legitimacy of the desire for inclusion, as an experience stemming from instituted normativity, was accompanied by discourses of denunciation and vindication that brought to light the historic injustices suffered by colonised countries. At the same time, these discourses emphasised the value that colonised countries could bring into the world, sometimes from their historically constructed experiences and at others from a firm identity construction that bordered on essentialism.

This process went in parallel with other contestations. Over the previous centuries, various groups had come to the forefront vindicating their logical access to a legal framework regulated by the Western logic of rights – by thus becoming rightholders – through the most basic of them, the recognition of the right to have rights (Arendt [1951] 1973), from which many were (and still are) excluded. Some of those struggles had had their first battles decades earlier, but they re-emerged precisely in the 1960s and 1970s with different features to those of traditional labour movements, and many of them appealed to identity issues in order to fight discrimination based on race, gender, origin and language. They were thereby called new social movements, and included anti-colonial struggles, the struggle against black oppression, the struggles of American Indians or the Beurs, the civil rights movements, feminism, pacifism, environmentalism and anti-nuclear environmentalism. All these struggles to overcome inequalities and achieve the political recognition of oppressed and/or marginalised groups are either more or less exhausted or were energised almost half a century later in anti-establishment struggles.

Many of them have gradually been incorporated into the agendas of traditional political parties. One of the most noticeable dangers is that which relates to the homologating and normalising capability of power. Despite the distances between them, the basic experiences shared by these groups and their members can perhaps be read quite easily in light of Mary Wollstonecraft's dilemma: the feeling of the legitimacy of their desire to take part as equals in the game of privileges of those who hold political, economic and cultural power, and the difficulty of becoming part of this system without being assimilated and betraying the cause. The history of recognition as the assimilation of the other has also been outlined in recent decades as the mechanism used to set the imperialistic constitution of the colonial subject. Liberalism has acted differently – although still neutralising differences: by assuming the whole ensemble within its (pseudo)-universal Man, it made invisible those differences that were in fact being negatively valued and hierarchically organising society. It is becoming increasingly clear to these historically minoritised groups that asking to be recognised as human beings and, therefore, as legal subjects with human rights is not enough, and that their specific differences are the ones in need of full recognition (equal value, equal dignity). And this is something that has to be carried out in both the legal and symbolic spheres.

The tight theoretical net created around this axis has come to be called 'the [epistemological] paradigm of the other' (Mignolo 2003: 20). Although focusing more on cultural aspects – sometimes to the detriment of economic ones – these theories not only presented arguments but also justified the demands of the Southern countries for a fairer geographical rearrangement of economic, political and cultural power, as well as for inclusion into governance and global trade spaces and mechanisms.

This process of empowerment is recognised, for example, by the incorporation of emerging countries into the G20, but also in reviewing the status of the South as a whole of poor countries, and especially in the creation of an effective narrative of horizontality, cooperation, solidarity and respect for sovereignty able to garner international good repute.

As we mentioned, since the 1990s the take-off has been impressive and it has helped these countries to consider themselves as economic powers, bringing emancipation at this level to a considerable degree of fulfilment. But they have also succeeded in transforming their identity and international legitimacy into that of political actors to be taken into account. Although economic growth appears to have slowed since 2012 and the gaps according to indicators of per capita income and individual well-being in comparison with the North persist, it is already a fact that the SSC has questioned the hierarchical division North–South. In particular, it has done so on policy issues of cooperation and development by creating its own systems and institutions (with the Bank of the South and the New Development Bank undermining the role of the North and the OECD in this area and at the same time challenging the legitimacy and vertical forms of governance that have been hegemonic).

However, after all these years, the 'Southern identity' – as a promise for something other than multilateral power in the face of Western or US unilateralism – seems to be compromised. The political and ideological emphasis on structural change has shifted towards objectives of greater participation in the forums that define development agendas and a more equal distribution of power, yet without laying much stress upon social and environmental justice issues, at least not more than that which the North does in terms of its sustainable development agenda. It is not known to what extent these developments signal the rise of an alternative normative power. Moreover, the UN's universal Agenda 2030 seeks to innovate on a large scale with a paradigm shift regarding the Millennium Development Goals and, in general, the paradigm of aid and North–South cooperation as it has been known so far. As its self-definition as 'universal' indicates, and unlike previous agendas, it is not a small group of donors from the North that decides what the development model implemented by the South must be. Rather, universality must be the criterion for both the creation of the agenda (made from a transnational participatory process) and the concept of development itself that targets all countries through the idea of a framework of local governance of development that has a global effect. The development concerns the whole of humanity and the planet, while the development concept itself is intended to be rearticulated from a global perspective.

In addition, the economic practices of some of the most powerful countries of the so-called Global South – such as Brazil and China, *primus inter pares* – seem to be under suspicion due to their recent past (Estrella Faria 2005; Woods 2008; Strange et al. 2013; Gray and Murphy 2013; Gray and Gills 2016). More and more critical voices observe that after the anti-hegemonic discourse – still in force when projecting their image abroad – their foreign economic policy is reproducing neo-liberal policies and strategies of domination over the resources and people of some of their partner countries – such as sub-Saharan African countries – under the pretext of assistance and cooperation. Some voices speak of southern neo-colonialism and sub-imperialism (Gray and Gills 2016).

Hence the interpretive crossroads between on the one hand, those who suggest that this is in fact creating a new South-South dependency system and others who, on the other hand, see an asymmetric interdependence system being created, as part of a project against dependency where what is gained by each party in the exchange is necessarily different due to the heterogeneity of Southern countries (money earned as a result of trade or obtaining more intangible benefits such as experience, knowledge and cultural exchange, capability building, diplomatic solidarity, the promotion of human rights and the visibility and recognition of the South). Hence the calls to revive the spirit of Bandung or the old Third World drive (Santos 2000; Echart 2016).

In terms of domestic politics, the state, which seemed to have aligned with social movements in previous decades, has ignored them in decision-making – instead taking legal action against them and infantilising them for their lack of realism. The argument stating 'you cannot make an omelette without breaking eggs' still prevails (de Sousa Santos 2008; Wallerstein 2002).

In summary, we are witnessing a rather thorny dispute concerning interpretations. In fact, the question of whether the South is fulfilling or will fulfil its promise is closely linked to a broader debate about whether the phenomenon of emerging powers is considered indicative of a shift in the locus of the economic and political power of Southern countries, which would mean they have emancipated from the North; or whether it simply signals the co-option of a select number of key states in the Western-led neo-liberal world order, meaning there has not been an effective emancipation of the most economically developed Southern countries; instead, they would only be an instrument for managing the agony of American hegemony, supported by the Global North.

In other words: are we already at the end of hegemony as we used to know it, with BRICS now the vanguard – supported by the South – that will demonstrate its counter-hegemonic strength negotiating at forums and serving the interests of all Southern countries? Or rather, are the BRICS just the latest form devised by hegemonic power to prevail in its position and pursue its logic?

Moreover, what court has to judge and give authority to the fulfilment of the promise of the South remains an open question. Would it be the North reiterating its legitimising narratives? If the economic criteria available to quantify and analyse changes in the characteristics of poverty are increasingly questioned, a never-solved issue remains: how to measure and properly assess the rates of individual and collective self-realisation in social, moral and political spheres. What seems clear at this time of conflicting narratives, and struggles for interpretation and self-interpretation is the danger of interpreting the new, if there is any, with the criteria of the old.

We take the present moment as the provisory ending point from which to trace back a line that links it to a starting point: the moment in which we may find the pre-history of the North–South divide, that is, the moment of the encounter of the European seafarers with the inhabitants of the New World. To reach that point and then return

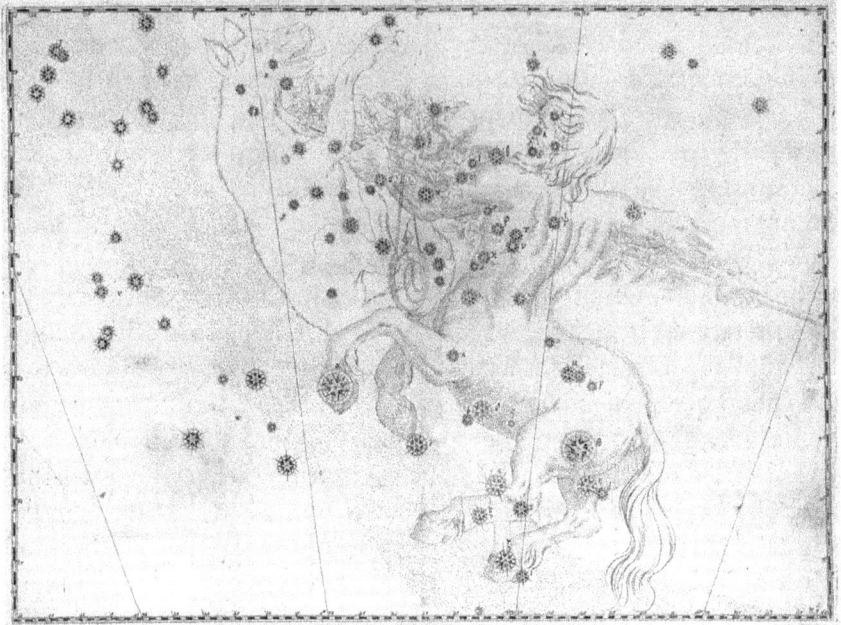

Figure 6.1 The Centaurus constellation, in Johann Bayer, *Uranometria: omnium asterismorum continens schemata, nova methodo delineata, aereis laminis expressa*, Augsburg: Christoph Mang, 1603.

progressively to our present, let us be guided by the constellation that was the most significant for both at that time: the Southern Cross. Between this past and our present mediates a progressive construction of an imaginary that allows us to read the dynamics between South and North as an ongoing struggle for recognition. In the next section its history will be re-presented through a print of that time.

Under the Southern Cross: a fragment of an early modern imaginary

The significance of the Southern Cross can be grasped in the fact that it is not displayed only in astronomical charts, but is the only constellation represented on the flags of a few Southern countries, and particularly on the flag of Mercosur, since it was founded in 1991. The Southern Cross has actually, and by extension, become the symbol of the Southern Hemisphere. Furthermore, if there is a distinctly 'modern' constellation, it is the Southern Cross: considered the most proper and primordial constellation for inhabitants of the Southern Hemisphere, between the fifteenth and seventeenth centuries it assumed an unparalleled relevance for sailors as a guide in unknown seas and lands. Described in diaries and letters by pioneers, poets and thinkers from diverse backgrounds, for many of them its disconcerting beauty was also related to its figure, the cross which inscribed their faith in the sky. So, without possessing a story linked to an ancient imaginary, it was originally baptised in a Romance language (*cruzero*), not in Latin, and was finally recognised as an independent constellation – a status that it holds until today (Room 1988; Kanas 2007).

In the Figure 6.1 we can observe it being represented as a Latin cross, absolutely Christianised and located to the south of Centaurus, but still not independent from the imaginary body of this hybrid being. The image is part of the *Uranometria: omnium asterismorum continens schemata, nova methodo delineata, aereis laminis expressa* by Johann Bayer, published in Augsburg (Germany) in 1603 and considered the first global representation of the celestial sphere in the form of an atlas.

Whilst the gaps in terrestrial maps had been completed in line with the great navigation experiences – carried out especially by the Dutch – celestial charts had not advanced significantly. Before the end of the decade, Galileo Galilei would present the diabolical contraption that was the telescope, which would make it possible to observe the skies and start the revolution of the universe.

Amongst Alexander Mair's superb fifty-one copperplate engravings symbolising the sixty constellations fixed by Bayer, and as it happens in the sky itself, the great southern constellation of Centaurus undoubtedly stands out. This constellation was already contained in Ptolemy's *Almagest*, and he circumscribed amongst its stars – particularly those in the lower part of the mythological animal's legs – four brightly shining stars which had been known since antiquity and which were easily visible at that time from North Africa and especially from Alexandria.[2] Those stars would be called the Southern Cross. However, the Centaurus constellation was not represented in isolation by Bayer, but in conjunction with the wolf constellation, Lupus. Furthermore, they are not juxtaposed but in interaction. In fact, they appear in a fighting position, at a moment when Centaurus has reached the wolf with its ornamented spear, which may be camouflaged with ivy.

The main reason why this print will be both the first fragment of our story and the constant reference of all the following argumentation is because it can be taken as an eloquent symptom of an imaginary that was under construction during the period between the fifteenth and eighteenth centuries. Luciferous stars guiding adventures into uncharted seas; different disorders that shake up the traditional orders; knowledge and techniques contributing to overcome the mistrust in human capabilities and in turn to control human freedom; bestial men – both masters and slaves – dance in the double imaginary of modernity, in its constitutive tension between autonomy and mastery (Arnason 1989; Castoriadis 1990; Wagner 2008).

Nevertheless, when European sailors first saw the Southern Cross, the dialectics had not taken that form yet, nor that first global dimension. What would happen was still only one of the possibilities to be determined. And when it effectively happened it was just the beginning of a great transformation.

It was determined as a fact in the form of an encounter with the new – and retrospectively for us as a *Faktum*. The novelty lay on both sides, voyagers and native Americans, and precisely because it was so it can be interpreted also as an experience of recognition, in the sense that all of them had to catalogue what the others were by placing them in the imaginary net of their own world (Pagden 1983: 12).

However, the classification of the others in those encounters was not immediate, univocal and symmetrical, as we can see in the documents left both by Europeans and native Americans (Guillén 1974; Pagden 1983, 1993). It became so progressively, through the political and epistemic practices that were established in the course of the encounters. In order to systematise and legitimate this *Faktum*, the way in which the encounter with the other effectively took place, the Western philosophy of history created an epistemological and normative frame that resolved the constitutive tension of modernity with a biased understanding of the concept of universality that pretends towards totalisation (Fuster and Rosich 2015). What is particularly dependent on the European experience of modernity is conceptualised either as the only possible experience of modernity, or as an instance of a universal concept of modernity to which one needs to conform if one wants to be modern (Wagner 2008). Those are issues that we have dealt with elsewhere (Fuster and Rosich 2015). What this chapter aims to go back to is the argumentative thread, in order to take it a little further and illuminate – through juxtaposition of some other fragments – other aspects of a possible forgotten history of recognition.

In the scene illustrated by Bayer and Mair, the struggle between those two beings, the centaur and the wolf, seems to be at the threshold moment between movement and immobility, the moment of suspension, the *standstill* of 'a constellation saturated with tensions' (Benjamin 1999: 475), the instant of motionless coexistence Theodor Adorno in his correspondence with Walter Benjamin tried to define as 'the moment of indifference between death and meaning' (Benjamin 1999: 466). This print arrests our gaze precisely due to the lightning quality of those dialectical images. By lighting up the now, the print contains an index or historical mark which from the past sends us to the present. In fact, this is the second reason why this image has been chosen, because it illustrates our present in its specificity. It represents the present instant as the pure now, in its innermost constitution, that of no longer and not yet. But it also represents the gap in which we significantly find ourselves nowadays when seen from the perspective of a progressive path to higher and better recognitions.

But before moving onto what the image tells us about our now and its past, let us pause step by step on the details of our illustration of this place in the celestial sphere. The fascinating intimacy between the astronomical and philosophical vocabularies we are mulling over will be pushed to its limits in order to outline – on the map – the surprising and deep meanings represented by our constellation saturated with tensions.

In the image, following the position of the sky from a geocentric perspective, Lupus is further north and Centaurus is southward. In fact, the physical power that propels Centaurus upward is none other than the animality of its hind limbs, precisely where we see the four brightly shining stars whose name in Roman times was that of Caesar's Throne, and which only after Andrea Corsali's Christianised baptism would come to be called the Cross.[3] The stars of the Cross, which at the time of Bayer's publication were already beginning to be treated as a separate constellation,[4] were the most important celestial guiding lights in the days when the South Seas were furrowed, guiding the great navigators towards the phantasmic Indies. Their nautical and terrestrial importance is essential because they allow for easily and accurately tracing the south cardinal point: the celestial south pole around which the celestial sphere and the geographic south seem to rotate. As soon as the North was left behind, the Cross was there to indicate the South. Its symbolic role is less clear, but it is quite easy to deduce that the Cross was a comforting sight for European sailors, and less easy to conclude that it was a symbolic ally and an alibi in terms of the legitimacy of the evangelising mission undertaken under the sign of the (Holy) Cross, as aborigines of the South already had their own interpretations of the Cross.

No European unveiled the four stars to the inhabitants of the South, who for millennia had used the astronomical knowledge necessary for their farming practices and vital activities in general by building on the observation of the small constellation that for some was the beginning of their sky (their north according to the representation of our maps). Despite the scarcity of sources, we know that – through fragmentary evidence, mostly oral and sometimes architectural – since the days of the great civilisations, those four stars were regarded as the most significant ones in the sky; so significant in fact, that in Andean cultures – under the Quechua name *chakana* and already seen as a cross – they were deemed to be an ascending or descending bridge or stairway, the intermediate reality linking the earthly world to the celestial world and the world of the dead. Its representation is the result of the condensation of astronomical observations and a cosmovision that confines its geometric harmonies within a stairway-shaped square cross, with twelve ends, whose oldest representation found so far dates back between 4,000 and 5,000 years. The *chakana* still appears today as a symbol of Andean indigenous cultures and a vindicating sign of the relationship of current cultures with their aboriginal past (Lajo 2002, 2006; Tone 2009). Other cultures – such as the Mocoví people – represented these stars as part of the *ñandú* – also called *súri* or *choique* – a sacred animal, stalked by two hounds, one on each side. It is common amongst other distant southern cultures (in Australia, Africa, New Zealand and the Pacific Islands) to interpret the shape of the stars as the image of a sacred animal (emu, possum, lioness), often stalked by human hunters, animals or even – repeatedly – the paw- or footprint of an animal, such as an ostrich or an eagle (Bhathal 2006; Norris 2008a, 2008b). In the end, these stars were at the heart of different cosmovisions and self-interpretations of southern societies, and some of them already interpreted their shape as a cross.

But these fifteenth- and sixteenth-century explorations – carried out under a particular interpretation of the Cross, that of Christianity, and science – eventually imposed a global shape and order onto celestial and terrestrial maps. These representations were the prelude to the modern world-system in which the different interpretations of the world tend to become one. In this frame of interpretation, while the Copernican revolution changed the understanding of our system, the North never stopped being at the top and the South at the bottom in cartographic representations.

As an independent constellation, the Cross was not represented until the publication of Jodocus Hondius Junior and Adrian Vaen's celestial globe in 1613, with the caption '*Cruzero hispanis, at Ptolemy Pedes Centauri*'. It was supposedly Augustine Royer who first publicly named it as *Crux Australis*.[5]

If we now examine the Greek mythological component involved in these constellations, the Cross itself does not possess its own history, as for the Greeks it was merely a part of Centaurus. On the other hand, the Lupus constellation is a constellation marked by the history of violence of a father, Lycaon – King of Arcadia – who kills his children for fear of them snatching power from him, later serving one of them to Zeus at a banquet. To punish Lycaon for his cruelty, Zeus transforms him into a wolf.

Chiron, the most famous of all centaurs, also had the archetypal devourer of children as a father: Cronus. While those of his kind were wild and violent creatures, the talents of this hybrid being included medical wisdom, knowledge of the stars, the arts and the use of the bow, which he learned from Apollo. In fact, it is usual to see him represented tightening a bow just before shooting an arrow, and it was precisely the wound caused by an arrow accidentally shot by his friend Heracles that caused such excruciating pain that in order to end his own suffering he decided to exchange his immortality for Prometheus's mortality. When he died – so the legend goes – Zeus placed him in the sky, and there he is, in the shape of a constellation (Sagittarius or Centaurus).

In none of Chiron's stories are we told about a fight with a wolf, so the scene represented by Bayer does not have a traditional reference. This is why it is interesting to understand the author's imaginative gesture: to link the centaur and the wolf through the dynamics of a struggle, replacing the arrow with a spear, covering it with ivy as if it were a ploy devised by the centaur to trick and capture the wolf, and finally turning the struggle into a fight to the death. The stars' layout did not compel Bayer to outline this profile: the only thing he had inherited from tradition was a Lupus and a Centaurus inscribed in the sky.

In the general political view prevalent in early modernity, shaped by the fear and violence of sea attacks, the wolf stands out as the most popular animal reference of an anthropology that developed at the same time as the Southern Cross entered modern history.[6] Man had already started – from the times of Plautus – being a wolf to man, but only through Thomas Hobbes – 'the twin of fear' borne by his mother's horror in face of the proximity of Spain's Invincible Armada – does it truly become one. First in *De cive* ([1642–3] 1983) and later in his

Leviathan ([1651] 2012), the representations of rulers are easily identifiable with a devouring father who has already swallowed his children. One could say this was done in order to protect them, or as the myth of Cronus already indicated, for fear of being dismissed by a new order they could introduce into the world.

Thus, the scene tells us – *unhistorically* – of a fight to kill the devouring father/bestial ruler, which is carried out by a hybrid creature, half-man half-animal, a joint paradigm of intelligence and power. By contrast, in regard to our present, Bayer's image historically points towards the time of suspension itself: the end of the fight is not consummated. It stops – significantly – between the 'no longer' and 'not yet': the wolf is not dead, but they have caught up with it. Will it stay that way forever? Never? That is perhaps the greatest question of the print, which is not immediately or easily noticeable. Is this (near) the end of formal domination (Wagner 2015)?

The unknown – as is almost always the case – is hidden in time. In the heat of the battle, we have failed to notice – perhaps – the peculiar object carried by the centaur on its left arm. It is in fact the only modern object in the whole scene: a pocket watch. Invented only a few decades earlier, in the second half of the sixteenth century, the watch displays the time that before was only shown by the stars, the ticking of *no longer–not yet*.

The struggle with the other as a forma mentis

A mere man or a mere beast, in all probability, would not have reached this point. The wolf is on top. In its dialectics, the image suspends – perhaps – the moment that is closest to the end of a struggle, a struggle to shake off that which rises above the individual from a metaphorical 'top'. A fight to avoid the (indeterminate) threat of power? The threat of physical integrity? The threat over freedom? Power configured in modern times swallows its children, it includes them in its social body (even as equally free) in order to ensure the liveability of life (non-death/freedom) (Butler 2004). Very often, it does so at the price of the difference potentially meant by that freedom. Only as a remainder: equality does not oppose difference, inequality does; difference finds its opposite in sameness or homogeneous identity.

Late modernity has also taught us that power does not swallow, it shapes bodies and souls. That which is left outside the scope of what swallows/shapes/recognises power is what is monstrous, deformed, unclassifiable, neither one thing nor the other (what is inter-). Therefore, the centaur's hybridity will be key to our reading. The juxtaposition of its body – which is not bending – is a triple formation that opens up to multiplicity: human–animal–cross. And as a cross: ladder–bridge–scale.

Machiavelli also, capitalising on the lessons learnt from the centaur Chiron for *The Prince*, advised the sovereign to be hybrid, double, to know how to divide or multiply himself – as a fox and a lion. Given the increasingly difficult governance of peoples, the Prince does not need to have such qualities, but must intend to have them in order to become recognisable as a prince and stay in the place which he knows is not entirely his (Machiavelli 2010: 69–70).

So who is the sovereign in the image? The wolf or the centaur? For there to be a struggle, it must virtually be both.

The self-governance and general governance manual that is *The Prince* is the best and clearest example of an era whose political space was organised around the question of how to rule, which was a predominant political concern in the fifteenth and sixteenth centuries, whilst the great navigations guided by the Southern Cross were taking place. According to Foucault, Western Europe at that moment was characterised by focusing both its thinking and practices precisely on governmentalisation. Thus, creating multiple governmental skills – in all fields – went hand in hand with the reversal of the question of how to govern: how not to be governed (in this way). In the eyes of Foucault, the experience of criticism institutionalised as an ethos of the Enlightenment can be read – therefore – as an experience of resistance in face of the authority that undermines the strength of the pillars of traditional legitimacy. The self-interpretation of humans as beings able to conduct valid interpretations – both in regard to the natural and supernatural (the Scriptures) dimensions – establishes an open space for the practice of criticism as both interpretation and transformation, 'the art of voluntary insubordination, that of reflected intractability [. . .] would essentially insure the desubjugation of the subject in the context of what we could call, in a word, the politics of truth' (Foucault 1997: 32, 39).

What Foucault calls historical critique, with its origin in the question about governmentalisation, allows us to discern and illuminate the four most significant historical points in the chronology that we are using: (1) the dawn of modernity, marked by religious wars and the discovery of the New World (fifteenth to sixteenth centuries); (2) the *Aufklärung* (sixteenth to eighteenth centuries); (3) the emergence of social control (nineteenth century); and (4) the world of today, emerged from the Second World War (from 1950 until the present) with its theories and practical critique of the complicity of power and instrumental rationality (a position in which Foucault situates himself, in proximity to the Frankfurt School).

If we go over our temporal contextualisation in parallel with the exposition of the governmentalisation question, it is important to note that it was precisely the European sailors who – in their encounter with the inhabitants of that particular South which is now America – experienced and laid the foundation of the modern question of equality, in terms of whether these beings (in their eyes, quite unclassifiable) were like them or not; whether they could be included in humanity or not (Pagden 1993; Fuster and Rosich 2015). Can they be included in 'us'? In the various determinations of 'us'? To do so, they must beforehand be categorised, to decide whether they belong to the category of humans or beasts. Or if they are an inter-. And based on that, to rule them or subject them. A symptom to keep in mind is that Bayer, in his twelve figurations of exotic animals for the twelve new constellations of the southern hemisphere, included the Indian (*Indus*). The successive interpretations of the question, the different answers and their practical implications, as well as the heated debates amongst the intellectuals of the day belong to the history of that *Faktum*. What is worth underlining is that the modern civilisational project, with its space–time configuration, initially legitimised both domination and the struggle to end it. These were not successive actions, but simultaneous ones.

But only from the perspective of a very advanced Modernity in which the different disciplines have systematised the meaning of the events into a universal project can Bayer's image be read as the future of the image of the encounter. What mediated between the two moments were normativities that were progressively assimilated into the modern imagination. They were registered especially through the revolutions of the end of the eighteenth century and their related institutions and practices, even in the post-revolutionary era (from the drafting of national constitutions to the knowledge represented – for instance – by modern political and moral philosophy). Equal freedom and the struggle to determine what this meant informed the main institutions of that period. Whereas being free had been declared a duty since Kant – and this duty was extended to everyone due to the systemised universalist matrix within philosophy itself – the possibility of a free future became a right, apart from being the challenge par excellence of all rational beings for breaking out of ignorance and passivity.

Thus, from the necessity of the *Aufklärung* – formulated by Kant as the attainment of the age of majority (from the tutelage of the other) – it is tempting – and almost natural – to see every confrontation as a struggle for emancipation, autonomy and equality. And we also understand every struggle for freedom – almost directly – in terms of a struggle for recognition (of being and the ability to be). We find it natural because we are still under the effect of the Hegelian figure of the master–slave (*Herrschaft–Knechtschaft*) fight to the death. This figure was his critical reinterpretation of Fichte's concept of recognition (*Anerkennung*) in *Foundations of Natural Right* ([1796/7] 2000). Hegel ([1806] 1977) underlines the moral component of the process of recognition that Fichte ignored and in a metonymical move abstracted from the reality of the Haitian Revolution, transforming it into a dialectic between a master and slave (Buck-Morss 2009). This is the climactic and explicit formulation of an implicit understanding that had been brewing since the institution of the philosophy of history (Fuster and Rosich 2015). Such a conception of the meaning of the struggle and its internal dynamics shocked the core of the philosophical and political imagination of the nineteenth century – but especially the general imagination of the late twentieth century – to such an extent that it has become a *forma mentis*.

Similarly, the North–South relationship as an oppositional dialectic is at this point a *forma mentis*, and not only for its opposition on the map. In fact, it is easily legible in terms of a struggle for recognition because these geographical positions are the contemporary names of two poles of a history through which is forged the logic of the relation with the other that shapes the heart of the theories of recognition. The meeting of the North with the geographical and metaphorical South constitutes progressively and asymmetrically the master and slave poles, transforming the previous experience of this relation forever. This is the experiential and conceptual core of the theory of recognition that has shaped the contemporary grammar of politics and has become our *forma mentis*.

But let us pause on Hegel. As is known, in the Hegelian theory of the constitution of a universal consciousness, consciousness alone can emerge through the recognition that is granted to it by another – formally equal – consciousness. The dynamic modality is that of a struggle between life and death of two non-self-realised consciousnesses, which – in turn – are internally divided between the will to be free and the will to be dependent. This is not the kind of dialectics found in Benjamin's dialectical images, where the relationship takes place in a juxtaposition that establishes analogies, but an asymmetrical dialectic whose inner logic leads to improvement. Neither is this the logic of the experience of recognition that took place during the encounters; instead of an openness to the will to meet an other who is as other as possible, there is the rush to subsume its novelty, to control it and neutralise it. The struggle for recognition, although not presented by Hegel as belonging to the political dimension, when transferred to it, dislocates the paradigm – created by Hobbes – that understands human action as a struggle for self-preservation. However – from the beginning – the confrontational spirit of this conception of politics is present: in order to be, we need the other. Not the equal other, but the originally equal other that has been historically subjugated (Negroes, indigenes, women, the South, and so on).

On the other hand, the struggle for recognition is a fight that does not seem imposed on everyone with the same force of obligation, as hinted at by Hegel when referring to Napoleon as the 'world spirit on horseback':

> When Napoleon said before the Peace of Campo Formio 'the French Republic is no more in need of recognition than the sun is', his words conveyed no more than that strength of existence which itself carries with it a guarantee of recognition, even if this is not expressly formulated. (Hegel [1819] 1991: 366–7)

Nor can everyone enter the struggle of their own free will, because it is an asymmetric fight between peers. If in the master–slave dialectic what established the dynamic situation was always the open possibility for the slave to become someone worthy of being a master (through education, revolution or a prospective entry into the middle class), then for a person who is unable to access their self-recognition, even the possibility of fighting is forbidden (the figure of the Negro and the uncivilised or barbaric nation).[7]

Therefore, the attainment of the express statement of that recognition is, however, what seems to be implicitly guaranteed by mere existence, which will become a normative horizon in Hegelian philosophy. The expression of personal courage is not enough; there is also a need for a positive evaluation from others of what one claims as one's own. Its meaning surpasses Kantian 'respect' – the basis of society and morality – and also tolerance, 'refraining from using power against strongly disapproved of important deviations' (for a distinction of the three terms, see Khomyakov 2013).

In its discriminatorily inclusive capacity, the concept of recognition had an immediate influence in the legal field, especially in international law, between the nineteenth century and the mid-twentieth century (Parfitt 2016). In the absence of a conceptual history of the term 'recognition' – as there is for other closely related terms like 'freedom' or 'emancipation' (Koselleck and Presner 2002) – if we look at recent studies in the legal field we can conclude that the use of the term 'recognition' in this context is precisely that which was referred to by Napoleon: validating or denying the statute of nation-states in the field of intra-European discussions (they had internal sovereignty, but they needed the recognition of other nations to have an international legal identity). Yet that was just the beginning. Over time and through different stages, recognition went from being a theoretical tool of individualisation and inclusion to a powerful instrument of exclusion of what was non-European, by means of identification, cataloguing, minoritisation and social control of communities and individuals, which would legitimise and facilitate colonial imperialism between the last quarter of the nineteenth century and the fall of the British Empire in the 1950s (Clark 2016).[8] Hence, symptomatically, after the collapse of imperialism, the framework of recognition was discarded, since its exclusionary ability was no longer in use.

It is therefore in the new experience of the imperialist encounter – when the normative power of Europe has already constituted itself as such – that we discover that there is no obligation to behave towards the other following the moral and political patterns that govern the land we come from. With the aim of eliminating both the internal and external obstacles to the expansion of capital, imperialism – and the new encounter fostered with the other – has become characterised by the term 'horror' (Joseph Conrad). The unmitigated horror that causes that *other-that-is-no-other* legitimises the horror that may be committed when there are no containment barriers or reciprocal pacts, which are so distinctive of nation-states. Under certain conditions, the elimination of the other proves to be a respectable policy. With this epistemological framework of recognition, imperialism exceeds its economic motive to go deeper into the geopolitics of a world divided into 'master–slave races' (Arendt [1951] 1973).

We say *other-that-is-no-other* because it does not count towards entering the struggle for recognition, but at the same time it does not count not for being radically other, but precisely for not being so as much as expected. What is awful is realising that the other – seen from Western recognition frameworks as brutal and barbaric – is not so different to us, is not inhuman, and shares the colonisers' humanity. Moreover, what is terrifying is realising that the idea of humanity (Christianity, civilisation, progress) is a social construction, and it wobbles when going beyond borders. Proximity without the protective distance offered by a civilising creation is horrific. It is the dissonance between identity and difference that marks the emergence of the category of race, which will partner with the mechanism of bureaucracy in the encounter of the Boers with South Africa (belonging to a cataloguing bureaucracy of recognition). Racism is not the expression of rejection towards difference, but an effective prophylactic against an experienced similitude (Arendt [1951] 1973).

But we insist on the fact that the functional epistemic framework for determining the encounter was not created in the encounter of the nineteenth century: it had already been created as a result of the colonial experience of the fifteenth century. Therefore, every encounter with the other – with what remains to be found – will again be chilling, but it will quickly be reduced to the same layout: barbarism, uncivilisation, bestiality.

What has been a progressive novelty is its increasingly ontological coherence, more and more rooted in humankind's own way of being. Had another determination been possible – something contingent, only one possibility amongst those possible – a theorisation of recognition would take place as the only constitution of humanity at an individual, social and political level. The maximum effectiveness of the theory is achieved through ontologisation, the maximum power of persuasion. But that was still to come.

In fact, the obsolescence of the term 'recognition' seems to have lasted only four decades, yet this time with a specular use. Its resurgence is a recent event of the end of the 1980s, and especially of the 1990s, hence the risk assumed by our interpretation. The concept of recognition resurfaced vigorously, again with Hegel as a reference, although the egalitarian Hegel of *Jena Writings* is the most preferred version (Honneth, Siep), as opposed to that of *The Phenomenology of Spirit* (Butler, Taylor).

Although the Hegelian concept of recognition has been at the heart of other authors' thinking (Taylor 1994; Butler 2004), it did not become a proper recognition theory until it was systematised and developed, especially by Axel Honneth ([1992] 1995), who sees the constitutive intersubjective dynamics of identity and otherness outlined by Hegel under the influence of the object relations psychoanalytic theories of Donald Winnicott and Jessica Benjamin's relational psychoanalysis (Benjamin 1988). Configured this way, the contemporary theory of recognition has demonstrated its strength for over two decades. This strength is due not only to its power as an ethical and political normative theory, but also to its heuristic capability: it satisfactorily unravels, interprets and explains the operational and legitimising psychological, ethical, social and political mechanisms of our world today. In addition, the most recent scientific contributions – such as the discovery of mirror neurons – seem to reinforce this strength, to which the old psychological and psychoanalytical theories on personality formation in children can be added, preferably as a complement.

With no big debates surrounding the meaning of the term, the core of the social struggles of the last decades has been structured around this concept, also with little resistance. The main task of the current theory of recognition – in line with the critical theory methodology to which most authors working in this framework adhere (the most significant exceptions are again Butler and Taylor) – is to analyse the hurdles to freedom and social justice in terms of social domination, as along with the social conditions of individual and collective self-realisation. That is, recognition is addressed primarily from the perspective of cases where there is misrecognition or a lack of recognition altogether. In other words, not from the top down, but from the bottom up.

Perhaps part of the success and validity of the term 'recognition', especially in association with the term 'struggle', is due to the fact that it proves to be really intuitive, and it reveals as well that individual and collective identity are intersubjective phenomena that are formed when we relate to others, that is to say, they are dependent on otherness. It is therefore not surprising that many of the claims and discursive productions of recent decades – also from the South – use the concept of recognition to articulate their demands for justice. In the Declaration of the Bandung Conference, the term 'recognition' appeared – in an inclusive sense – in principle 3: 'Recognition of the equality of all races and the equality of all nations large and small' (Ministry of Foreign Affairs 1955: 168). Even though it does not seem to have any technical significance, its field of use follows the lines we mentioned previously: the equal sovereignty of nations and groups, based on racial criteria.

The frameworks for the management and enunciation of political discursive spaces have changed considerably, but now, because this principle has become normatively grounded, when talking about other globalisation possibilities from the South in terms of recognition – and also of redistribution and situated knowledge (de Sousa Santos 2014) – principle 3 forms part of the basis.

From the general perspective of the modern emancipatory project, recognition is a concept capable of dealing with the issues of inter-subjectivity, historicity and contingency of the formation of individual and collective subjects. Unlike other democratic narratives in political theory, it does not do so from a presupposition of conflict – that characterises the relationship of the self with the other (litige and agonism) – but from an inclusivist perspective that corrects the most exclusionary and asymmetrical features of the Hegelian concept. It is also, and above all, a concept that addresses the question of freedom and equality through the phenomena of individualisation and inclusion, which are crucial to social change and analysable from a social science perspective.[9] Furthermore, it can be productive for carrying out an analysis of social institutions.

The impregnability demonstrated by this theory prompts us to consider the hypothesis that the theory of recognition has become a true paradigm in the Kuhnean sense. The level of detail of discussions is steadily increasing and authors – especially Honneth – keep updating the theory, yet it has not lost the formal elegance and elasticity that characterise it. It is a paradigm because it seems to be sustained by the agreement of the social scientists at different levels and with different degrees of involvement.[10]

Beyond the community of social scientists, we find those whose lives unfold against the backdrop of the paradigm's validity. In regard to this last point, it could be argued that the theory of recognition went beyond the walls of academia a long time ago, to become a kind of *sensus communis* or, as we said at the beginning, a *forma mentis*. It is an interpretive framework through which citizens make their own private and public behaviours intelligible, and therefore all our actions may be susceptible to (self-)interpretation as part of a determined struggle for recognition, which may itself consist of several intersecting recognitional struggles and may entail changing the frameworks of recognition.

The main criticisms levelled at the theory of recognition could be classified as follows: (1) it ignores the strictly economic dimensions of social injustice, which may work in favour of the injustices caused by neo-liberalism (Fraser, de Sousa Santos); (2) it can reify (assimilate, homogenise, stigmatise), essentialise and individualise identities (Fraser, Benhabib, Butler); (3) it reduces the intersubjective relationship to an appropriative relationship of domination (Levinas, Pagden, Fuster and Rosich); or, on the contrary, (4) it ignores the fact that the self–other relationship is always a relationship where power dynamics are present, constructing identity (Butler, McNay); (5) when objective inequalities are taken into the body and naturalised as subjective dispositions, the capacity for political agency can be subtly eroded (McNay); and finally, (6) an amendment to the whole would entail recognition theory being called an ideology, following Rousseau's idea of inauthenticity as the outcome of aiming to please others (Althusser, Neuhouser).

To offset the limitations and fill in the blind spots highlighted by these criticisms, various arguments have been developed, and they have contributed to refining, clarifying and incorporating perspectives (at an intra-paradigmatic level, the Honneth–Fraser discussion (Fraser and Honneth 2003) is of particular interest, and at an inter-paradigmatic level the same is true of the Honneth–Rancière discussion (Honneth et al. 2016), although its impact so far has been more limited). With regard to the meaning of the term 'recognition', we can observe a kind of general consensus. In intra-paradigmatic terms, the Hegelian notion, understood as the intersubjective dynamics of the constitution of the subject, is preserved – a notion that is based on mutuality, which, however, is no longer as asymmetric as it was in the master–slave struggle and, also, is based on the exchange of positive assessments. This agreed definition accounts for the criticism concerning the suitability of potentially synonymous terms like 'identification' or 'acknowledgement'. It would seem therefore that this term – unlike most political terms – is not open to contestation, and in order for it to be deployed this minimal meaning would suffice.

We shall return to the subject of this apparent conceptual profile – not open to contestation – in the final section of this chapter. For now, it is important to stress that at an intra-pragmatic level the struggle for recognition is not considered amongst the possible forms of relationship with the other, but as the foundational dynamics of the individual and social psyche. Let us go back to the struggle of the centaur and the wolf, to propose a reading linked to the present.

The centaur's watch: what is beyond the paradigm of recognition?

We said that the mystery contained in the print in Figure 6.1, which is not immediately noticeable, lay in the suspension of time. The centaur's watch will have stopped between a no longer and a not yet. Or maybe it is the only thing in the scene that retains its relentless beat, but the watch's case blocks our view. We also said that Bayer's image challenges us because it illuminates something inherent to our present: the 'no longer, but not yet', in which many of the struggles of our time seem suspended. Amongst them, as noted before, is the struggle for the geopolitical organisation of our world-system.

As easily as in a dream, this question turns into another, which could become the political question of our time: can we leave the North–South behind? With its variations: can we leave the North–South behind if we come from the South? And the North? Can we leave the North–South behind if we come from the North? And the South?

It may be the form of a question articulated from the Souths of existence, wherever they may be, close or far away from the North. To understand the specificity of our time, we need diagnoses that establish differences and also live up to appearances. Even if it is counter-intuitively and provocatively. If we look at the present from the vindictive background of the years when the North–South discussion was forged, especially from the 1970s onwards, we can take distance from the most absolutising, negative interpretations that can lead to immobility or paralysis. Taking into account the indicators and criteria available (economic, legal) to measure historical evolution or what used to be called progress, we would have to say that the levels of recognition at an individual and collective level – and hence of freedom and material welfare – have increased globally. After a transformation of the orders of recognition, the gap between established principles of freedom and justice and their actual realisation is decreasing.

These considerations and the attempt to discriminate between forms of domination are the origin of Peter Wagner's provocative thesis, which we had announced as a question and left suspended with Bayer's image: our present is the time of the (near) end of formal domination. We understand formal domination as 'a kind of domination that justifies hierarchy of one group over another and enshrines such hierarchy in formal rules that, among other elements, determine who dominates and who is dominated' (Wagner 2015: 19). We have reached its (near) end because we have left behind the legitimation and possible legitimacy of the domination of one group over another or the exclusion of one group from participating in determining the rules of socio-political organisation (Wagner 2015: 19). It is not a question of there being no domination (the end of formal domination is not the end of domination), but rather that old dominations are no longer sustainable at a justificatory level and find resistance everywhere. Nonetheless, many of these dominations – beyond the legal scope, but here as well – actually remain valid on different scales in all corners of the globe.

But does this (near) end signal that we are near the equator? Can we see the Southern Cross from here? Have we left the North behind as José Martí wanted?

Is the question relevant despite the paradigms of the North–South relationship being declared obsolete or – precisely because of being declared obsolete – does the question arise due to the possibility of truly leaving these logics of power relations behind, to start new ones? We realise that declaring the death of a principle of world order does not mean that the ghost of the deceased exerts no power or domination (capitalism, colonialism and patriarchy are only some examples).

The invocation of the name of the South during the last few decades did indeed attempt to contest an order. After the political liberation brought by national independence processes, the accusation of injustice made by the South against the North went far beyond the notion of human slaughter and economic spoliation. In an increasingly coordinated manner – whether under the theory of liberation or not – its demand was presented as a demand for the recognition of a historic injustice perpetrated in the cultural, symbolic and epistemic realms.

The anti-capitalist challenges featured in the origins of the debate gradually disappeared, and as we said, if during the years after the Second World War *distribution* was the key word of social struggles, after the emergence of the new social movements the key word changed to *recognition*. The policies associated with this framework of understanding – and policies of recognition – but also identity policies and policies of difference, possessed logics that could be valid locally or could be articulated with the existing universal normativity and be claimed as global policies. However, overlapping social equality with political equality imposes an imperative of normalisation of differences. Equality is not an innate quality that arises from differences, but a relational framework artificially created through politics and law. This legal framework originally bore the seed of utmost inclusiveness, and this is what it progressively aims for (Arendt 1958). Precisely for this reason, it is worth remembering that not all invocations of differences 'disturb and generate conflict against the vocation of order' (Birulés 2015: 46). The current emphasis on differences is just the other side of the homologating universalism formulated in the obsessive modern identity language, since these occur – very often – only as unyielding identities (Birulés 2015: 46). Faced with a thorny dialectic, between denial and the 'victimisation of victims', many groups demand recognition for the diverse tones of their discourses and undertaken initiatives, while simultaneously tending towards a strong internal differentiation as various forms of domination are identified between the subgroups that compose them.

Perhaps, the teaching of the centaur is not to allow oneself to be reduced to identity and to make only a strategic use of it: to give oneself the chance to be more than that which is presented to the wolf for the sake of presentability – what is given to the hegemon to recognise as being recognisable – having a stronghold of unpredictable otherness that is the price not to be paid for being included. It is from this stronghold that it gets its elan, its hind legs, the stars of the Southern Cross. By losing them, it will only be a disabled centaur, mired in pain and wanting to exchange its immortality for a lenitive death.

Other voices said, before the framework of interpretation – from which the universal Agenda 2030 stems – was established: the North–South divide must be left behind. 'On the contrary, the South seeks an undivided world [a truly interdependent world] in which there would be "no" South and "no" North', stated *The Challenge to the South*, the document published by the South Center Commission in 1995 under the chairmanship of Julius Nyerere, former President of Tanzania (South Commission 1995: 9–10). 'And because it is the people of the South who more urgently need change in the present world order, it is they who have to take the initiative to make this vision of the world a reality' (South Commission 1995: 10).

This vision of the South is the overcoming of the dialectic; a vision of reconciliation that would be resolved through new geopolitics, which would render the North–South geographical categories metaphorically useless. Would it even change the orientation of the sky vault?

Milton Santos spoke about this revolution at the beginning of our century when, citing Nyerere and stating the convertibility of globalisation into *another possible globalisation*, he said that history had not ended, but that instead it was about to begin: 'The movement of the world reveals a single pulse, although the conditions are different depending on the continents, countries and places, which are valued for their form of participation in the production of this new history' (Santos 2000: 74, 83).

The World Social Forum (WSF) framework initiated in Porto Alegre, which is trying to capture this spirit, at once conciliatory and revolutionary, insists on these transnational alliances at the level of a civil society and anti-systemic movement, under an alternative world view:

> Importantly, the WSF seeks to bring together movements from the North and the South within a single framework. The only slogan, as yet, is 'Another World is Possible'. Even more strangely, the WSF seeks to do this without creating an overall superstructure. (Wallerstein 2002: 37)

But for some years a different voice has been raised: that which certainly seems the most unlikely option is that the new geopolitical figure resulting from reconciliation will be able to enjoy the forms and levels of well-being that characterise the North today. Everyone seems to agree that the North cannot be expanded: the production and consumption system that is dominant today in the United States, the European Union and Japan is not universalisable because there are insufficient natural resources and ecological space on the planet to allow for a similar expansion elsewhere they affirm.

Perhaps precisely because of this we are facing a situation in which the 'no longer' and 'not yet' do particularly give us cause for thought. In theory, much has been done, and what is yet to be done is only a matter of time, especially if we think of time as a line that leads us on the right track. But perhaps the perplexity of the 'not yet' is more evident because what is on the horizon – seen through the lens of the Anthropocene – is not very rewarding. Finite beings, as ever, in a world that is more finite than ever before in their history. It is not only a new philosophical conundrum, which in the best of cases can push us into taking an incalculable leap, like that which Oedipus took over the old Sphinx's shrewdness. Nor is it the announcement of a setback, but rather a clue for us to grasp that there will be a future reorganisation (or an unparalleled disorder) in which perhaps the universalist and progressively inclusive logics turn out to be a beautiful remnant. Not of what we were, but of what we someday expected to be.

Is history about to begin or is a certain history about to end? Why are we about to leave the North behind? The South? The North–South?

We said that in most legal codes the traces of formal discrimination have disappeared, although they may continue working at an empirical level and new forms of domination may be created. We also mentioned the fact that formal or controlled inclusion has been the perfect move to continue excluding without any scandals, to sustain the position of the master. Nor is it the first time there has been domination under conditions of formal political equality.

We also said that there is a possibility that the South is fulfilling its promise of another normativity. Then, within the paradigm of recognition, what seems logical is for the struggles for self-determination, for freedom, to be understood as struggles that continue. They continue in the name of reshaping the frames of recognition, of making them more and more inclusive, making them fuller forms of recognition. They go on beyond the achievements in the formal level, reshaping effective practices until a fuller justice, a fuller freedom, will be achieved.

But there is a discontent that persists beyond the fact of being legally and symbolically recognised. It is a discontent we keep calling the urge for freedom, and we do not know if it is due to a social pathology derived from historical injustices with present consequences. Here we wonder whether it has been caused by the very understanding of the social and political aspects of a struggle against historical injustice in terms of the struggle for recognition, where the struggle for redistribution is already included for the purpose of completing the paradigm of justice. We cannot rule out the fact that it may be due to the very constitution of humanness as the incompleteness from which desire emerges. But that desire re-emerges as a desire for freedom or a justice that would allow us to live in freedom.

What is apparent from some of the Southern existences is that even when we feel recognised and included, we continue experiencing underestimations and exclusions that are identifiable at an empirical level of life, but others are not even legible. It is not only that there is no outside of power, but also that it is already understood as a constitutive dynamics. What is nurtured is a deep-rooted suspicion that by participating, and allowing ourselves to be recognised so much and so well (also through the identity construction practices favoured by new social networks in the context of the identity obsession that was already occurring), we are perhaps dancing to the tune of new forms of voluntary servitude or the sophisticated versions of old ones.

In any case, it is difficult to understand what happens to us when we inhabit the gap that is our present. We struggle to understand if it is just the desire to be like the other, to be the other, because we understand that that is the only way to really be. We do not believe this is the answer. We also find it difficult to grasp in what new ways, different from the struggles for recognition within reciprocity, the response – the resistance to remaining and emerging dominations – is being formulated: in the self-recognitions of different sovereignties?

In fact, we have difficulty understanding how the new normativity will be articulated, a normativity that will enable the discomforts arising from the relentless attempt to collapse some hierarchies – almost always the same and which do not cease – to stop once and for all. And for others to be created, surely.

What seems indisputable is the fact that – despite the few positive expectations evoked by the future – we remain installed in a messianic normative conception. We have before us an elusive horizon that serves as a criterion for evaluating our actions and their achievements. This is the case, as has been said, if we accept that we still have a horizon ahead to direct our steps. But at the same time and perhaps precisely because of this, emancipatory discourses – from the classical discourse of progress to the discourses disputing it, from feminism to postcolonialism in its most anti-liberal versions – seem to have lost their validity in the eyes of many. They seem to repeat old ideas that have already been normalised and institutionalised, when not outgrown. That is why it is tempting to think in terms of a renewed experience of critical impotence. A renewed experience of the impatience of freedom. The question besetting us may not arise from any other experiences; we in fact believe it besets us almost without realising it: is there a chance to experience and reconceptualise our relationship with others, with ourselves, with what is happening and is about to come, from outside the idea of a recognition that imposes geographies of one, the other, the margins? Are the possibilities of resistance still found in knowing how to extract creativity from our desire to be beyond the other, that is, the complement of the Same? From exploring within our being the otherness of that other? The reluctance to be recognised, catalogued, reduced and normalised can be seen in the vindication of the category of transition, of a persistent non-identification as a vocation, as a condition. But our new histories of migrations, refugees, displaced and stateless people show us that in the current political margins these imposed nomadic modalities are unliveable. This does not mean that the force of resistance inherent to what attempts to be unrecognisable is negligible.

On the contrary. In the experiences of freedom made from desires that do not attempt to win recognition for themselves – whether voluntary or accidental – there may be an effective lever in terms of the questioning of our frames of self-understanding. It is from that questioning that we utter the bemused question: can we leave the North/South behind from the paradigm of recognition? The retrieved fragments of the forgotten history of recognition seem to point out that there is a close dangerous liaison between the divide and the paradigm to understand it.

But can we leave the paradigm of recognition behind? Taking this question seriously would involve stepping into a conceptual darkness and passages full of ambiguity. This is the reason why maybe only the reflected light of the Southern constellation's brightness – before the creation of the North–South dialectics – would be able to guide us. But by not taking this step we may end up curtailing those hind legs made of stars from which the centaur gathers momentum.

Notes

1. Its logo represents the world map as an equidistant projection made from the North Pole, surrounded by two olive branches. The representation is thus a direct inversion of what we would see if the projection had been taken using the Southern Cross as its zenith.

2. It has been claimed – since Amerigo Vespucci (letter of 1499), not without great controversy – that the stars mentioned by Dante in Canto I of the *Divine Comedy*'s 'Purgatory' were the only ones seen by the first humans, Adam and Eve, since paradise – according to the poet – was located in the opposite hemisphere to his, that is, the Southern Hemisphere. It is also speculated that the Southern Cross was in fact the star that guided the Three Kings to Bethlehem, for it was visible in Jerusalem.

3. There is controversy surrounding the question of who the first person to give it that name was, but in the 'Lettera di Andrea Corsali allo illustrissimo Principe Duca de Medici, venuta dell'Indis del mese di Octobre nel XDXVI' we have an early testimony (written on 6 January 1615). Interestingly, although the Cross first found its rightful place in Bayer's celestial maps, it is shifted about 45 degrees to the left due to the fact that, when positioning it, he continued using the *Almagest* instead of using the information gathered by the Dutch, which is a symptom of the authority granted in the West to the opinions of the ancients, especially the Greeks, often undermining what had been discovered with new scientific methods.

4. Bayer seems to ignore that it is thus and does not seem to know the name *Southern Cross* either, calling it 'moderis crux'. The ratification of Crux as an independent constellation was not formalised until the 1930s by the International Astronomical Union (IAU).

5. Shortly afterwards, Julius Schiller Christianised the constellations in his *Coelum Stellatum Christanum* (1627), replacing the pagan figures with saints and apostles.

6. Hobbes writes wryly: 'Fear and I were born twins. My mother hearing of the Spanish Armada sailing up the English channel gave premature birth to me' (Hobbes 1839: LXXXVI).

7. As is known, Hegel denied uncivilised individuals and groups the possibility of having personality of any kind due to the fact that they were unable to distinguish between themselves as individuals and their essential universality, which meant they could not enter the struggle for recognition. In addition, he believed that civilised nations could treat as barbarians other nations that were not as advanced as they were (Hegel [1819] (1991): §13, 376).

8. According to Clark, this development proceeded in four steps: (1) (1800–80) Generalised accounts of the criteria of recognition that are fixated almost solely on intra-European diplomatic disagreements gradually emerge. (2) (1871–85) Recognition begins to incorporate ideas of Christianity, civilisation and progress to exclude non-European political communities from entry into the international community. (3) (1885–1914) This orientation towards progress proceeds further into the period of late colonialism and the 'Scramble for Africa', shifting the focus of recognition to the technicalities of government and territorial control and, eventually, to a state-centric account that normalises civilisational inferiority into 'difference'. With the emergence of the fourth and final step (1915–50), recognition becomes a basic concept in international law, reflected in intense debates over its meaning and its use to advance or undermine a range of political projects within the League of Nations, including the universalisation of international law, changing modes of imperialism, and the constraint of state action through law.

9. Individualisation has also been called autonomy, and this comes to signify 'that human beings can develop their life-projects on their own, without being conditioned or determined by others', whilst inclusion means that 'human beings – individuals or groups – become members of a society with equal rights in relation to all other members' (Wagner 2015: 58).

10. Especially interesting for our case are Gregor Sauerwald's conciliatory attempts to make the Honnethian theory of recognition productive in terms of analysing the conditions and demands of Latin America. He does so through demonstrating the shared purposes – despite the difference in their vocabularies – of liberation theories and other vernacular philosophies through which the theory of recognition has been renamed as 'contextualist universalism' (Sauerwald 2008: 20). He wants recognition for the theory of recognition and also for theorists to recognise the value of Latin American thought. However, it seems to have worked in one direction more than in others. Despite the reluctance described by Sauerwald, the concept of recognition has also penetrated the discourses of the South.

References

Arendt, H. [1951] (1973), *The Origins of Totalitarianism*, New York: Harvest

Arendt, H. (1958), *The Human Condition*, Chicago: University of Chicago Press.

Arnason, J. P. (1989), 'The Imaginary Constitution of Modernity', in Giovanni Busino (ed.), *Autonomie et autotransformation de la société: La philosophie militante de Cornelius Castoriadis*, Geneva: Droz, pp. 323–37.

Benjamin, J. (1988), *The Bonds of Love: Psychoanalysis, Feminism and the Problem of Domination*, New York: Pantheon.

Benjamin, W. (1999), *The Arcades Project*, Cambridge, MA: Harvard University Press.

Bhathal, R. (2006), 'Astronomy in Aboriginal culture', *Astronomy & Geophysics*, 47: 5, 5.27–5.30.

Birulés, F. (2015), *Entreactos. En torno a la política, el feminismo y el pensamiento*, Buenos Aires and Madrid: Katz.

Buck-Morss, S. (2009), *Hegel, Haiti and Universal History*, Pittsburgh: University of Pittsburgh Press.

Butler, J. (2004), *Precarious Life: The Powers of Mourning and Violence*, London: Verso.

Castoriadis, C. (1990), *Le Monde morcelé: les carrefours du labyrinthe III*, Paris: Seuil.

Clark, M. (2016), 'British contributions to the concept of recognition during the inter-war period: Williams, Baty and Lauterpacht', in R. McCorquodale and J.-P. Gauci (eds), *British Influences on International Law, 1915–2015*, Leiden and Boston: Brill Nijhof, pp. 110–44.

de Sousa Santos, B. (2008), *A Gramàtica do Tempo: Para uma Nova Cultura Política*, São Paulo: Cortez Editora.

de Sousa Santos, B. (2014), *Epistemologies of the South: Justice Against Epistemicide*, New York: Routledge.

Dussel, E. (1973), *América Latina, dependencia y liberación. Antología de ensayos antropológicos y teológicos desde la proposición de un pensar latinoamericano*, Buenos Aires: Fernando García Cambeiro.

Echart, E. (2016), 'El Sur Global, más allá del Estado', *Open Democracy*, 15 February, <https://www.opendemocracy.net/democraciaabierta/enara-echart-mu-oz/el-sur-global-m-s-all-del-estado> (last accessed 15 January 2017).

Estrella Faria, L. A. (2005), 'La política exterior de Brasil: ¿Dónde queda el Sur?', *Revista del Sur*, 161, 3–6.

Fichte J. G. ([1796/7] 2000), *Foundations of Natural Right. According to the Principles of the Wissenschaftslehre*, ed. Frederick Neuhouser, Cambridge: Cambridge University Press.

Foucault, M. (1997), 'What is critique?', in *The Politics of Truth*, ed. Sylvère Lotringer, New York: Semiotext(e), pp. 23–82.

Fraser, N. (2000), 'Rethinking recognition', *New Left Review*, 3, 107–20.

Fraser, N. and A. Honneth (2003), *Redistribution or Recognition? A Political-Philosophical Exchange*, London: Verso.

Fuster, À. L. and G. Rosich (2015), 'The limits of recognition: history, otherness and autonomy', in P. Wagner (ed.), *African, American and European Trajectories of Modernity: Past Oppression, Future Justice?*, Edinburgh: Edinburgh University Press, pp. 55–74.

Gray, K. and B. K. Gills (2016), 'South-South cooperation and the rise of the Global South', *Third World Quarterly*, 37: 4, 557–74.

Gray, K. and C. Murphy (2013), 'Introduction: rising powers and the future of global governance', *Third World Quarterly*, 34: 2, 183–93.

Guillén, E. (1974), *Versión inca de la conquista*, Lima: Editorial Milla Batres.

Hegel, G. W. F. [1806] (1977), *Phenomenology of Spirit*, Oxford: Oxford University Press.

Hegel, G. W. F. [1819] (1991), *Elements of the Philosophy of Right*, Cambridge: Cambridge University Press.

Hobbes, T. [1642–3] (1983), *De Cive*, Oxford: Clarendon Press.

Hobbes, T. [1651] (2012), *Leviathan*, Oxford: Clarendon Press.

Hobbes, T. (1839), 'Thomae Hobbes Malmesburiensis *Vita Carmine Expressa*', in *Opera philosophica*, vol. 1, ed. Sir William Molesworth, London, pp. LXXXI–XCIX.

Honneth, A. [1992] (1995), *The Struggle for Recognition: The Moral Grammar of Social Conflicts*, Cambridge: Polity.

Honneth, A., J. Rancière, K. Genel and J. P. Deranty (2016), *Recognition or Disagreement: A Critical Encounter on the Politics of Freedom, Equality and Identity*, New York: Columbia University Press.

Kanas, N. (2007), *Star Maps: History, Artistry, and Cartography*, New York: Springer Praxis Books.

Khomyakov, M. (2013), 'Toleration and respect: historical instances and current problems', *European Journal of Political Theory*, 12: 3, 223–39.

Koselleck, R. and T. S. Presner (2002), *The Practice of Conceptual History: Timing History, Spacing Concepts*, Stanford: Stanford University Press.

Lajo, J. (2002), 'Principios de la filosofía andina: la dualidad complementaria y la oposición proporcional', in *Qhapaq Kuna . . . Más Allá de la Civilización*, Cusco: Asociación Pachawaray, pp. 58–79.

Lajo, J. (2006), *Qhapaq Ñan: La Ruta Inka De Sabiduría*, Ibarra: Abya-Yala.

Machiavelli, N. (2010), *The Prince*, Chicago: University of Chicago Press.

Mignolo, W. (2003), *Historias Locales/Diseños Globales: Colonialidad, Conocimientos Subalternos y Pensamiento Fronterizo*, Barcelona: Akal.

Ministry of Foreign Affairs, Republic of Indonesia (ed.) (1955), *Asia-Africa Speak from Bandung*, Djakarta: Ministry of Foreign Affairs, Republic of Indonesia, pp. 161–9.

Norris, R. P. (2008a), 'Emu dreaming', *Australasian Science*, 29: 4, n.p.

Norris, R. P. (2008b), 'In search of Aboriginal astronomy', *Australasian Sky & Telescope*, March/April, 20–4.

Organisation for Economic Co-operation and Development (OECD) (2011), *Perspectives on Global Development 2012: Social Cohesion in a Shifting World*, Paris: OECD Publishing.

Pagden, A. (1983), *The Fall of Natural Man: The American Indian and the Origins of Comparative Ethnology*, Cambridge: Cambridge University Press.

Pagden, A. (1993), *European Encounters with the New World: From Renaissance to Romanticism*, New Haven, CT: Yale University Press.

Parfitt, R. (2016), 'Theorizing recognition and personality', in A. Orford and F. Hofmann (eds), *The Oxford Handbook of the Theory of International Law*, Oxford: Oxford University Press, pp. 583–99.

Prebisch, R. [1948] (1998), 'El desarrollo económico de la América Latina y algunos de sus principales problemas', in *50 años de Pensamiento en la CEPAL*, Santiago de Chile: Fondo de Cultura Económica, pp. 63–130.

Quijano, A. (1972), 'Imperialismo y capitalismo de estado', *Sociedad y Política*, 1: 1, 1–5.

Quijano, A. (2000), 'Colonialidad del poder, eurocentrismo y América Latina', in E. Lander (ed.), *La Colonialidad del Saber: Eurocentrismo y Ciencias Sociales. Perspectivas Latinoamericanas*, Buenos Aires: CLACSO, pp. 122–51.

Room, A. (1988), *Dictionary of Astronomical Names*, Routledge: London.

Santos, M. (2000), *Por uma Outra Globalização: Do Pensamento Único à Consciência Universal*, Rio de Janeiro: Record.

Sauerwald, G. (2008), *Reconocimiento y liberación: Axel Honneth y el pensamiento latinoamericano. Por un diálogo entre el Sur y el Norte*, Münster: LIT Verlag.

South Commission (1995), *The Challenge to the South: The Report of the South Commission*, Oxford: Oxford University Press.

Strange, A., B. C. Parks, M. J. Tierney, A. Fuchs, A. Dreher and V. Ramachandran (2013), 'China's development finance to Africa: a media-based approach to data collection – Working Paper 323', Washington DC: Center for Global Development, <http://www.cgdev.org/publication/chinas-development-finance-africa-media-based-approach-data-collection> (last accessed 8 February 2017).

Taylor, C. (1994), *Multiculturalism: Examining the Politics of Recognition*, Princeton: Princeton University Press.

Tone, E. F. M. (2009), 'Identidad Latinoamericana como *chakana* en el marco de la filosofía intercultural desde Josef Estermann', *Cuadrantephi*, 18–19.

United Nations Development Programme (UNDP) (2013), *The Rise of the South: Human Progress in a Diverse World. National Human Development Reports*, New York: UNDP.

United Nations General Assembly (1960), *Resolution A/RES/1514(XV): Declaration on the Granting of Independence to Colonial Countries and Peoples*, 14 December, <http://www.refworld.org/docid/3b00f06e2f.html> (last accessed 15 January 2017).

Wagner, P. (2008), *Modernity as Experience and Interpretation: A New Sociology of Modernity*, Cambridge: Polity.

Wagner, P. (2015), *Progress: A Reconstruction*, Cambridge: Polity.

Wallerstein, I. (1974–89), *The Modern World-System*, 3 vols, New York: Academic Press.

Wallerstein, I. (2002), 'New revolts against the system', *New Left Review*, 18, 29–39.

Woods, N. (2008), 'Whose aid? Whose influence? China, emerging donors and the silent revolution in development assistance', *International Affairs*, 84: 1205–21.

7

On Spaces and Experiences: Modern Displacements, Interpretations and Universal Claims

Aurea Mota

Introduction

THE TENDENCY TO spatially displace imaginaries of societies and their specific historical development is not new. The interpretation of a space based on geographical orientation has indeed seldom been based on any natural idea of what the space is (Gregory 1994; Garfield 2013). Recently, though, much attention has been devoted to the discussion of space as a political and historical entity. It has been rediscovered as a privileged object for the analysis of different historical processes largely crystallised in different parts of the globe.

As part of this volume, in which the reader will find a variety of issues related to how spatial categories can be taken as 'useful' concepts for the inquiry into problems of the social world, this chapter addresses a relatively unexplored aspect of modern experience with space. This aspect concerns the relation between displacements of people in different spaces and the production of knowledge/interpretation. It argues that the South, understood for now simply as a specific localisation of historical relations, has always been a space where general trans-regional theories and concepts have emerged. As with so-called 'Northern theory', 'Southern theory' shares similar pretensions of universality and also proceeds by exercising similar gestures of historical erasure. Hence, from this point of view, there is not a strong purely intellectual distinction that could split Northern and Southern thought.[1] However, an important aspect constituting what could be regarded as something that does split a Northern from a Southern intellectual tradition is that the former has departed from the idea of spatial neutrality as a condition for the production of theories, as Mignolo (2011) has shown; and the latter, on the contrary, has interpreted itself and its place in the world through what is called here a critical localisation of argument.

This critical localisation of discourse is done without any prejudice against the production of universal claims. Henceforth, this chapter highlights what could be an important difference detected between the 'Northern' and 'Southern' intellectual traditions, but argues in favour of the existence of similar claims of universality despite the location of knowledge/interpretation. That is probably due to the difficulty of clearly specifying *where* things happen in the modern world. It is so because of the argument, also developed in this chapter, that it is in the movement of people crossing spaces/times and the displacement of established societal self-understandings that modern thought has emerged and has distinguished itself. The aspects of the transformation on a larger scale of temporal and spatial orientation have been well explored. This chapter will raise some questions related to the problem of modern thought and the experience of space.

In this introduction, it is also worth summarising the arguments that the discussion below intends to call into question. There are two lines of argument. The first line refers to what could be a sort of essentialisation of spaces that involves a radical dualism and sometimes antagonism between different parts. In this view, space became historically crystallised into entities that are used as explanatory categories to think about the historical development of the world and the relations of its different parts. The representation of the relation between the West and the Orient can help us in elucidating the issue. During much of the early modern period (roughly from the 1500s to the 1800s), Western thought and art portrayed the Orient as an exotic realm to be experienced and explored (Said 1985; Behdad 1994). The metaphor of a wise but somewhat decadent West as the observer of a very intensive and novel but also ancient world suits this relation well. With a change of focus but retaining the same analytical perspective, in some contemporary approaches the South is seen as the place for the exercise of lively alternatives for the future (Santos 2009; Connell 2007). It seems like the South has replaced the Orient as the place in which creative innovations developed and imagined in whatever this socio-spatial category might be are more interesting and effective than modernisation perspectives and allied views could have expected. The difference is that now Southern actors have a voice and play a central role in such representation themselves. In both perspectives, however, the North is still portrayed as a sort of wealthy and powerful old man whose success can be easily attested, and whose examples could elucidate a lot of current problems, but whose uneven trajectory has produced more problems than it has solved. This man is exhausted and not able to represent himself as a paradigm for the future. He has become the image of a past and remembered more for his mistakes than his glories.

This leads us to the second line of argument against which this chapter was developed. Following from the previous representation, it has been wisely attested that the main mistake of this man – the North in this image of world regions to which outstanding structural power has been attributed – was the development of colonial and neo-colonial global capitalism. The works that have recently appeared under the umbrella category of 'Global South' highlight the colonial structures of power as that which is responsible for the crystallisation of the North as the site of accumulation of capital and the South as the site of exploitation (for more about this topic, see Pinheiro in this volume). Geopolitical relations of power are taken as the focus of these approaches that mainly analyse the historical aspects of political and economic mutual and unequal dependency of centres, peripheries and semi-peripheries for the development of capitalism (Wallerstein 1974; Quijano 2005). The problem with this perspective does not reside in the assumption that the history of colonialism is the main causal factor in the consolidation of the world system as we find it today. The problem concerns the issue of attributing strong structural powers to places that act as rational actors.

The first line of argument above highlights more the aspect of the *representation* of a space by agents acting in specific cultural and historical scenarios. The second line could be regarded as based on a more *empirical conception of global history* and of economic development in the era of capitalism. In both accounts, however, the idea of antagonistic interests of spaces as historical entities predominates. Places, above all from the North, are understood as actors that exercise a large measure of control over the course of their actions by subjugation and/ or imposition of their desire wherever they want. From an analytical point of view, those studies could not have been done by taking a long distance from what can be regarded as a classical sociological approach to talking about the other separated in time and space. In classical approaches, the localisation of the space occupied by different groups is not an explanatory factor in the analysis – as it appears in Durkheim's work ([1912] 1995) about how the fundamental notions of thought found in the 'simplest' form of religious life could elucidate the way knowledge and theories are produced. Durkheim's others were synchronically separated in time and space. But space in itself does not appear as the main fact that explains the difference in the forms of social knowledge and of religious life. It is the different forms of organisation of systems of belief that determines their place in history. Pursuing a different argument, but retaining some lessons learned from such classical approaches, in this chapter we want to be able to show that subjects are not determined by their place of origin. As important as the determination of the milieu is the understanding of the diverse forms of displacement that mark a subject's life and thought.[2]

In order to show the limitations of the perspectives criticised above, we will develop an argument about the relation between, on the one hand, the specific character of modern displacements and, on the other, the interpretation and the consolidation of universal claims. For that, we will proceed as follows. In the next section, I provide a general overview of the discussion of space in modernity. A brief inquiry into the forms of representation of space and its relation to different historical developments will be also offered in order to understand the relation between displacement and knowledge in modernity. After this section, the focus will move to the discussion of two authors and intellectuals whose displacements share what we regard to be a critical localisation of universal discourse: Simón Rodríguez and Isabelle Eberhardt. They lived in different times and moved through different spaces. One is a man, the other a woman. The man was devoted to the human sciences, was involved in tremendous political activities, and made an impact on history; the woman had strong literary pretensions but had some difficulty in becoming recognised as a writer during her lifetime.[3] They both help us to elucidate the argument about the difficulty of splitting Northern and Southern thought in a very clear way when it comes to the absence of a pretension to universality and the absence of 'unavoidable' historical events. The discussion concludes with some remarks that summarise the proposal to look at space in the social sciences as conforming to no pre-established cartography in order to overcome the problems of essentialisation and of spatial determination.

Space, representation, displacement: reviewing ideas to build an alternative approach

Space has been interpreted as a phenomenon related to the formation of nation states; it has been seen as a key concept for understanding the formation of the new modern *urbis* and the reproduction of old societal problems along with the creation of new ones in its spaces; it has also been viewed as part of the formation of centres and peripheries in the global system (Anderson 1991; Mbembe 2000; Lefebvre 1991; Wallerstein 1974). The broad theoretical understanding that those approaches offer is the relation between space and the formation of capitalist and colonial societies, as it appears very clearly in the work of Harvey (1985). From this perspective, the issue of space in modernity has been mainly connected with places and territorial transformations, understood as the political and economic physical space determined by changeable boundaries and its uses. The nationalist reading of this process tended to crystallise the image of modern space as self-contained units that could be compared and hierarchised (Menon 2010).

Since the end of the twentieth century, space increasingly has been viewed as represented and interpreted according to the perspective that humans beings give to it and the recent revival of space can be seen as a new concern with this older approach (Gregory 1994; Massey 2005). As with the definition of societal borders, the nationalist conception of territories has been revised by the proposal for more interpretative cultural-historical categories such as 'world regions' (Lewis and Wigen 1997) that aims to emphasise the different paths found in larger geospatial categories of thought. Those approaches lose sight of at least two other different ways through which spaces are formed: the movement of people across space that creates new meaningful worlds that would not exist without the action (the movement) itself; and the analysis of how the imaginary representation of a space is a key variable for thinking about different historical trajectories of social, economic and political development. Most of the discussion about the 'South' in contemporary critical thought tends to emphasise empirical evidence that shows the consequences of unequal economic and social development for the constitution of the global order. In this chapter the argument is that space has been experienced and transformed by the action of human beings, not only by institutions or by the large territorial transformation of the modern state and the *urbis*. There are other societal movements that need to be regarded as productive forces in themselves.

In terms of spatial representation of societal imaginaries, it was only by the seventeenth century that geographical representations started to become less concerned about the display of a 'fantastic' picture of societies and more concerned about what places are in terms of their physical structure, form and politically determined spatial boundaries. However, there was still no scientific progress in cartographical representation regarding the neutrality of perspective of the observer (Brotton 2013). This transformation was a product of the incorporation of so-called 'Oriental' knowledge, the development of new techniques of navigation and orientation over sea and earth, as well as the achievements of the polycentric sources that led to the scientific revolution of the Renaissance. In light of our argument, it should be said that the difference between the pre-seventeenth-century representation of the world and those that started to appear in this period was due not only to scientific advancement, but also to the increasing impulse for displacement and a desire to know, interpret and represent the unknown. It is this spatial and temporal discontinuity that gives form to the perspective of human beings moving across spaces and creating new epistemic orders of a new era. The development of new exploratory expeditions to Africa and America, the development of new routes to Asia and Oceania, and the participation of writers and scientists in those travels can be seen as the basis of this transformation in the early modern period. From the nineteenth century on, through different means, the movement of people, knowledge and the creation of a new imagined global order come to be even more important despite being little understood. That is what allows us to understand the difference between the increased significance that displacement has in the modern era if it is compared with, for instance, medieval travels, the Viking sagas and classical odysseys (Labarge 2005; Ross 2000).

Yet in the early modern period there was a major transformation in the way that spaces were represented in maps, globes and atlases. What remained unchanged from the sixteenth to the beginning of the nineteenth century was how narratives based on the movement of people across the globe – as 'travels' and 'exploratory missions' – were positively welcomed in the literary and scientific world. In the early modern period, travel literature was a widespread and lively activity that became important also as a source of ethnographical materials (Talbot 2010). The vivacity and importance of travel writings in this period becomes even more important if one bears in mind that it was first recognised as a specific literary genre only in the eighteenth century (Cristóvão 1999). From the sixteenth to the eighteenth century, travel writings were largely used as reliable material to inform different ways of interpreting and knowing the world(s). John Locke, for instance, was a prolific reader of travel literature, above all of authors who went to the New World – a space that empirically informed his political and philosophical approach (Mota 2015).

It also was in the early modern period that individual entrepreneurs and intellectuals started to travel for personal reasons. This whole process is not limited to overseas trips from Europe. The ideas of spatial displacement and the production of a representation of the other marked by a hierarchical structure of domination have been strongly emphasised by studies that associate modernity with the consolidation of the Western/coloniser perspective on the other and colonised subjects of the South and of the East/Orient (Said 1985; Behdad 1994; Pratt 2008). Those approaches try to understand the issue of the representation of the other mainly by analysing travel writings. However, the implications of the movement that they analyse should not be seen as a one-way process or something that was used only to impose the European perspective. Displacements of persons from other parts of the 'dominated' world to Europe also formed a not-yet-scrutinised colonised perspective on the structure of domination and their place in it. The claim that the 'natives did not travel' (Appadurai 1988) as well as the idea that the colonial perspective crystallised only in the perspective of the coloniser (Pratt 2008) both need to be strongly challenged. The same can be said about Euben's (2006) proposal to see travel as a 'necessary condition' for the production of theory, which is for her the main manifestation of knowledge. Her argument is not ultimately convincing because of a narrow conception of what knowledge is and a failure to see the spaces where people travel as a source of experience and knowledge per se. For us, the experience of foreign spaces and the interpretation of them in light of specific historical developments express the way that modernity has been understood as a phenomenon of universal significance in different times and places.

This spatial experience is possible only through movement (transformation) and imagination and it is one of the main sources of modernity in itself. The sociological and historical literature that focuses on travel writings and the object/subject represented in it have not paid attention to the fact that the movement from fiction to the sciences of the discourse on the other and us shows how knowledge started to be regarded in the modern world. That is why for us it was not by chance that social science stabilised itself at the same moment when travel literature began to be disregarded as a reliable source for an interpretation of the world(s). The fact that there was a considerable decrease in the generation and public relevance of travel writing in the nineteenth century can be interpreted as an expression of the new epistemic order that was created in modernity: the transition to science as the legitimate field in which the discourse on the other and us should take place.

As modernity started to consolidate into a global imaginary, the desire to know and transform the world through displacement has changed with regard to the role of spatial displacement as a public condition for the production of knowledge and of modern space itself. Displacements that gave rise to scientific interpretations became hidden (or assumed as a secondary fact) for human knowledge to accomplish orders of universality in what has been regarded as Northern thought. In this space, this is the basis of the process of divergence between, on the one hand, a philosophy of experience, meaning and the subject and, on the other hand, a philosophy of knowledge, of reason and of concepts (Foucault 1985, 2001). However, as we will see in the following section with the discussion of Simón Rodríguez and Isabelle Eberhardt, which retain similar pretensions to universality, displacement and knowledge/interpretation occupy a very explicit place in what we can regard as Southern thought. It is exactly the explicitness in localisation of the discourse that makes us able to see a difference between 'Northern' and 'Southern' thought. Displacements, movements, disconnections and discontinuities in time and space made by human beings are an important force in the transformation of the modern world and reveal that its epistemic-spatial form is not easily crystallised in any unchangeable representation of spaces and of intellectual traditions. Before moving forward it is worth explicating better what modernity means in our approach.

Modernity in philosophical and sociological terms can be understood as the process of the acceleration of 'historical time' and by the idea of 'to be in one's own time' (Wagner 2008; Bayly 2002; Koselleck 2004). From this perspective, it is possible to see how difficult it is to relate modernity to a single temporal and political understanding. However, European authors did not have much problem in agreeing on the place of a specific revolutionary process that became an important point of reference for understanding the modern ruptures. In Koselleck (2004) this place and time is very clear. For him it was during the *Neuzeit* – understood as a 'new time' that emerged around the time of the French Revolution – that the idea of progress and the future became connected in a very specific form. What is important to bear in mind is Koselleck's idea that it was in light of the transformations of the *Neuzeit* that three aspects crucial for the understanding of modernity emerged: the idea of autonomy is connected with the possibility of a positive transformation, the acceleration of time, and its increased separation from the space where life flows. The emphasis on the orientation of time – towards the future – is based on the 'space of experience' (Koselleck 2002). However, this space is not scrutinised deeply enough in this approach (Pickering 2010).

In a similar vein, for Giddens (1990), time and space distantiation is what distinguishes the rhythm of change in modern societies, making them different from traditional ones. Giddens sees the 'pace of change' of modernity as something that happened because of the separation of time and space and their recombination in forms that permit the precise 'time-space zoning' of social dynamics. For Giddens, what he sees as 'pre-modern societies', spaces and places tended to be the same.[4] In modern societies, on the contrary, spaces became detached from their locales. What he calls the 'mechanisms of embedment' are responsible for the reorganisation of social relations in a situation of large time-space distances in modern societies. It is due to this large separation that one of the consequences of modernity is the formation of an 'empty space' in which social life happens (Giddens 1990). In Giddens, modernity had its beginning in Europe from roughly the seventeenth century and then spread worldwide, a process accomplished in spite of the imposition of a European perspective on ways of representing the world. He very much believes that 'the progressive charting of the globe that led to the creation of universal maps, in which perspective played little part in the representation of geographical position and form, established space as "independent" of any particular place or region' (Giddens 1990: 19). In our view, this approach is based on a conception of the modern representation of the world as able to leave behind a privileged perspective of the representation of lived space and time. Thus in Giddens's perspective, despite its European origins, modernity acquired the form of a non-local phenomenon because of the novelty that it possessed in terms of space and time separation. In doing so he is probably the first to unintentionally theorise the idea of spatial neutrality as a feature of modern Western thought.

Against the view that modernity and its specific representation of shared space as an equal globe have emerged in an insulated space – as the West – and spread later on throughout the world, it is sustained that the modern experience was made by the synthesis of practices, experiences and interpretations that cannot be easily reduced to the central areas of the North/Western world (Wagner 2012). The rise of a modern imaginary around the idea of the autonomy of human beings as individuals and collective persons and in relation to the possibility of making changes in the world in the name of this imaginary is completely connected to the experiences of displacements of persons and thoughts from and to different parts of the globe. This idea challenges not only the notion that modernity emerged in an insulated area but also the idea of the 'emptiness' of the space where life flows.

To be sure, Mignolo (2011) has been theorising the modern/colonial space and offering an alternative approach to the established Northern perspective. His approach starts out from Schmitt's (2006) attempt to relate the geopolitics of the organisation of the world and the birth of European international law, and from Wallerstein's (1974) world-systems approach as a way to replace the traditional focus on nations and societies as almost closed entities. Mignolo (2002) tries to understand the modern space departing from, but going beyond, both approaches because in his view they do not address the issue of 'coloniality the power' – a phenomenon that was previously analysed by Quijano (1998). Mignolo (2011) highlights the fact that 'we are where we think', but only the European system of knowledge was built on the basic premise 'I think, therefore I am'. However, his thesis places too much emphasis on the establishment of a fundamental division between Europe and the non-European world. In his view, the new decolonial subject should be able to say, 'I am where I think,' and by doing so show the Europeans that they also are the same. The author is right when he says that 'I think, therefore I am' is a premise adopted by the modern European system of knowledge. However, he is wrong in saying that it is a prerogative of the modern European system. As in our perspective time and space are not absolute categories, we all think, therefore we are and where/when we have been and how we have imagined ourselves.

The focus on displacement, the transformation of social imaginaries and interpretation all point to another view of modern/colonial history. This view challenges proposals that address the issue of the modern global configuration based on crystallised geographical images that aim to explain *how places think* (see, for instance, Burawoy 2009; Connell 2007; Santos 2009). By saying that the spatial dimension of modernity is based on the experience of displacement and knowledge, I mean to indicate that to experience a different way of seeing the unknown or of seeing what it was already known with different eyes is a way that human beings can situate themselves in a world(s) that has become transformed because of their own action. It also makes it possible to articulate modernity in terms of a meaningfully connected history of peoples and the concrete but also imagined routes they created in their movement.

Simon Rodríguez and Isabelle Eberhardt: different forms of critical localisation of universal claims

This section analyses aspects of the life and work of two authors that lived in different spaces and times of the modern world: Simón Rodríguez (1769–1854) and Isabelle Eberhardt (1877–1904). By different means, they both express what can be understood in our argument as the critical localisation of universal claims that are very strongly connected to the displacements they undertook during their lifetimes and help us to discuss some aspects of what has here been called a modern experience with space. Analysing their life and intellectual contributions together is a way to challenge the idea both of spatial determination and of the necessary adoption of spatial neutrality for the production of universal ideas in modernity. By doing so, I also hope to elucidate the argument about displacement and modern thought and how we can understand it in relation to the discussion about Northern and Southern intellectual traditions. From the very beginning, it is important to notice that both authors adopted different names that would be used for them to insert themselves in the new environment in which they found themselves: Simón Rodríguez became Samuel Robinson and Isabelle Eberhardt became, along with a number of other names, Si Mahmoud Saadi. Simón Rodríguez remained a male with an English name; Isabelle Eberhardt became a male with an Arabic name. The use of pseudonyms and of assuming a different character meant for them to open doors that otherwise would have remained closed. The change in names was also a way to remind themselves that displacement means something more than only a spatial condition.

Simón Rodríguez is one of the main intellectuals and protagonists of the many groups that took part in the struggles for emancipation in America. He was closely linked to Simón Bolívar and other emancipators who fought in the struggles against the colonial system in Venezuela, Nueva Granada and in the Viceroyalty of Peru. Going into exile after he was appointed as one of the leaders of the *Conspiración de Gual y España* (1797–9), he left his home in Venezuela for Jamaica in 1797. From there he travelled to parts of the United States, Europe and Eastern Europe.[5] Unlike his brother, Cayetano, who was regarded by everyone close to them as the 'good one' and the 'exemplary Catholic' that had never left his home, Simón Rodríguez showed from an early age an interest in learning from experiences with different spaces and thoughts (Rumazo Gonzáles 2006: 12).[6] He was already versed in philosophical and political texts from abroad when he left America. But it was when he lived in the Northern part of the world that Simón Rodríguez developed most of his ideas.[7] The main subject of his thought was how America would become free and constitute itself as a new and original political order in a world increasingly connected (Rodríguez 1840, [1830] 1971). To think about America, he based his approach on his own experience of getting to know domination in many parts of the world – he wrote about slavery in Turkey, Russia and Prussia; exclusion of Jews in many parts of Europe; and the marginalisation of manual workers, such as craftsmen and farmers, from political life (Rodríguez 1840: 6–7).

In his opinion, the new nations of America did not share with Europe and the East the addictions of being old political traditions based on a strong hierarchical conception of life in society. This was due to the fact that in America the political challenge was to create something anew, not to reform an older order as would be the case in the other civilisational forms of life he found in Europe. Despite this important historical difference, the formation of enlightened governments would show what is right for any society. It could be done in spite of historical contingencies, cultural orientations and civilisational backgrounds. For Rodríguez, in America it should be easier to develop an emancipated political life suitable for the new era emerging in the nineteenth century. But it would not be done if the vanguard of his time were not able to learn from the experiences of diverse parts of the world in an attempt of find the best solutions for solving the problems of social and political organisation. This is what he calls 'competition of faculties'. For him, curiosity and knowledge would together create the conditions for any society to find a way out for problems related to the formation of modern republican political life (Rodríguez 1840: 15; Rumazo Gonzáles 2006: 56). His idea of knowledge is one based on the idea that to know better you need to compare what you know with what others know about similar problems under different conditions. If this formula is followed, this sort of cosmopolitan imaginary developed by Rodríguez could be easily converted into institutional arrangements that could be applied everywhere (Mota 2012). For him, universal knowledge is possible by the incorporation of experiences of any societal groups otherwise apart in time and space.[8]

America had a central role not only for the creation but also for the maintenance of the new political imaginary emerging in the nineteenth century (Rodríguez [1830] 1971). The struggle for emancipation in the United States of America, the successful Andean break with colonial ties, the revolution of black slaves in Haiti, and the formation of the Pan-Americanism movement of the beginning of the nineteenth century were events that attested to the political vivacity and desire to change the colonial condition in this part of the world. He also regarded the French Revolution, and even more importantly the experience of the *Les Enragés* for the consolidation of the 'utopian socialism' in Europe, as evidence of the desire for change everywhere. All of those experiences should be followed for the implementation of the ideals of rights of property, freedom, republican education[9] and knowledge to all (Rumazo Gonzáles 2006).

At the time when Rodríguez was actively working, the division of the New World into North and South America and the formation of an idea of a successful North and the failed South did not exist as fully consolidated phenomena. The process of calling the America stopped in time by 'South America' and 'Latin America' is a production of a division within the New World that was happing at this moment (Mota 2015). Simón Rodríguez's main work, *American Societies*,[10] is a book that shows exactly how the continent was seen at that moment, as a place with similar problems and dilemmas but with different historical trajectories that were not strong enough to be regarded as something existing apart in time and space. The 'American divergence' of the nineteenth century and the formation in the New World of the meaningful idea of the North as the place where important developments are observed and the South as a place that did not get away from its past problems was understood through a process that might be called the *paradigmatisation of historical events* (Mota 2015). This is a process through which many revolutions, reforms and emancipatory movements do not play the same role as other similar events for the analysis of the formation and transformation of the modern world and the new emerging conception of space and time. Important intellectuals of this time, such as Alexis de Tocqueville, had become part of this process of divergence in America, of creation of a specific idea of North and South and its relation to modern developments. Simón Rodríguez died in 1854, probably too soon for him to able to reflect on the consequences for Latin America of its historical creation.

Simón Rodríguez was concerned about the state of the political developments in Europe and America at the beginning of the nineteenth century. But he did not try to reflect upon those developments and the relation between the New and Old Worlds using spatial ideas such as North and South to describe what he was experiencing. It seems that for him those categories could not establish anything of substance about the meaning of the relation between those parts of the world and their development in history. Unlike Simón Rodríguez, Isabelle Eberhardt used the reference point of the South as a meaningful category to represent her desired desert (the Maghreb), for her the projected space of liberty and self-realisation. In her *Visions du Moghreb*,[11] the South appears as another word to express a space 'without political boundaries' compared with the Western world, which is the place of imprisonment and of unescapably forced exile.[12] This is for her the main characteristic that split Europe, her birthplace, and the South, her chosen place of rebirth. From her writings it is quite clear that Eberhardt saw from a very early stage of her life that freedom could be realised only away from her cultural milieu (Abdel-Jaouad 1993).

The South appears in Eberhardt's writings as a space in which one can have a true experience of autonomous action – to decide to what or to whom one wants to be subjected. Going against what anyone would expect from a person that was born in a family with strong anarchist ties,[13] she decided to convert to Islam. It is because of her freedom that she felt she could choose to convert to a religion of submission. When she moved to Algeria[14] she joined a group of Sufist Muslims who placed great emphasis on the mystical experience between God and the believer. For Sufism, suffering and pain are not seen as negative feelings. They are part of the experience of a full submission of someone to God, enabling them to see the other as more important than oneself.

For her, the fact that the Maghreb was so close to Europe without Europeans knowing anything about it revealed Europe's self-imposed blindness. The Maghreb was geographically nearby but completely faraway when it came to the knowledge that the Western world had of it. It was a place that Europeans saw as fit only for exploitation and the imposition of an absolutely unfair way of ruling collective life. That is why she became obsessed with finding an Algeria that existed before colonisation. She wanted to experience a space that had remained untouched by the Western powers.[15] To think about Isabelle Eberhardt as an intellectual that helps us to elucidate the point about the South as a space of production of knowledge that shares similar pretensions of universality to 'Northern' thought, as we have done with Simón Rodríguez, we need to understand her political struggle against the colonial structure developed in the North of Africa. For her, contact with Europeans meant the destruction of every form of non-Occidental life (Eberhardt 2000: x). That is the basis of the strong anti-colonial critique that appears in Eberhardt's works. Anticipating later postcolonial and decolonial thinkers, Eberhardt sees the development of modernity and of coloniality as a process of destruction of forms of non-European 'traditional life' by foreign Western forces.

We can look at Eberhardt's writings as a contribution to the critique of Western colonialism everywhere in the world, not only in the North of Africa (Eberhardt 2000, 2008). Abdel-Jaouad (1993: 102) observes this when she says that Eberhardt's work expounded a general sociology of 'colonialism and oppression' that in the Francophone world would only later be highlighted by the works of Frantz Fanon and Albert Memmi. She has immersed herself in the colonial world of North Africa, and it is from this specific locale in a specific time that she builds her universal critique of Western colonialism everywhere else. Her strategy of radical critique is built on the use of language(s) as tool for subversion of reality and she masters this tool in an outstanding way. She uses French as the main language of her writings, but uses her polyglotism[16] as a form of transgression of the French colonial world. The elements of her strategy of criticism can be summarised in the following extract:

> By intertwining oral and written literary materials and incorporating indigenous ethnographical and anthropological elements into her fiction, Isabelle deterritorialized [. . .] the content of her writing completely and radically. She was the first to experiment and use polyglotism as a device to undermine the hegemony of 'monolanguage', one of the principal pillars of the colonial orders. She was the first to present the Maghrebian ethos from the inside, using consistently the Arabic name 'Maghreb' when the current and official term was North Africa, and first also to introduce indigenous words into the French language, beginning thus a long process of disenfranchisement of the dominant language. (Abdel-Jaouad 1993: 116)

In her texts one can easily discern that her refusal to translate key words that express feelings and experiences is connected to her critique of the imposition of monolanguage in the colonial world. Language and gender were not fixed categories of Eberhardt's thought – they were means of displacement through different worlds she wanted to inhabit. They were the main means she used to deterritorialise herself and make her universal claims about the unfair relations established in the neo-colonial world.

According to Connell, the 'Northernness' of Northern social thought has been produced by the use of four basic textual moves: 'the claim of universality, reading from the center, gestures of exclusion, and grand erasure' (Connell 2006: 258). In this text, Connell analyses the work of three late-twentieth century authors, James S. Coleman, Anthony Giddens and Pierre Bourdieu, to show how they all proceed by the idea of producing theories that do not have a place of origin. They all come from the North, but try to present themselves as supporting 'Northern' intellectuals' claims to the eyes of the reader. Proceeding by a similar path of looking at how intellectuals have produced their ideas and what their ideas mean in terms of temporal and spatial orientation, we have taken authors that are not widely known that have transited between Southern and Northern spaces at specific moments of transition in modernity. What unite those different moments and spaces, however, is the struggle against colonialism and the creation of imaginaries of emancipation. Problematising the argument developed by Connell, I wanted to show that Southern thought shares at least two of these textual moves that she identifies as key structures of the Northern thought: one related to the argument's pretensions to universality, and the other related to the gesture of historical erasure.

Both Simón Rodríguez and Isabelle Eberhardt claim the universal relevance of their ideas, struggles and remedies for the problems of domination. They both also talk only about the history they know. In this way, they also have deleted for critical readers that know other histories equally important alternatives that should have figured in their proposals. Simón Rodríguez is clear when he creates the basis for the formation of a shared programme of universal political and social emancipation that could be applied everywhere. The history that he knows and talks about is the history of domination in America. Although he had long experience of living in Northern countries, this space and its histories appear in his analysis only when it comes to comparing similar examples of domination developed inside the North. He does not talk at all about what was going on in others parts of the world at the same time. Using literary means, Isabelle Eberhardt also offers us a strong critique of Western colonialism. She did not have any pretensions to be recognised as a social scientist. However, even without sharing this idea of producing a general theory that should be free from personal impressions and fictional characters, she is able to make universal claims about how different forms of social life have been destroyed by the imposition of colonial monolingualism, religion and power structures. As with Simón Rodríguez, she did not incorporate what she knew about other realities into her writing. She constrained herself to what she wanted to let us know. Both intellectuals have kept everything they regarded as peripheral to their main idea away from the centre of their analysis.

Concluding remarks

In this chapter we challenged two mainstream ways of looking at how history and imaginaries of spaces merged together in the formation of the modern world. On the one hand, we tried to problematise the naturalisation of the idea of Northern – very often treated as a synonym for Western – societies and their role in the formation and consolidation of the modern world; on the other hand, we tried to understand some limitations of the self-proclaimed anti-Western traditions that attempt to construct a strong distinctive Southern tradition of thought. Simón Rodríguez and Isabelle Eberhardt were taken in this chapter as authors whose life and work cannot be easily analysed by the tools of these two available conceptions of how to think about the experience with space and of displacements, and the structure of knowledge and interpretation, in modernity.

In the social sciences, the only studies that combine empirical investigation with theoretical analysis about the life in displacement of intellectuals and the changes in their interpretations are offered by Offe (2005) and Scaff (2011). Both authors develop different approaches about how 'America' has played an important role in the work of some European thinkers. The focus of Offe's (2005) study is how for three European authors – Alexis de Tocqueville, Max Weber and Theodor Adorno – who went to the United States in different periods, the European path to modernity would become comparable to (or overtaken by) the one developed along the North American path. However, Offe (2005) does not pay attention, first, to the fact that spatial displacement in itself was a source of knowledge for those intellectuals and, second, that the meaning of 'America' for each one of those authors is different because of the transformation historically brought about in the 'New World' in its relation to the 'Old World' (Mota 2015). It is fair to make this criticism because of the prominent role played by those three individuals in forming an understanding of the making of modernity. It should be mentioned that Scaff (2011) has offered a very detailed and descriptive account of Max Weber in the United States. Nevertheless, as in Offe's approach, the author did not consider movement as part of the knowledge process, quite apart from almost ignoring the importance of Weber's companion Marianne Weber in this process. The cartography that marks the meaning of South and North America for that matter was also created by the movement of those intellectuals.

The argument that we have developed is built upon the idea of looking at the specific kinds of displacements that modern subjects have made themselves or displacements that they have been subjected to, to think about the constitution of modernity itself. The discussion about Isabelle Eberhardt and Simón Rodríguez has hopefully helped us to elucidate the space of action in modernity as something that cannot be taken as a pre-established cartography. The modern experience with space is instead one which links time and space by displacement in the following way: to think about where you are, you need to displace yourself to the unknown in time – to a future – and in space – out of one's own place. It is a temporal and spatial discontinuity that constitutes the way human beings experience societal transformations. The imaginary of emancipation in modernity emerges from this exercise of displacement. It does not refer only to spatial displacements but also to historical transformation that leaves in suspension our certainty about the social world. What remains as an open agenda to critical social sciences is the analysis of the modern 'need' to understand foreign spaces and to interpret them in light of specific historical experiences. In our argument, it is by such means that modernity has been understood as a phenomenon of universal significance in different times and places.

Notes

1. As it appears, for instance, in the work of Santos (2009) and Connell (2006, 2007).
2. Displacement in this chapter means not only the concrete movement of someone from a point in space to another point. It also means the displacement of a societal imaginary that affects the way that societies can understand themselves. The American divergence of the nineteenth century that led to the creation of the idea of South and North America can be taken as an example of a displacement of a

societal imaginary (Mota 2015).

3. Isabelle Eberhardt was an intellectual who started to write very early in her life – her first writings were published as *Visions du Moghreb* when she was eighteen years old. Following a strategy that became part of the way she constructed herself as a person and intellectual, she used a male pseudonym to publish it. As Abdel-Jaouad (1993: 106) observes, it is unlikely that *Visions du Moghreb* would have been published if she had not used her male pseudonym of Nicolas Podolinsky. This is so because, first, she was talking about a topic that in her time 'concerned only men' – French colonialism in the Maghreb – and second, because the text was very critical of French colonialism and was to be published in a journal quite enthusiastic about the 'French mission' in North Africa.

4. For Giddens, spaces should be understood as the abstract sphere of physical relations and space as the area of social life.

5. The places Simón Rodríguez visited during his exile are: 1797 Kingston, Jamaica – where he changed his name to Samuel Robinson; 1798 Baltimore; 1801 Bayonne and Paris (France); 1804 Vienna; 1805 Paris, Lyon, Chambery, Milan, Venice, Ferrara, Bologna, Florence and Rome – where he made a famous oath with Simón Bolívar at the Monte Sacro on 15 August; 1806 Paris; 1807 Prussia, Poland, Russia and Paris; 1823 London and Cartagena, where he also readopted his name Simón Rodríguez (Rumazo Gonzáles 2006: 137⊠9). After coming back to America he kept travelling, fighting and working in different places. He moved around until the very end of his life, but he did not leave America again.

6. Before he went into exile, Simón Rodríguez worked as a mentor for young students and he wrote a book about public education and political emancipation in America. In his first book he started to develop his method of education and writing, which would be regarded later as his main working approach: first 'criticism' and then 'creation' (Grases 1954: 5–27).

7. Nonetheless, his writings start to appear just after he returned to America, especially by 1828. As has been argued by his main commentator, his thought cannot be located in any specific time or space. It was unsystematically produced, in many parts of the world and in different times (Rumazo Gonzáles 2006).

8. The author exemplifies the change in thought that is created by contact and movement with a personal analogy: 'The fortune of my compatriots brought me to patriotism; patriotism brought me to Europe and Napoleon; Napoleon brought me to Bolívar [Simón Rodríguez met Simón Bolívar in France]; Bolívar brought me to Venezuela [thinking about his homeland again]; from there I started to see America, and in America I found the republics that torment me' (Rodríguez 1840: 16).

9. Republican education means to Simón Rodríguez that which produces a public authority and not a personal one. It is based on the principle of popular sovereignty and opposed to the idea of personal desire (Rodríguez 1840: 88).

10. The first edition is from 1828, but the book was published in other important editions in the course of the 1830s.

11. One of Eberhardt's first writings – see note 2 for more details.

12. Isabelle Eberhardt was born in Geneva as a Russian *Heimatlose*, a stateless refugee. This condition marked her earlier life with the impression of being a stateless refugee from a country in which Russian emigrants were seen as 'suspicious' (Abdel-Jaouad 1993: 95). In one of her first writings, a short story published

using the male pseudonym of Nicolas Podolinsky in the *Nouvelle Revue Moderne*, she expresses her condition of being *Heimatlose* in Europe and projected a vision of the Maghreb as a place of autonomy and self-realisation.

13. According to Ortega (2008), Eberhardt's tutor, who is regarded as being her real father, Alexander Trophimvsky, was a personal friend of Bakunin. He was a philosopher who had escaped from Russia because of his ideas and lived in exile with Eberhardt's mother and brothers. In their place close to Geneva, a house called *La Villa Neuve*, many people who escaped Russian Czarisms for political reasons found shelter. Isabelle Eberhardt was raised in this milieu, which strongly marked her view about exile, political boundaries, and the role of displacement and thought in the human imaginary.

14. In 1888 Augustin de Moërder, Isabelle's brother, joined the French Mission in Algeria. By this time Isabelle had become increasingly interested in Arabic culture. In 1897 she went to North Africa with her mother Nathalie Moërder – she adopted a male name and male clothes to insert herself as she wanted into the Maghreb. Her mother died in Algeria. Isabelle came back to Europe when her economic situation deteriorated in North Africa. In 1900 she would go back to Algeria again but had to leave in 1901 because of her involvement in political activities against colonial rule. She returned to Algeria one year later, after marrying Slimane Ehnni, an Algerian man to whom she had been a partner for a long time.

15. One could also take the view that Eberhardt wished to do as Durkheim did in his search for a place where religion had been experienced in its most pure form. Following this approach, one would be able to look at her displacement to the Maghreb and her conversion to Islam as a sort of anthropological strategy of immersion to know the other and to be able to make herself part of the object of analysis.

16. She was fluent in French, Russian, German, Italian and Arabic. She could also read Latin and Greek.

References

Abdel-Jaouad, H. (1993), 'Isabelle Eberhardt: portrait of the artist as a young nomad', *Yale French Studies*, Post/Colonial Conditions: Exiles, Migrations, and Nomadism, 83: 2, 93–117.

Anderson, B. (1991), *Imagined Communities: Reflections on the Origin and Spread of Nationalism*, 2nd edn, London: Verso.

Appadurai, A. (1988), 'Putting hierarchy in its place', *Cultural Anthropology*, 3: 1, 36–49.

Bayly, C. A. (2002), *The Birth of the Modern World*, Oxford: Blackwell.

Behdad, A. (1994), *Belated Travellers: Orientalism in the Age of Colonial Dissolution*, Cork: Cork University Press.

Brotton, J. (2013), *A History of the World in Twelve Maps*, London: Penguin Books.

Burawoy, M. (2009), 'The global turn: lessons from southern labor scholars and their labor movements', *Work and Occupations*, 36: 2, 87–95.

Connell, R. (2006), 'Northern theory: the political geography of general social theory', *Theory and Society*, 35: 2, 237–64.

Connell, R. (2007), *Southern Theory: The Global Dynamics of Knowledge in Social*

Sciences, Cambridge: Polity.

Cristóvão, F. (1999), *Literatura de Viagens*, Lisboa: Edições Cosmos.

Durkheim, E. [1912] (1995), *The Elementary Forms of Religious Life*, New York: Free Press.

Eberhardt, I. (2000), *País de Arena: Relatos Argelinos*, Madrid: Ediciones del Oriente y del Mediterráneo.

Eberhardt, I. (2008), *Los Diarios de una Nómada Apasionada*, Barcelona: BackList.

Euben, R. L. (2006), *Journeys to the Other Shore: Muslim and Western Travellers in Search of Knowledge*, Princeton: Princeton University Press.

Foucault, M. (1985), 'La Vie: l'expérience et la science', *Revue de Métaphysique et de Morale*, 90: 1, 3–14.

Foucault, M. (2001), *The Order of Things: An Archaeology of Human Sciences*, London: Routledge.

Garfield, S. (2013), *On the Map: Why the World Looks the Way It Does*, London: Profile Books.

Giddens, A. (1990), *The Consequences of Modernity*, Cambridge: Polity.

Grases, P. (1954), *Escritos de Simón Rodríguez: Compilación y Estudio Bibliográfico*, Caracas: Imprenta Nacional.

Gregory, D. (1994), *Geographical Imaginations*, Cambridge: Blackwell.

Harvey, D. (1985), *The Urbanization of Capital: Studies in the History and Theory of Capitalist Urbanization*, Baltimore: Johns Hopkins University Press.

Koselleck, R. (2002), *The Practice of Conceptual History: Timing History, Spacing Concepts*, Stanford: Stanford University Press.

Koselleck, R. (2004), *Future Past: On the Semantics of Historical Time*, New York: Columbia University Press.

Labarge, M. W. (2005), *Medieval Travellers: The Rich and Restless*, London: Phoenix.

Lefebvre, H. (1991), *The Production of Space*, Oxford: Blackwell.

Lewis, M. W. and W. E. Wigen (1997), *The Myth of Continents: A Critique of Metageography*, Berkeley: University of California Press.

Massey, D. (2005), *For Space*, London: Sage

Mbembe, A. (2000), 'At the edge of the world: boundaries, territoriality, and sovereignty in Africa', *Public Culture*, 12: 1, 259–84.

Menon, D. (2010), 'A local cosmopolitan: "Kesari" Balakrishna Pillai and the invention of Europe for a modern Kerala', in S. Bose and K. Manjapra (eds), *Cosmopolitan Thought Zones: South Asia and the Global Circulation of Ideas*, London: Palgrave, pp. 131–58.

Mignolo, W. D. (2002), 'The geopolitics of knowledge and the colonial difference', *The South Atlantic Quarterly*, 101: 1, 57–96.

Mignolo, W. D. (2011), *The Darker Side of Western Modernity: Global Futures, Decolonial Options*, Durham, NC: Duke University Press.

Mota, A. (2012), 'Cosmopolitanism in Latin America: political practices, critiques, and imaginaries', in Gerard Delanty, *Routledge Handbook of Cosmopolitan Studies*, London: Routledge, pp. 491–503.

Mota, A. (2015), 'The American divergence, the modern Western world and the paradigmatisation of history', in Peter Wagner (ed.), *African, American and European Trajectories of Modernity*, *Annual of European and Global Studies*, vol. 2, Edinburgh: Edinburgh University Press, pp. 21–41.

Offe, C. (2005), *Reflections on America: Tocqueville, Weber & Adorno in the United*

States, Cambridge: Polity.

Ortega, A. G. (2008), 'Preface', in Isabelle Eberhardt, *Los Diarios de una Nómada Apasionada*, Barcelona: BackList.

Pickering, M. (2010), 'Experience as horizon: Koselleck, expectation and historical time', *Cultural Studies*, 18: 2–3, 271–89.

Pratt, M. L. (2008), *Imperial Eyes: Travel Writing and Transculturation*, London: Routledge.

Quijano, A. (1998), 'La colonialidad del poder y la experiencia cultural latinoamericana', in R. Briceño-León and H. Sonntag (eds), *Pueblo, Época y Desarrollo: La Sociología de América Latina*, Venezuela: Editorial Nueva Sociedad, pp. 27–38.

Quijano, A. (2005), 'Colonialidade do poder, eurocentrismo e América Latina', in Edgardo Lander (ed.), *A Colonialidade do Saber: Eurocentrismo e Ciências Sociais*, Buenos Aires: CLACSO, pp. 227–78.

Rodríguez, S. (1840), *Las Sociedades Americanas, Luces y Virtudes Sociales*, facsimile of the Valparaíso edn.

Rodríguez, S. [1830] (1971), *El Libertador del Mediodía de América y sus Compañeros de Armas, Defendidos por un Amigo de la Causa Social*, Caracas: Cromotip.

Ross, M. C. (2000), *Old Icelandic Saga and Society*, Cambridge: Cambridge University Press.

Rumazo Gonzáles, A. (2006), *Simón Rodríguez: Maestro de América*, Caracas: MCI.

Said, E. (1985), *Orientalism: Western Conceptions of the Orient*, London: Penguin.

Santos, B. S. (2009), *Una Epistemologia del Sur: La Reinvención del Conocimiento y la Emancipación Social*, Buenos Aires: Siglo XXI Editores, CLACSO.

Scaff, A. L. (2011), *Max Weber in America*, Princeton: Princeton University Press.

Schmitt, C. (2006), *The Nomos of the Earth in the International Law of the Jus Publicum Europaeum*, New York: Telos.

Talbot, A. (2010), *The Great Ocean of Knowledge: The Influence of Travel Literature on the Work of John Locke*, Leiden: Brill.

Wagner, P. (2008), *Modernity as Experience and Interpretation: A New Sociology of Modernity*, Cambridge: Polity.

Wagner, P. (2012), *Modernity: Understanding the Present*, Cambridge: Polity.

Wallerstein, I. (1974), *The Modern World System*, vol. 1, New York: Academic Press.

8

The South as Exile

Nathalie Karagiannis

What will we do without exile and the long night that stares at the water?
Mahmoud Darwish, 'Who am I, without exile?'

Sur, espejismo, reflejo.
Federico García Lorca, 'Suite del agua. Sur'

Figure 8.1 William Kentridge, drawing from 'Felix in Exile', 1994, charcoal and pastel on paper, 120 × 150 cm / 47-1/4 × 59-1/16 in. Courtesy of the artist and Marian Goodman Gallery. Copyright: William Kentridge.

IN THE DRAWING in Figure 8.1, Felix looks into the mirror and faces Nandi through a double-ended telescope, while the blue water of memory is pouring into his room. The striking film, from which this still is taken, was made on the eve of the first general elections in South Africa and its explicit purpose was to reflect on the past as a necessary part of the present and perhaps as something that threatened to be obliterated.[1] The poignancy and apparent confusion of the events/ pictures of the film are the direct expression of the poignancy and confusion with which Felix, who is in exile in Paris, apprehends events in his homeland. Pausing a little bit longer on this picture compels one to see that, contrary to conventional thinking that makes of exile and home opposite poles, *exile is the dynamic approximation of home.*

Indeed, exile is not the opposite of home. Reversing María Zambrano's intuition that the true homeland creates exile, I will explore in convoluted ways the idea that *exile creates the homeland or, in essence, that exile is a homeland.* During this exploration, it will emerge that between utter alienation and feeling/being at home, there is a very vast middle ground occupied by a variety of experiences, some more intimate, others more collective,[2] which are all likely to be described by the notion of exile. The paths we will follow in this exploration lead into various areas: poetry, philosophy, psychoanalysis. Each of these accounts presents interesting particularities, and I look out for what they have in common. Exploring such paths partly captures the complexity of that which is otherwise currently called the refugee crisis. Each individual whose survival or death we hear of as pertaining to a number is likely to have gone through some of the experiences that are subtly but relevantly described by poets, philosophers and psychiatrists below. Accordingly, the dark South, which is explored in the last section, can be turned on its head: for those coming from Syria, it is called Europe.

In the particular light of this chapter, *the South indicates the direction home*, just as in the picture by Kentridge. It goes without saying that not all homelands are situated in the South. But the South is of central interest here because of very specific features such as juxtaposition, sharpness of contrasts and simultaneity, which will be detailed in the last section. The point here is one which speaks of an imaginary South: this imaginary serves as a direction through which loss and disorientation are reconfigured into home. It is in this sense that the feature that Edward Said ascribes to exile in his famous essay 'Reflections on Exile' (2002) takes on its full meaning: it is *'strangely compelling'*, because just as strangeness and compulsion are centripetal and centrifugal and nev-ertheless cohabit spontaneously in this phrase, exile and home cannot but exist together, not apart. If the South is the reconfiguration of exilic loss (and disorientation) into home, then the South is an equivalent for return, which is a *topos* of any discourse on exile, as we will see later.

Let me then make clear that 'the South as exile' is a shorthand for the idea that *the South means return from exile*, that is, the tantalising remedy for the irremediable loss that characterises any exile. As such (as a shorthand, but also as its explanation) it is an idea that one has to undergo – as Jorie Graham would propose for a poem – as a journey. I grant the reader that there is nothing self-evident in what I propose; on the contrary, it is a deeply personal series of intuitions that stem from personal experience. One good example of this is the structure of this chapter: even though I claim that the South gives exile its direction, it only appears at the end of the exploration of exile. The main reason is that I want to show, physically as it were, how disorienting exile is before bringing the South to it – as a possible solution? (But the reader is warned from the very first line of Mahmoud Darwish in this chapter that one might feel lost without exile, whereas Federico García Lorca speaks about how the South may prove illusory.) Another example of the personal nature of this journey is the homage paid to the writers, almost all of them poets, in exile who have expressly struggled with this idea (and sometimes with the idea of the South too): each section bears one or more names, irrespectively of the significance of their visible contribution to this chapter.

One last word of caution: before starting this short but twisted journey, I would like to briefly dedicate a few preliminary lines to the relation between the exile and the foreigner. Talking of exile is one side of the coin; talking of the foreigner is the other. Thinking around exile centres on the relation between the movement towards somewhere and what (place) has been left behind. Thinking about the foreigner centres on the relation between the movement towards somewhere and what (place) has been encountered. Thinking about exile means thinking, among other thing, about solitude; thinking about the foreigner means thinking about, among other things, grouping people. Thinking about exile means thinking from rootlessness, thinking about the foreigner means thinking from a clear-cut space, that for which the person is foreign. Exile: escape. Foreigner: hospitality. These are the differences of the two sides: the coin is one and the same.

Let me now indicate that in the first three sections of this chapter, I look at three issues for which I could not easily find answers elsewhere: the connection between blindness and exile, the antagonism between exiles and those who stay, and the contemporary changes in the *topos* of return from exile. I then dedicate a section to María Zambrano's thought on exile, because this extremely fruitful thought is not known by Anglophone readers and because it is María Zambrano who made me think of the many borders within exile. The next step the chapter takes follows naturally María Zambrano's thought: in section 5, the psyche (lost and found and lost again and found again) is looked at from various angles: poetic, psychoanalytic, philosophical. Finally, in the last section, the South comes in to offer some direction.

1. Being blind and knowing: Oedipus (and Antigone) and Adam (and Eve), and Roberto Bolaño

> I don't believe in 'exile', especially when the word sits next to the word
> 'literature'.
> Roberto Bolaño, 'Literature and exile'

> True exile is the measure of every true writer.
> Roberto Bolaño, 'Exiles'

The word 'exile' was first offered to me by a Spanish-Swiss psychoanalyst who had lived formative years in Argentina. It seemed to perfectly fit the need of the moment: to make sense of the mismatches between everyday life and experience and (cultural) expectations, and whereas it began as a satisfactory description, it later turned into a useful tool and then into a theme worth exploring as such. I have now come full circle and have lost my attachment to the idea of exile, and this might be the best position from which to write about it – as its emotional charge has lessened and been exorcised in a poetry book entitled *Exorismos* (Karagiannis 2016b), a word that has fallen out of usage in Modern Greek but that phonetically brings together the Modern Greek words for exile (εξορία) and for definition (ορισμός).

The trajectory of exile through the centuries retains a few unsolved ambiguities. It is often thought that death was a lighter punishment than exile in ancient Athens. The Socratic option for death in the stead of exile has consolidated the intuition that exile must have been taken to be the worst fate one could face. Set practically in the context of the not always amiable relations between city-states and of an infinitely more reduced world in terms of language and communication, as well as against a code of honour which tightly related the person to the community, we can imagine the gravity of the punishment of exile.

However, mentions of exile in ancient Athens usually focus on the moment of punishment itself. Being condemned to exile meant, in a second step, being given another opportunity to build a life in a community – even though this community would not be the one into which one was born. The practical difficulties of exile cannot be underestimated, but what I now want to underline is that exile was not devoid of dignity. Taking distance from the place where the wrong was done allowed the recovery – for the wrongdoer – of dignity (just as it allowed the victims to remain dignifiedly in the same place, without facing the outrage of the wrongdoer's presence). As Richard Sennett points out, Oedipus is an exile who retains all his dignity throughout the ordeal: indeed, Oedipus introduces a moral dimension into the very act of displacement, showing himself to be a stranger of tragic grandeur rather than an unwanted foreigner of lesser position (Sennett 2011: 109–10).

In such a context, it is amusing to read Roberto Bolaño's claim that Adam and Eve must be thought of as the first exiles.[3] Among the many classic depictions of Adam and Eve's expulsion from the Garden of Eden, Masaccio's is certainly one of the most expressive. Eve hides her breast and pubis and mourns desperately, with the mouth open, and an upward-cast gaze. As for Adam, he hides his face in his hands, sobbing. The desolate, dramatic effect of the fresco has often been commented on. I am struck by the discrepancy or non-continuity of the movement between the figures of Adam and Eve, which adds to their sense of desolation and, mostly, solitude and separateness, as if by being separated from God they also become separated from one another. But what is centrally at stake here is the similitude of the movement between Adam and Oedipus, who also brings his hands to his face, in several early Renaissance depictions – in order to blind and then hold his wounded eyes. It is no coincidence that both prototypical exiles hide their eyes. A great part of the exile that is about to happen features the blind spot (of knowledge) – both as origin and as consequence. Until he ate the fruit of the tree of knowledge, Adam was ignorant of his ignorance, or blind to it. The fruit opened his eyes and made him fall into disgrace. Leaving the Garden of Eden condemns him to not seeing it again, ever, until . . . he closes his eyes at the time of his death. As for Oedipus, his prior knowledge does not prevent him from committing the crimes that are his destiny – his knowledge has a blind spot. Horrified by his understanding when the time comes, he blinds himself and becomes an exile, who is never again to see his native land. There is a strong sense that exile goes hand-in-hand with some form of blindness.

The exilic fate of Oedipus and Adam is a fate we (can) share as humans, with respect to our lack of control over the hybristic moment or the moment of the sin, the fall, and so on. Thus, the emotions that their exile stirs up in us are empathy, pity, perhaps some kind of relief that is related to *catharsis*. We do not view these archetypical men as contemptible or indeed shameful wrongdoers but as beings whose dignity persists throughout the divinely sanctioned or simply hazardous ordeal.

2. Going and staying: Ovid

What would have happened if Eve hadn't been involved in the story of the tree of knowledge? What would the relation between the exiled Adam and the non-exiled Eve have been? This is not a feminist counterfactual. Neither do I want to think about the marital relations across borders, even though this is a very interesting theme – from, for instance, the way Ovid's relation to his wife while he is in exile passes through the highs and lows of trust and jealousy[4] to, closer to us, that of the parents of Greek poet Michalis Ganas (2007), whose father stays in Greece while the mother moves to Hungary with the children.

Rather, I would like to point out the ambiguous relation between the exiles and those who stay. Talk of brain-drain and massive exodus of the young and talented – a mild form of exile – is an everyday issue in journalistic and public discourse in current Greece under crisis. Indeed, a lot of younger people have left the country in recent years – even though surviving chronic corruption and tax evasion has been a problem long before the so-called crisis hit the country. The public discourse associated with this phenomenon mostly takes the form of a lament, regretting the situation, and so on. However, there are cases – in music and texts[5] – where exile is seen as a weak stance, one that does not offer resistance to the dangers and threats of the crisis. By opposition, staying in the country means truly and courageously resisting, and is the highest form of action. The same antagonism is palpable in accounts of political resistance to the 1967 coup d'état in Greece. Those who stayed often covertly accuse those who did not stay of cowardice, lack of political dynamism, lack of vision, and so on.

This antagonistic relation between those who leave and those who stay hinges on the ambiguity of the obligation of exile. Is it clear that a politically active member of the resistance to a putsch, for instance, cannot stay in the country? Is she obliged to leave the country – assuming that if her activities or herself were found, she would be arrested, tortured, killed? Or is she rather obliged to stay, in order to be closer to the 'battlefield' and by her example encourage others to fight? If most reasonable respondents would now allow our fictive resistance to become an honourable exile, such a response may not always have been evident, in particular not under communist discipline. Economic exile involves the same problems: after what threshold is one honourable in choosing exile? After almost starving to death? After remaining unemployed over six months, a year, two years without other resources? Or after simply coming to the realisation that the obstacles that everyday corruption brings to one's path are unacceptable or cannot be reconciled with an ethical life?

3. Impossible return (not any more?): Ossip and Nadezhda Mandelstam, Julio Cortázar, Edward Said, Faiz Ahmad Faiz, Melpo Axioti, Michalis Ganas

Perhaps the main problem in the relation between those who stay and those who go is the intimate conviction that they share and seldom speak out: that return from exile is impossible. The rupture that exile produces is such, both within the individual and between the individual and that which he has left behind, that even if there is a physical return, there cannot be a return to the social reality which was there before exile. Social relations are by definition mutable, but few things have the destructive power of exile, as Raymond Williams has pointed out (Williams 1961).[6]

Oedipus and Adam archetypically act out this irreversibility.

Said's 'Reflections on Exile' (2002) refers eloquently to this as a condition of *terminal* loss. Terminality signifies an end, a threshold that cannot be crossed the other way around. And indeed, it is this sensation of terminal loss which differentiates exile as it has been lived for two millennia and the current understanding of exile.

For the condition of exile is nowadays much more ambiguous than it used to be with regard to the impossibility of return. Means of technology – mobile phones and the internet and, within the internet, emailing, Skype and social networks – have entirely changed the conditions under which exile is lived. The constant stream of communication by writing, the possibility of relating across borders instantly, the possibility of seeing each other on a screen while being miles apart have transformed earlier exile's feature of severe rupture into an apparently much greater back and forth movement between the 'home' and the new place.

There is a host of studies about cyberspace and virtual reality and their consequences for the people who spend a lot of their time in those spaces and realities. For exiles, that space is as vital as it is illusory. They owe to that space that exile is not the irreversible rupture it used to be. Not only is it not irreversible any more, but also one could say that exile does not/cannot happen any more like it used to: the exile is in constant relation to those she has left, she can see and hear the land (cannot smell it, though, which as the first phrases of Proust's magnum opus have come to symbolise, must mean a certain loss of memory), she can see and hear – and some would say: know – all that which the exile before globalisation could not.

Technology has changed exile, but so have numbers. The amount of exiles, refugees, émigrés, displaced and uprooted people (let us not make any distinction between them for the moment) has increased exponentially in the last decades. Be it because of war, climate change which changes the job markets at 'home', or simply because transport has become so much cheaper, settling into a different country than the one where one was born is hardly an exceptional phenomenon any more.

The increased number of displaced people and the technological means available to them have a profound influence on two fundamental and interconnected aspects of exile: language and isolation. In the essay mentioned above, Said recounts a meeting where Faiz Ahmad Faiz, a Pakistani poet, meets another Pakistani in Lebanon. Only when the poet is able to speak his language at last does he 'seem to overcome his sense of constant estrangement', that 'solitude' which the exile 'experience[s] outside of the group' (Said 2002: 138, 140). Not being able to speak one's language (normally, on an everyday basis, publicly) used to be one of the hardest ordeals of the exile: technology has changed this to a great extent. Almost anybody can now be connected to the internet and through it to local television and radio stations; almost anybody can speak on the phone or on Skype with their people for free. The possibility of constantly using the home language has changed the perception of extreme isolation or desperate solitude that was earlier associated with the condition of exile. Think, by contrast, that the only companion of Adam was Eve, and the only companion of Oedipus was Antigone; think of Nadezhda Mandelstam who memorised Ossip's work in order to keep it alive until publication became possible.

So perhaps it is not so much that return has become more possible (many times it remains impossible because it is too dangerous), but that it is not as dearly desired as it used to be. The creation of the intermediate, technological state along with coexistence with a multitude in the condition of exile has perhaps rendered the return less urgent. Reading black British poet Kwame Dawes's (2011) interesting reflections on 'The Pleasures of Exile' confirms that if younger people, and especially writers, are concerned with their exilic condition, they have dynamic means of dealing with it – and feel that many are in the same situation.

In a 1983 TV interview, Julio Cortázar talks about the massive exile of Latin American writers and finishes by saying that 'in the end, we will all come back'.[7] Apart from the poignant irony that grips today's spectator who knows that Cortázar died a year later without, of course, returning to Argentina, what strikes one is the need to reassert (the desire for) the possibility of a highly improbable return.

The improbability of return in this striking example invites us to think in the direction of a trope of the return in exile, which is constitutive of the latter. I mean that, no matter how improbable the return might be, and no matter how irreversible the condition is supposed to be and often actually is, the discourse of/on the return is part of what makes the condition itself. One could push this even further and say that if it is because of its very irreversibility that exile is such a desperate human condition, then that despair is always and constantly undermined by the idea of the return to the 'homeland' – at the same time the despair is cultivated and enhanced by the same, never accomplished, always postponed return.

There is a softer condition than the one just sketched, which raises other kinds of questions: that of the effective return. In *Mitria Patrida*, Michalis Ganas (2007), an established Greek poet, talks about the forced move of his family (his mother and sibling, grandparents and aunts but, importantly, not his father), partly due to a political misunderstanding, from northern Greece to Hungary, where a special refugee status is created for Greek refugees. Even though the conditions there are difficult, the return is depicted as even stranger, precisely because of a supposed familiarity and cultural and social continuity. When they come out of the boat which transported them back to Igoumenitsa, the narrator (the boy Ganas) says that everybody comments on how well dressed he and his brother were, as if they had not seen the photos sent to them during exile. The rift between exile and the return, between the reception of those who stayed through the virtual reality of the photos and the 'real' perception cannot be bridged. Where there was a 'patrida', a fatherland, there is now a 'mitria', a stepmother.

Melpo Axioti's (2015) *Kadmo* is another very interesting example of a description of an effective return. Contrary to Ganas's family, whose head (the grandfather) had sided with the right wing and travelled to Hungary only due to a misunderstanding, Melpo Axioti was a political refugee, belonging to the Communist Party since her youth. Kadmo, the author's barely hidden autobiographical character, keeps a tight balance between past memories (of the origins, of exile) and the grim present of return. Flashbacks and fragmented versions of the present succeed each other, while the text is delivered by Kadmo as a narrator or spoken to Kadmo in the second person of the singular, in the harrowing realisation that exile is death (Kadmo 2015: 84) and that this death will accompany every effort for a new life.[8]

Just as in the case of the never-achieved return, the effective return is part and parcel of the exilic condition. Because even after one has returned, one remains an exile.

4. The implacable promise of exile: the liminal thought of María Zambrano

One hypothesis about why this is so can be derived from the radically transgressive thought of María Zambrano, for whom exile creates home.[9]

Even though her work is little known outside Spain, María Zambrano is one of Spain's foremost twentieth-century philosophers. She lived between 1904 and 1991; she spent forty-five years in exile, which began in 1939 because of the end of the Spanish Republic and the Second World War. One of the most important characteristics of María Zambrano's work is the style of her thought, which is poetico-philosophical: she called it 'razón poetica',[10] as it is understood to enrich reason by intuition and revelation.

Zambrano never wrote systematically on exile, even though it is very clear to all that her life and thought were indelibly marked by the condition of exile. She did, however, think of a book that would be called *Desde el exilio* (*From Exile*), and to this end she took down notes and wrote a couple of longer texts on exile. This project never saw the light in a finalised form, but this is where I have looked for her thinking (these texts were fortunately brought together in a book called *El exilio como patria*[11] [*Exile as Homeland*], published in 2014), along with her book on Antigone and a couple of pieces of secondary literature. Because her work, and especially the excerpts I look at here, is not easily available in English, and the phrasing of her thought is extremely open to interpretation, I have loaded this section with quotations in the original and in English translation. That may prove cumbersome, but I think it is both useful and unavoidable.

'There are some journeys of which one starts knowing something only upon return' (Zambrano 2014: 58).[12] In trying to capture the development of a thought that scrutinised exile in an elusive way, if this can be said, let us start from what she says about exile after her return to Spain and slowly work our way towards what she says further into the past. After having come back to Spain, she writes: 'Exile has been like my homeland or like a dimension of an unknown homeland, which once it is known, cannot be renounced' (Zambrano 2014: 58).[13] There are two important points to be immediately made here: first and foremost, the assimilation or embracement of exile as home; and second, that the exile, that unknown – or imaginary – home cannot be renounced – by opposition to the real homeland one has renounced. And she goes on by admitting that in the end she had to renounce this non-renounceable home and that left her more than naked, without a skin: 'I admit . . . that renouncing my forty years of exile has demanded a lot of work . . . from time to time it hurts, no, it's not that it hurts, it is a sensation of having been flayed, like Saint Bartholomew, an unintelligible sensation, but which is there' (Zambrano 2014: 58).[14]

In what terms does she describe this homeland that exile is? One can discern three categories along which María Zambrano's thinking develops. In terms of space, exile is a desert, a home without frontiers and without a kingdom,[15] but also elsewhere 'that kingdom, that field, that source of tears'.[16] The hesitation between the idea that exile may be a kingdom and that it may not be indicates her ambivalence about the role of the person in exile: is she a king of this desert or can the desert not have a king? Is the exile standing at the centre of something powerful, just as a king would be, or is she, as it is traditionally seen, wandering in something which, having no limits, is undefinable . . . and therefore lacks substance? The strictest contradistinction to the 'normal' homeland is indeed made through the absence of borders.

The idea of the border touches, in María Zambrano, upon another theme, which was mentioned earlier: blindness. Indeed, here, exile is a place which allows one to see and prevents one from doing so at the same time,[17] 'because the exile has only horizon. But paradoxically the horizon is at the same time the condition of visibility, of the confine of the visible and the invisible orders' (Zambrano 2014: 51).[18] In the quasi-mystic understanding of María Zambrano's exile, the invisible – that to which we are blind, and which is accessed through exile – is on the other side of an unending emptiness or line that is the horizon. One could imagine that she beheld a *ligne de fuite* as that horizon which both set free and kept the invisible at a distance, until the revelation.

Another spatial inversion she operates regards the countries that have welcomed her and that share Spanish as a language: there, she writes, the strangers like herself feel outsiders (*extraños*), and insiders (*entraños*, a neologism derived from *entrañas* – the entrails of an animal) because they feel within themselves a lost inside.[19] The coincidence of the Spanish language in Spain and in its former colonies allows the deployment of the thought that exile actually becomes the inner part, the core, but one that is lost. Bringing it close to the metaphor of desert that she also uses, it is possible to say that María Zambrano's effort is directed towards imploding the significance of the border in the creation of exile, either by blowing it up as much as in a desert where there are no visible borders or by shrinking it to the inner core of the exiled self, so that exile becomes a part of oneself. This two-directional strategy allows her to bring out the home-generating capacities of exile, rather than its destructive effects.[20]

Finally, the metaphor of the islands of exile is used by Zambrano (2014: 39, 41) to significant effect. The autopoietic capacity of exile is most manifest here, since these islands appear by virtue of the presence of the exile, where they did not exist. This is a metaphor that I find particularly interesting because of its explicit use of water (which surrounds the islands) and a much greater concreteness or body given to the exile.[21]

Time is a second category according to which this thinker's understanding of exile can be described. The 'interrupted dawn' ('la alba interrumpida') (Zambrano 2014: 31) is a recurrent trope of her work. As one commentator says: 'All Zambrano's thought wants, in fact, to be dawn-like, that is, born into light from within the obscure insides of existence' (Trueba-Mira 2012: 152, n.17). Especially on exile, the philosopher writes: 'When it [the homeland] *dawns* in history, when one can minimally see it – actually it is enough for it to be announced – it creates the exile of those who, having seen it and served it even minimally, have to go away from it' (Zambrano 2014: 48)[22] – the liminal moment of dawn corresponds to, on the one hand, the moment when the announcement touches the coming-into-being and, on the other hand, the springing of light from within obscurity. It is a liminal moment (but perhaps all moments are, by definition, liminal) that separates two very different, clearly perceptible, states – and we perceive how close this idea is to the one of the horizon, mentioned above, which separates the visible from the invisible. Zambrano's reiterated idea of Cronos being the only god without a shape and without a mask is related to the significance she gives to the (Faustian) suspension of the moment. But this is also what she thinks of the exile: she does not have a shape, a face or a mask and that may turn her into an omen (like the dawn).[23]

Dawn is an indestructible moment, for Zambrano, and there lies its utility in terms of thinking exile. The fact that it is interrupted suspends it in time, having the effect of crystallising a past that is never gone, of keeping the past in the present (Zambrano 2014: 31). I see this as the other side of the theme of the impossible return – the radical destructive power of exile, in the sense that nothing will ever be the same upon return. Here, the moment of entering into exile is magnified and glorified, so that the homeland can be ultimately saved.

Zambrano's deployment of spatio-temporal metaphors regarding exile takes another form, which brings together one moment and its various components. On the one hand, she has a sense that one finds oneself in exile suddenly, without prior announcement, without possibility of choice: one wakes up in exile.[24] On the other hand, she establishes a clear distinction between two stages in exile: (1) abandonment (and expulsion), which is followed by the desert and (2) achievement. However, from the chronological-experiential point of view that Zambrano adopts, I do not find clear indications of a distinction between expulsion and abandonment. On the contrary, they both importantly point out the border-like existence of exile: it starts before it has even started, it already starts when one stands at the edge of it.[25]

Indeed, the role expulsion plays at the beginning of exile is straightforward. By contrast, the role abandonment plays is a little bit less so. On María Zambrano's double register of the Greek and Judaeo-Christian traditions, abandonment is the disappearance or the silence of the gods. Take the cue from what she says about Antigone: 'Antigone's passion happens in the absence and the silence of gods'[26] and Sophocles' tragedy (the gods do not intervene), which is general-ised as a feature of all tragedy.[27] Likewise Oedipus, whose destiny was announced to him and whom no divine power descended to help.[28] The nature of abandonment renders the gaze and judgement of the gods absent, and the only thing that comes to the fore is dispossession.[29] Referring to 'the Father' too – which is the mediation, at the same time as the family, the native city, and so on – she comes to the same conclu-sion.[30] A loss of the gods that is attached to a loss of their gaze brings us indirectly back to the theme of blindness,[31] and vice versa, but also to the lack of voice, and the need to raise the human voice, which are both crucially relevant for poetry, as we shall see in the next section.

When the acute sense of abandonment subsides, the desert opens up not as expulsion but as exile. Exile's desertic features are the absence of borders, the immensity, the fragmented encounters with other home-lands. The loss takes on the form of the infinite. So, 'in order not to get lost [in it] one has to lock the desert within oneself, [. . .] interiorise it, in the soul, in the mind, in the senses, sharpening the ear rather than the eye so as to avoid illusions and hear voices' (Zambrano 2014: 40).[32] The exile dispossesses herself of all demands.

This internalised desert produces several consequences, which express an achieved exile.

The most dramatic of those is the fact that the exile will never settle down into any other homeland. No place or circumstances will ever be able to fully tempt her into putting down roots – and of that, Zambrano says, the exile will be accused (Borgna 1996: 55).[33] Conversely, achiev-ing exile means the discovery of the real homeland. In a deeply ascetic understanding, the thinker expresses her certainty that entirely renouncing the homeland is that which allows its authentic appari-tion.[34] (The same kind of movement – renunciation of love of God, in order to attain that God – is what characterises the common question posed by the mystic thinkers whose work is explored by Anne Carson, discussed in section 5 below.) Then and only then does the homeland become unavoidable. And coming full circle, she reverses the adventure of the exile towards her always-elusive homeland: the true, unavoidable homeland, she writes, creates exile.[35]

There is an unresolved ambiguity in the direction of the relation between exile and homeland but I ultimately think it is of little impor-tance. Rather, it is worth keeping in mind the aspect of creation, or of generation in the sense that one is generating the other, and that they are intrinsically tied together. Another aspect which we should recall is that of interruption of dawn, because it suggests something very strong about the state of suspension (of parenthesis) that is caused in the condition of exile. Finally, the recurrent mention of the lack of borders in exile, which is the same as the infinite horizon and the non-seeing, should be brought together with a theme with which we started and that we will find soon again: blindness.

5. The exiled soul: Federico García Lorca, Odysseas Elytis, Anne Carson, Pascal Quignard, Derek Walcott, Etel Adnan, Vladimir Nabokov

approbation had turned me into an exile
Derek Walcott, *The Prodigal*

Just as Zambrano thematised her experience of exile into poetic reason, others in other fields have treated exile both as a field of human experience and as artistic practice. Indeed, the theme of exile haunts the arts of the twentieth century to such an extent that one could call that period the century of exile. The great critic George Steiner has proposed that 'extra-territoriality' is the defining condition of modernism (Steiner 1971).

Rather than thinking of how exile has been represented in poetry and psychoanalysis, I would like to propose that the poetic fact and the psychoanalytic space are constituted by elements that can be discovered in the constitutive conditions of exile, in other words, that these are ontologically similar.

El hecho poético: jump and mystic

In a 1928 conference on 'Imagination, inspiration, evasión', Federico García Lorca writes:

> Imagination supports and creates a poetic ambiance and inspiration invents the poetic fact. The poetic fact cannot be controlled by anything. It must be accepted as the rain of stars is accepted. But let us be happy that poetry can run away, escape from the cold claws of reasoning.[36]

Like every other human being, the poet lives in a social and political space, a space where relations are constantly at play and where she herself is constantly at the centre of these relations, as partner, daughter, mother, friend. However, the poet does not write while cooking, while attending the children, while paying the bills, while reading an academic text. The poet can write about all of these, but in a space which is different from all of these, and which is not coextensive with them. The non-coextensivity of the everyday (called 'the real' below) and the other space, this jump between them, is constitutive of the poetic. For the moment, let us say that there is a jump between the poetic space and what it is not.

In that poetic space, the poet writes against or simply despite the (social, political, everyday) laws, she continually transgresses the laws, the laws of the fatherland and the laws of the language, and is thus, de facto, an outlaw. In the poetic space, the poet listens to and sings a language, which is not the everyday language, even though it uses everyday words. Thus the mysterious, liminal result: the poem is not an everyday object even though the material from which it is made is everyday, recognisable material.

Two apparently contradictory examples can be used to describe the poetic space as exile; they are both indebted to the gnostic tradition. The first example is that of the Greek poet Odysseas Elytis, whose references to exile as an ontological condition of the poet are to be found repeatedly in his opus magnum *Axion Esti* (1989).[37] As his French translator and commentator says,[38] the retrieval of the essential instinct of Eros and its articulation, its turning into Logos, infringes the laws of the city and makes of the poet an exile. But where does the decision to do so come from? There are a few beautiful pages in the introduction to the French translation of this work where Xavier Bordes (1996) develops Elytis's gnostic influences.

Gnosticism was the cultural matrix of the Mediterranean in the third and fourth centuries CE. Its most relevant element here is that of the foreign soul, a soul which has forgotten whence it comes, that it is a lost fragment of God, one of many lost fragments. These fragments of soul forget their name, forget what or who they are and cannot be called back (by the angel messenger), even when God wishes so, and thus are condemned to perpetual suffering. The foreign soul has distanced itself so much from its origin that it has lost its identity (Galimberti 1996). So subjectivity passes from God to the humans and history is created; the event acquires meaning.

According to this narrative, the poetic space is located in the vertical space between the soul and God or the gods: it is a recuperable *ascension*.[39]

Unexpectedly, Anne Carson's concern with *Decreation* (Carson 2006) can be likened to this ascension, but the other way around, as the neologism 'decreation' (coined by Simone Weil) signifies. Indeed, in one of the essays included in the book, 'Decreation: How Women Like Sappho, Marguerite Porete, and Simone Weil Tell God', the poet and classic scholar explores the ways these three writers attempt to draw out the coincidence between 'telling', which must always start from the self, and God, who is silent[40] and whose love can only truly be known and experienced when the self is annihilated. All three authors, Carson argues, understand the essential contradiction between being an authorial self and having access to God and in order to resolve it, invent a 'dream of distance', which attempts to both retain at a distance and bring close that which is most desired. As James Pollock points out in an excellent review of *Decreation*, 'God' is another word for the sublime (Pollock 2008), and it is the sublime Elytis is also after in *Axion Esti*.

Even though Carson does not thematise exile as such, in this book, a title like: 'Every Exit is an Entrance' or the piece on Antonioni express a direct concern with similar themes. Most relevantly, I think her thought around the FarNear, that she translates from Marguerite Perote, is akin to Elytis's recuperation of the sublime in the homeland through the assertion of exile, and to María Zambrano's intuition about the intrinsic tie between homeland – the God, the sublime – and exile.

In the silence, the forgetting and abandonment of the humans by the gods or God, which implies the forgetting of one's own identity as derived from the god/s, as godly, the poet speaks, she *raises* her voice ... Does the poet remember? Is she the messenger (*Hermes*, άγγελος) or the foreign soul? And is this remembrance, the prophecy, the reconstitution of the past that indicates the way forward, to come? For indeed prophet means she who speaks in the stead of/in place of (God). But, as Michaux says, the poet is not master at home (Michaux 1969). And speaking of poetry as a new beginning, he compares it to the first human beings who invented fire. The link we can create to the myth of Prometheus points directly to the substitution of the gods, that for which the humans are punished: attempting to annihilate the self would then be a plausible solution.

Mother-tongue, fatherland

Odysseas Elytis, in a section of *Axion Esti*, repeats the verse: 'My only concern was my language.'[41] In a Heideggerian echo, Jacques Derrida writes in *Of Hospitality*:

> 'Displaced persons', exiles, those who are deported, expelled, root-less, nomads, all share two sources of sighs: two nostalgias: their dead ones and their language ... [they] often *continue to recognize the language, what is called the mother tongue, as their ultimate homeland,* and even their resting place .... That was Hannah Arendt's response on one occasion: she no longer felt German except in language. (Derrida and Dufourmantelle 2000: 87–9)

The reason for this is that 'speech, the mother-tongue isn't only the home that resists, the ipseity of the self set up as a force of resistance, as a counter-force against these dis-locations. Language resists all mobilities *because* it moves about with me' (Derrida and Dufourmantelle 2000: 91). There are exceptions. In *Kadmo*, Melpo Axioti mentions the story of an isolated man, an exile, whom nobody spoke to out of negligence – so that he had neither the occasion to remember his tongue nor the opportunity to learn a new one. So, she says, this was a man – from the very few existing – who had no linguistic instrument (Axioti 2015: 45). However, the more frequent view is that language is that which can never be taken away from the exile. Even when she is in exile, the exile finds herself in her tongue, in her language. But if that language is the mother-tongue, why does it come from the fatherland? There is feminist literature on why the fatherland should really be the motherland, but for our purposes, I would rather ask whether exile is mother or father. What are the archetypes on which the different civilisations feed themselves with regard to exile? On the one hand, it seems clear that the land is female in many languages, so that the movement away from the land would be under the guise of the father. In general, the travel – as initiation, as search for resources, as hunting – belongs to the masculine. However, *la patria, η πατρίδα* are feminine nouns that originate in the collapse of an adjective and a noun into one. The word *terra, γαία* is obliterated in favour of the signifier 'of the father', the land where the father is born and is buried.

These questions lose significance in the numerous cases where people decide to live, and authors to write, in another language than their 'own', like, to take two famous examples, Vladimir Nabokov or Etel Adnan.

The psyche in exile

Felix Post's . . . recent studies of creativity and psychopathology found that among writers the highest rates of severe affective disorder occurred in poets.
Rosin Kemp and Josephine Loftus, 'Beckett: portraits of the artist in exile'

Twenty years ago a group of Italian psychoanalysts wrote on the very particular theme of therapies where the analysand and the analyst did not share the same mother-tongue. I found the reference in an article by a psychoanalyst who described his own exile as a passage from mother-tongue to father-tongue, that is from oneself to the Other. But is the mother-tongue not the tongue of the other already for every newborn?

The idea of the 'internal exile' does not only address psychiatric patients or psychoanalytic clients. It is more and more widely accepted that there are forms of exile that are intangible, that are connected in a linear or immediate way to the actual experience of displacement (Galitzine-Loumpet 2011). Thus:

> Exile does not appear only in the form of a concrete, external expe-rience of a lost homeland, but also as the experience of an internal homeland that we have lost and for which we go back and look desperately. In the psychotic *Lebenswelt*, [. . .] the acute and elusive experience of this being-in-exile, being-foreigner, without a home-land emerges anew [. . .]. (Borgna 1996: 54)

Eugenio Borgna, who wrote these lines, is a psychiatrist who has dedi-cated his life to the phenomenological approach to treating patients and who in the article quoted uses María Zambrano's thought around the features of exile – abandonment, border, etc. – in order to under-line the profound mutation of the perception of space and time that takes place in exile. The non-recognisability of the 'old' space or the 'old' people (who turn strange, threatening) but also of the new space;[42] the very strong sense of a break of time with no possibility of project-ing oneself into the future; finally, the difficulty of defining the border between the medical condition and the 'normal' condition, which goes hand-in-hand with a very difficult return to the old configurations of time and space, all speak of a great similarity of the experiences of the internal exile caused by psychic illness and of the physical exile as described by María Zambrano.

Additionally, it has been noted that in the work of Zambrano herself, the mad, along with the poor, children and women, can be subsumed under the category of the exile, given the fact that they have been buried or ignored.[43]

Exiting the extreme suffering of such illnesses, and entering the more usual realm of a psychoanalytic exploration without psychotic expressions, it is worth observing the particularities of the time and space of the psychoanalytic session. Henry Bauchau, a novelist and psychoanalyst of renown, wrote: 'The time of the sessions appears to be an island, that is surrounded by the beyond and beneath of the time of the session that form around it one, unique ocean' (Bauchau 2000: 107). One cannot but be struck by the use of the same metaphor that María Zambrano used. It is certain that similar accounts can be found easily, and such is also my personal experience. The absence of an experiential relation to 'the real' – the suspension of time – renders clear the closeness of the supposedly pathological and the supposedly less pathological.

However, this suspension of time in the guise of the island is, in another interesting account, the account of Julia Kristeva, 'scandalous'. Based on Freud's qualification of the unconscious as *zeitlos*, this is 'a fault, a breach, a frustration' (Kristeva 1997: 48)[44] in the linear time of consciousness, which at the one end expresses the pleasure principle and, at the other end, the death drive. In that view, the impossibility of integrating this a-temporality within the linearity – in its several forms – may be a feature of psychopathological states. Kristeva herself likens this scandalous *Zeitlosigkeit* of the unconscious to the *nunc stans* of medieval mystics, which must, in turn, be compared with the women thinkers Carson writes about, to Carson herself, to Elytis and Lorca.

Apart from the language that obviously stands between them – unites them – a final note on the correspondence between the poetic and the psychical underlines the dynamic movement of the 'soul': ascent – effacement – in the case of the mystical and the gnostic traditions; descent in the case of the discovery of the unconscious. Both could be pointing to the South.

6. The dark light of the South: Frédéric Pajak, A. Vigoleis Thelen, Evgenios Aranitsis, Johan van der Keuken, Isaki Lacuesta, Víctor Erice, Carlo Levi

> Everyone receives his inner sense of North and South at birth.
> Whether an external polarity comes with it is not terribly important.
> Jean Paul, epigraph to A. Vigoleis Thelen, *The Island of Second Sight*

At this point, we dispose of several spatial metaphors with regard to exile: desert, island, limit or border. Why introduce the idea of the South (and the concomitant ideas of the North – the loss of the North – and disorientation)?

As was hinted at in the introduction, the South is the direction home, an answer to the question that exile poses, a remedy to a loss which is considered irremediable. Even though it appears at the end of this chapter, one could consider it as foregrounding the main body of it ('Sur, espejismo, reflejo'), just as the idea of return foregrounds the experience of exile. During the preparation of a collective poetry book on *The Quest of the South* (Karagiannis 2016a), invited poets were told that the expression 'the quest of the South' refers to the quest of the imaginary South. It refers to a South that is the object of a pursuit, a South that is perhaps never reached, and is thus not a determined, physical or geographical place or space. It is an imaginary horizon, in the sense that it defines a limit, an end: of the world, the journey, the imagination. The quest refers to a journey, which can be circular – the starting point is the same as the end point, like in the Odyssey – or linear – where the two points are different, like in Rimbaud's flight to Abyssinia. The quest can be thus either nostalgic or romantic – or other things. The South is thus malleable, emancipative and resistant to imposed interpretations.

Looking for the South necessarily poses the question of the North. Drawing on Tacita Dean's astounding work,[45] Tania Kovats says:

> To lose your North Star implies confusion, or madness [. . .] The North Star is one of the brightest in Ursa Minor, and is one of the few starts in the night sky that most people can point to. [. . .] As you advance towards the idea of the north, the true north seems to move further away. Disorientation, losing your way, a space of 'unbelonging', a place of uncharted possibilities, no man's land and the ultimate test. (Kovats 2014: 57)

But one can turn the expression 'perdre le Nord' (which also means 'we have become mad') around and assert it positively. It is possible to refuse to see the North as the point whose loss leads to loss of mind or, slightly differently, that the loss – by extension, loss of orientation, void, gap – contained in the imaginary South is a loss that is worth referring to and out of which we can make a reference.

Thus, there is a rather straightforward line, I think, between loss of orientation and the quest of the South. In the book *The Quest of the South*, I proposed a scheme of disorientation going backwards in time, as it were: from destinations(/destinies), to transitions, to losses, to origins. The uncertainty of destinies, the concreteness of transitions succeeding the necessary and unavoidable sense of loss and, lastly, the always-reconstructed origins seem to fit both the quest of the South and exile, matching almost perfectly.

One could object that there are some formally differentiating features between exile and the South as categories.[46] Indeed, exile is a liminal category: it concentrates on the border, on the limits, on the horizon. It can only be thought as something which allows a position astride situations. On the other hand, the South is an indeterminate category: if it is clear that it is defined by its opposition to the North, it is also clear that it does not have any consistence, neither materially/factually, nor schematically in the sense of a shape. Furthermore, exile contains the blindness which is necessary to knowledge (of the origins: the homeland); whereas the South always shines with (dark) light. Exile refers to distance, whereas the clichés of the South underline closeness, warmth, etc. Additionally, in terms of direction, the South is about disorientation; exile is simply about loss. And finally, being in the South is a matter of phantasy, with all the nuances that can be found in the phantasy between the intentional and the non-intentional: the imaginary is the strongest element at play and it modulates experience. Being in exile is due to a jump, a sudden finding oneself at a loss.

Nevertheless, I would propose that to see in the South the irreducible element of return makes up for all other difficulties. All of exile's features, such as blindness, distance and liminality, tend dynamically towards home. However, exile's core element of loss is reconfigured into home through the *topos* of return; and this, we proposed, is the South: the South as the tantalising or tempting or promised remedy to the irremediable.

Before describing in more detail how this is so, I would like to mention, though not underline, that there is a factual, historical premise to the South as site of exile (and thus, survival), which starts first of all in the Europe of the troubled 1930s. The southern areas of Europe, islands like Mallorca and Ibiza, but also Latin American or African countries, all became destinations for those fleeing the rising threat of Nazism and the war. The creation of Israel itself can perhaps also enter this picture as an extreme case – where destination espouses destiny, indeed, and exile is turned upon its head by creating an entirely new homeland.

Innumerable amounts of intellectuals and artists fled the north of Europe towards its south or northern Africa: if one of the reasons was certainly the impression that one was not entirely leaving the continent, that one could easily come back (by opposition to going to the US, for instance), another one has to do with the South. The way the South is imagined varies, of course, according to the different sensibilities and interests of the exiles.

Film and literature provide us with many examples. The filmography around the South is so extensive that it cannot be mentioned here in a satisfactory way. One must nevertheless at least mention films as different as *Casablanca* or *The Snows of Kilimanjaro* because, in them, in different ways, the South takes the guise of exile and plays a fully dramatic (active) role in the post-war period. I will take a few more lines for four films where both South and exile are negotiated.

The opening scene of *Cristo si è fermato a Eboli*, the 1979 filmic adaptation of Carlo Levi's autobiographical account of his political exile in southern Italy, shows us an aging Levi (Gian Maria Volonté) seated in a couch and thinking about 'his' peasants of the South. The first phrase – off – is strikingly poignant and pertinent to our purposes, as it mentions the promise of return Levi has made to *i contadini* and which he now knows he will never be able to keep. The film takes off from there, as a flash back, a long journey of memory and imagination, in contradistinction to the Levi sitting there, old, immobile and surrounded by his own paintings of the South and its people. The element of the promise which ties the future (see Arendt 1958) is an essential element of exile, as we saw in Zambrano. Without the promise (either of return or of freedom), it is impossible to think of exile, we might as well renounce hope. It is, however, interesting that in *Cristo* the promise was made to the place of exile and it is now, from the vantage point of the present, surely broken. If this chapter were about literary theory, we would point out the different layers of the broken promise (are not the book which is being written, and before it, the paintings depicted in the surrounding of old Levi, the realisations of a promise that is deemed broken?); however, what interests me more here is the promise to return *to* (instead of: from) exile, which turns exile into home. And indeed, the film is a journey in the experience of the exile, discovering home in exile, or dynamically appropriating home in the South.

By contrast, the South is the unambiguous place of origin of the protagonist of Víctor Erice's beautiful 1982 film *El Sur*. However, contrary to *Cristo*, we never see the South in this film, which takes place entirely in a fictional North, a dark and cloudy North. In *El Sur*, the narrator is the young daughter of a man that has the gift of making magic tricks and that is, otherwise, quite absent. One day, the girl discovers that her father is connected to the South by the ties of romantic (not only family) love: the South is the other woman. Here again, the tenses of time are merged: the South belongs to the past, but a cinema theatre (called *Arcadia*!) brings it to life in the present, since the father's lover was a film actress and her films are shown in the North.

The Way South by Johan van der Keuken (1981) and *El Cuaderno de Barro*, by Isaki Lacuesta (2011), two documentaries, both take the South as their aim and object of reflection. In the first movie, the director films his descent from Amsterdam to Cairo, passing through Paris, Rome and Calabria. Johan van der Keuken was a Dutch documentary film-maker whose reputation in the essayistic documentary milieu and fame among a large audience are inversely related. He belongs to a tradition of politically committed documentarists, who matured with the idea of an exploited South or Third World. This film is extremely interesting, not only filmically, but also in its depiction of a troubled, poor South (Cairo, where people whom he tries to interview elude him or lie to him) or also of a South in the North (the long interview with the Maghreb worker who cannot find a job after an accident in Paris), and certainly a frustrating and disorienting South, which resists the Northerner's eye and ear. If one decides to watch another movie by van der Keuken, *The Film-maker's Holiday* (1974), one gets a rounder idea of what the South might mean for such a figure: in this second movie, the South is a sweet, family summer in the sun of France. If the first film exudes trouble, fight and frustration, the second shows rest and a meditative contemplation of beauty – and whereas in both films there is an acute sense of transience, as brings the condition of exile, its participants also represent resilience, another of exile's features (Kristeva 1994).

Van der Keuken's work is one of the strong influences on Isaki

Lacuesta, a contemporary Spanish film-maker who works between fiction and documentary. *El Cuaderno de Barro* documents the work of Miquel Barceló, the famous Mallorcan painter, in Mali. The film was made on the occasion of the performance *Paso Doble*, by Barceló and the dancer Josef Nadj, which involved entering parts of their bodies or their whole bodies into a huge wall made of clay. The *Cuaderno de Barro* follows the ways that Barceló has found of working around the obstacles and difficulties the natural environment imposes on him in the twenty-five years he has worked in Mali. The South is here, certainly, a return to the origins, to the earth, to uncontrolled nature, to a time that corrodes everything at a quicker pace than elsewhere but which seems eternal, at the same time. The consequences for this encyclopaedic painter's work are of great use: the natural destruction brought upon the work (for example, the eating of drawings and paintings by termites) is recuperated as part of the work, the importance of technical means diminishes (use of bleach, nails), and so on. In other words, destruction and poverty are reconfigured into art. Among the most striking scenes of the movie are the sittings for portraits of albino people that Barceló makes. The impoverishment of technique that Barceló may be seeking meets the poorest, in the sense of most under-valued, diminished individuals. Painting portraits of them restores dignity – but to whose eyes? When the painter suggests in front of the camera that one albino should have his eyesight corrected, the figure of the rich, well-meaning, patronising *muzungu* forcefully, and unwittingly, appears.

Straying away from movies, I would now like to keep the white and black of Barceló's albino portraits, in order to take a look at *Manifeste incertain 2*, the extraordinary book by Frédéric Pajak (Pajak 2013), which follows Walter Benjamin's journeys from the North to the South of Europe, and his stays on the island of Ibiza. Apart from its evident closeness to the theme of the South as exile, and to the underlying constant reference to exile in general, through the figures of James Joyce and Samuel Beckett, this absolutely singular book unveils, as it performs them, two major characteristics of the imaginary South: juxtaposition and sharp contrasts. First, juxtaposition is the making of the book as it brings together large drawings, underneath which come a usually short text. Image and text are not always related in a strictly logical, explicative or illustrative way. Most often, they are juxtaposed in a way which creates poetic resonances throughout the book. Usually, be it in a *cabinet de curiosités* or in poetry,[47] juxtaposition is the companion of fragmentation. And indeed, matching Benjamin's own preferred mode of thinking and writing, Pajak's book functions as an irreverently assembled collection of fragments, which are all the more poignant for being just that.

The second feature of the South which is clearly 'embodied' in this book is the sharpness of the contrasts. Like other graphic books, this book is in black and white, but most of its parts play up the contrast between full light and darkness, intense sun and very deep shade. The black-clad women in Sicily (which are referred to with nostalgia in the text), the blinding white of the houses, the immobility of the paths in contrast to the presence of the sea, which is immutable, all contrive and manage to give a sense of past and future merging into the present, an inescapable, as it were, present (which, all along, is a present one has arrived at) and of the porous limits between the external surroundings and the internal musings of the writer and his characters as well as of the conjoined threat of death and Eros. Thus, under the drawing of an ancient temple and the arid landscape that surrounds it, a text says: 'The atrocious marvels of creations are marvellously atrocious precisely because they do not originate in creation. They are' (Pajak 2013: 91). And inscribed on the sun clock of the beautiful cathedral on Ibiza, the phrase: 'Ultima multis'.

An echo of that same immobility in time, of that hanging threat of death at midday, of the admission of the lack of control, can be found in a poetic text called *[South]* (*[Νότος]*) by Evgenios Aranitsis (2016), a Greek poet and essayist, whose work combines an extraordinary capacity of reflexion with deeply moving language. In *[South]*, he deploys the contrasting rhetoric between North and South in a poetic key, playing with the *topoi* of the North and the South, and indeed giving an account of what the South is, by contrast to the North, on the occasion of an invitation to write on this but also in the context of the generalised, political demands for accountability: 'the north is vast and iron, mercury and nitre belong to it / the south is limited, deep and secret, and gold and brass belong to it' (Aranitsis 2016: 70). Or, 'because it holds that you PAY for your errors in the north, whereas you owe them and one owes them to you in the south' (Aranitsis 2016: 72); 'in the north, summer is the object of desire, whereas in the south it constitutes both an object and a cause' (Aranitsis 2016: 72); 'the north is chronic / the south is eternal' (Aranitsis 2016: 78), which reminds us of Julia Kristeva's psychoanalytic *Zeitlosigkeit*. This exploration yields fascinating results regarding the features of the South: the unapologetic tendency towards fusion with the other (human being, elements of nature) – another way of admitting the lack of ultimate control over things – the darkness of light where death presides over any construction of meaning, South and mourning as synonyms, and the persistence of Eros/love. Adding to sharpness of contrasts and to juxtaposition, which he also performs, as it were, Aranitsis draws our attention on one last, determining feature of the South: simultaneity. In the imaginary of the South, he seems to be saying, things are like this *and* like that *at the same time* and without this being specified, given that this is what the South *is*. No attempt at rationalisation is made. Sometimes, the artistic form naturally merges contradictions into one entity, such as in his dark light of the summer.

In all these singular works of art, the motor of the imaginary is the South. One could also turn this around and say: the South is a potent motor for the imaginary, and this is due to the fact that while eternity, immobility, immutability seem to be pervasive in the substance of the (imaginary) South, on the other hand, everything that is contradictory, fragmentary, simultaneous or juxtaposed in its form gives phantasy a push, which sets it off in another direction. Is this why Federico García Lorca calls the South an illusion (created by the mirror, etymologically: *espejismo*), a reflection, in the poem cited as an epigraph to this chapter? Is or can the South be anything that reflects upon it?

A mirror is a reflecting surface, but as art and psychoanalysis well know, it actually has unfathomable depths. The South is deep, as deep as the mirror in the drawing by Kentridge, from which Nandi looks back at Felix and from which is poured the water of memory and the past. However, what inhabits the mirror changes according to Felix's gaze, the exile's gaze, just as his own imagination is pervaded by the South. The limits between the two are porous and set the imaginary alive. Nevertheless, at some point later in the film, Nandi dies and there is nothing Felix can do about it, apart from drawing. When he comes back to his homeland, Felix holds a bag full of drawings. These drawings are precious, just as the paintings of *i contadini* are precious to Carlo Levi from the vantage point of home. The representation of the South makes the exile hold out while in exile. Thus, the South (whether it is home or an exile-turned-into-home) offers itself as a remedy to exile and, while doing so, embraces all states of the latter: the poetic, the psychical, the philosophical.

Notes

1. '"Felix in Exile" was created in 1994, amidst ongoing public debates on the relationship between the country's division of ownership and the formation of identity which accompanied the first open elections in South Africa. The film tells the stories of Felix, a man living in exile in Paris, and of Nandi, a woman working as a land surveyor. The woman is Felix's alter ego. She stands for the longing for one's homeland, and how for his sake someone bears witness to the incidents in the new, democratic South Africa. . . . Nandi too, finds death. Felix, on the other hand, finds himself once again in the deserted landscape of his homeland, but now with a suitcase full of drawings' (Media Art Net n.d.).

2. As the focus of these thoughts is not political- or social-theoretical, I will not establish differences between refugees, displaced persons, exiles, and so on. See Edward Said's (2002) 'Reflections on Exile' for an attempt to do so. See also Alexis Nouss's (2015) work on 'exiliance' for an accent on the psychic *experience* of exile, which is common to the individual (often chosen) or collective (most often not chosen) situations of exile. Nouss's work is particularly interesting insofar as it insists on exile as a combination of material conditions and a conscience or a state of mind.

3. But see also Zambrano (2014: 51).

4. Ovid wrote the *Tristia* (sorrows) while in exile from Rome.

5. See, for example, <http://www.kathimerini.gr/863565/gallery/epikairothta/ellada/apo-to-vrain-drain-sto-brain-gain> (last accessed 16 January 2017).

6. An expanded version of this article will contain a chapter on the unavoidable transformation of the body (Kristeva 1994) which makes return impossible as well as a section on regret, the regret of exile, as it is, for example, expressed here by Zambrano (2014: 56): '¿Por qué no me quedé, Señor, por qué no me quedé y aquí corrí la suerte de los que quedaron por amor?' ('Why did I not stay, Lord, why did I not stay and live here the fate of those who stayed out of love?') Here and below, all translations from Spanish, French and Greek into English are mine.

7. 'Julio Cortázar sobre los beneficios del exilio (1983)', available at <https://www.youtube.com/watch?v=diXQ1aCypxA> (last accessed 6 February 2017).

8. I am extremely grateful to Yiorgos Axiotis, Melpo Axiotis's nephew, whom I met on a plane to Athens in 2016, and who gave me one of his own copies of the book. Our common attachment to Greece and literature and our realisation that we have both lived longer out of Greece than in it made us start a dialogue between strangers. Let him be thanked as a friend. For a wider view on the literature of political refugees, see Apostolidou (2013).

9. In opposition to Said's or Sennet's dialectic relation between nationalism and exile.

10. See, for example, Zambrano (2012: 154).

11. While feminists in Latin-language countries have criticised the paternalistic roots of the Spanish word 'la patria' (like the Greek 'η πατρίδα'), which means 'fatherland' in English or 'Vaterland' in German, they have not pointed out that it presents the particularity of being a female noun ('la', also like in Greek: 'η') while having centrally to do with a male entity (*pater*, πατήρ). This interesting feature complicates the critical viewpoint. A similar point will arise in the later discussion

of 'mother-tongue'. In any case, here I will use the word 'homeland' for 'patria', trying to avoid these ambiguities. See Zambrano (2012: 61) on Mother Fatherland: 'la madre patria'.

12. 'Hay ciertos viajes de los que solo a la vuelta se comienza a saber.'

13. 'El exilio ha sido como mi patria o como una dimensión de una patria desconocida, pero que una vez que se conoce, es irrenunciable.'

14. 'Confieso . . . que me ha costado mucho trabajo renunciar a mis cuarenta años de exilio . . . de vez en tanto me duele, no, no es que me duela, es una sensación como quien ha sido despellejado [flayed], como San Bartolomé, una sensación ininteligible, pero que lo es.'

15. 'desierto, patria sin frontera y sin reino' (Zambrano 2014: 55).

16. 'ese reino, ese campo, esa fuente de lagrimas' (Zambrano 2014: 51).

17. 'sin ver' (Zambrano 2014: 55).

18. 'El exiliado solo tiene, pues, horizonte. Mas el horizonte paradojicamente es al par la condición de la visibilidad, del ordén visible que confine con el invisible', the world after the expulsion from Paradise.

19. 'paises de habla española, sufridores del Imperio español y beneficiarios al par de algunos de sus innegables dones' ('Spanish-speaking countries, that suffered the Spanish Empire at the same time they benefited from some of its undeniable gifts') make the strangers not 'extraños' ('foreigners'), but 'entraños, el sentir en ellos como une entraña perdida' ('insiders, as they felt in themselves something like a lost inside') (Zambrano 2014: 49).

20. See also 'Julio Cortázar sobre los beneficios del exilio (1983)', available at <https://www.youtube.com/watch?v=diXQ1aCypxA> (last accessed 6 February 2017): however, 'Patria, casa, tierra no son exactamente lo mismo' ('Fatherland, home, land are not exactly the same') (Zambrano 2014: 36), which is why 'desterrado' (unearthed: literally, landless), 'refugiado' (refugee) or 'exiliado' (exile) are not the same (Zambrano 2014: 35). 'La Patria es una categoria histórica, no así la tierra ni el lugar' ('Fatherland is a historical category; not so the land or the place') (Zambrano 2014: 47). And we should principally see in this differentiation a varying degree of intensity in the taking leave of the homeland. See Nouss (2015) on the different combinations between the experience and condition of exile.

21. Let it, however, be noted that elsewhere she likens exile to an ocean 'sin isla alguna a la vista, sin norte real' ('without any island or any real North to be seen') (Zambrano 2014: 45). The absence of North points to our earlier mention of disorientation.

22. 'En cuanto auroréa en la historia, en cuanto se da a ver minimamente, en verdad basta con que se anuncie, crea el exilio de aquellos que, por haberla visto y servido aun minimamente, han de irse de ella. Y luego en la historia apócrifa sigue en los que dentro y bajo ella mas bien se despiertan un dia exiliados. No hay opción para ellos, o no se despiertan o se despiertan ya en el exilio.' That is why: 'Tiene la patria verdadera por virtud crear el exilio. Es su signo inequivoco' (Zambrano 2014: 47).

23. 'El tiempo, un dios sin máscara [. . .] Dios de la visión: esto se verá con el tiempo, se me verá, se verá mi razón con el tiempo, dice entre sí, y a veces balbucea el exiliado, y mientras tanto el tiempo lo devora, a él que, como el tiempo – ¿ a imagen y semejanza del tiempo? –, no tiene figura, rostro ni máscara alguna. [. . .] ¿Será él, el exiliado, un augurio?' ('Time, a god without mask [. . .] God of vision: this shall be seen

with time, I shall be seen, my reason shall be seen with time, the exile tells himself, and sometimes he stutters, and in the meantime times eats him up, him who, like time – in the image and resemblance of time? – does not have a shape, a face nor any mask [. . .] Could the exile be an omen?') (Zambrano 2014: 38). Regarding liminality, I think it can be said to extend to the most general existential terms regarding the exile, those of life and death: 'El filo entre la vida y la muerte que igualmente se rechazan. Sostenerse en ese filo es la primera exigencia que al exiliado se presenta como ineludible' ('The thread between life and death that repulse each other. Maintaining oneself on this thread is the first demand that presents itself as inescapable to the exile') (Zambrano 2014: 36). It cannot but be brought into comparison with Axioti's remark on death: 'Θάνατος είναι κι αυτός τώρα ο χωρισμός. Δεκαεπτά ολόκληρα χρόνια, μακριά από την πατρίδα σου. Θάνατος είναι κι ο διχασμός της ζωής' ('This separation now is also death. Seventeen full years, away from my homeland. This division of life is also death') (Axioti 2015: 84).

24. 'Y luego en la historia apócrifa sigue [la patria] en los que dentro y bajo ella más bien se despiertan un día exiliados. No hay opción para ellos, o no se despiertan o se despiertan ya en el exilio' ('And then in apocryphal history, the homeland continues in those that inside and under it wake up one day as exiles. There is no option for them, either they don't wake up or they wake up already in exile') (Zambrano 2014: 48). This can be compared with Cornelius Castoriadis's striking description of the form of *hybris*. And: 'el iniciarse del exilio en un instante único, sin separación, al modo como en las tragedias se realiza prodigiosamente este imposible dar un instante único en varias de sus vertientes o dimensiones' ('the beginning of exile is one unique moment, without separation, just as in tragedy this impossible taking place of one unique instant through its various sides or dimensions is prodigiously realised') (Zambrano 2014: 36).

25. 'El encontrarse en el desierto no hace sentir el exilio, sino ante todo la expulsión. Y luego la insalvable distancia y la incierta presencia física del país perdido. Y aquí empieza el exilio, al sentirse ya al borde del exilio' ('Finding oneself in the desert does not make one feel the exile, but mostly the expulsion. And then the unsavable distance and the uncertain physical presence of the lost country. And there starts exile, with the feeling of being already at the border of exile') (Zambrano 2014: 36). 'Comienza la iniciación al exilio cuando comienza el abandono, el sentirse abandonado' ('The initiation to exile starts when the abandonment starts, the feeling of being abandoned') (Zambrano 2014: 35).

26. 'La pasión de Antígona se da en la ausencia y en el silencio de los dioses' (Zambrano 2012: 154). 'Una soledad [la de Antígona] que únicamente el Dios desconocido, mudo, recoge' ('One solitude, which is taken up by an unknown and mute God') (Zambrano 2012: 162).

27. 'Y esa última dimensión de su condena, *la que caracteriza a la tragedia griega*, resplandeciente hasta el extremo en Antígona: el abandono, el abandono total de sus dioses' ('And this last dimension of her condemnation, *which characterised Greek tragedy*, is extremely illuminating in Antigone: the abandonment, the total abandonment by her gods') (Zambrano 2012: 152; my emphasis).

28. 'Bien es verdad que Edipo tuvo el anuncio de su destino y ninguna potencia divina bajó en sua auxilio a la hora de la desdicha' ('But it is true that Oedipus's destiny was announced to him and no divine power went down to help him at the time of his unhappiness') (Zambrano 2012: 152).

29. 'Mas la tragedia humana sucede bajo la mirada de los *dioses* y su sentencia. Y en el abandono no se siente esa mirada ni la sentencia, como por momentos se querría. En el abandono solo lo propio de lo que se está desposeído aparece, solo que no puede llegar a ser como ser propio' ('But human tragedy happens under the gaze of the gods and their say. And in the abandonment, one can feel neither that gaze nor the say, as one would sometimes want. In the abandonment, only that which is dispossessed appears, only that which cannot make it to be a being as such') (Zambrano 1990: 32).

30. 'Through the abandonment appears the immensity, and this causes the firmament to fall apart, which is otherwise normally firm and a medium, and which makes one feel the presence of the *Father* when he is hidden and sustains his presence when he appears' (Zambrano 2014: 44).

31. Regarding translation, the poet María Negroni notes that one of its imperative conditions is an exile, in which one advances blindly (Negroni 2016: 112).

32. 'Para no perderse, enajenarse, en le desierto hay que encerrar dentro de sí el desierto, hay que adentrar, interiorizar, el desierto en el alma, en la mente, en los sentidos mismos, aguzando el oído en detrimento de la vista para evitar los espejismos y escuchar las voces.'

33. This is a very rare reference to the debate between those who stay and those who go (see section 2 of this chapter).

34. 'Cuando ya se sabe sin ella, sin padecer alguno, cuando ya no se recibe nada, nada de la patria, entonces se le aparece' ('When one knows one is without the homeland, without any suffering, when one does not receive anything any more, nothing from the homeland, then it appears') (Zambrano 2014: 47).

35. 'El exilio es el lugar privilegiado para que la Patria se descubra . . .' ('Exile is the privileged position in order to discover the Homeland . . .') (Zambrano 2014: 47). There is an ambiguity between the title of this fragment and its first phrase: 'la patria no solo se descubre en el exilio' ('the homeland is not only discovered in exile') and 'El exilio es desde luego el lugar privilegiado desde el que la Patria se descubre' ('Exile is, of course, the privileged place from which to discover the Homeland') (Zambrano 2014: 47).

36. 'La imaginación lleva y da un ambiente poético y la inspiración inventa en hecho poético. El hecho poético no se puede controlar con nada. Hay que aceptarlo como se acepta la lluvia de estrellas. Pero alegrémonos de que la poesía pueda fugarse, evadirse de las garras frías del razonamiento.' See <http://federicogarcialorca.net/obras_lorca/imaginacion_inspiracion_evasion.htm> (last accessed 6 February 2017).

37. 'εξόριστε Ποιητή, στον αιώνα σου, λέγε, τι βλέπεις ; / τότε, μην έχοντας άλλη εξορία, που να θρηνήσει ο Ποιητής, την υγεία της καταιγίδας απο τ' ανοιχτά του του στήθη αδειάζοντας, θα γυρίσει για να σταθεί στα ωραία μέσα ερείπια. / Αλλά τα πράματα της καρδιάς τρόπος δεν είναι να χαθούν, έννοια σου, και γι ' αυτά οι εξορίες δουλεύουν. Αργά-γρήγορα κείνοι που είναι ναν τα βρουν, θα τα βρουν' ('Exiled Poet, what do you see in your aeon? / having no other exile to mourn, emptying the health of his storm from his open breast, the Poet, will return to stand in the beautiful ruins. / But the matters of the heart cannot be lost, don't worry, and exiles work for them. Sooner or later, those who are meant to find them, will find them') (Elytis [1959] 1989: 65).

38. '[S]a pulsion d'Éros, indicible en termes de droit, indicible par le citoyen qui, du

fait qu'il a transgressé la loi, s'est mis en dehors, dans l'enfer, en situation d'exil: en situation poétique' (Bordes 1996: 28–9) ('The pulsion of Eros, which is unsayable in terms of the law, which is unsayable by the citizen who, having violated the law, has situated herself outside, in hell, in situation of exile: in poetical situation'). '[T]out acte poétique naît de l'exil. Et le public pardonne mal à celui qui se tient hors de la cité' ('Every poetic act is born from exile. And the public does not forgive the one who stands outside the city') (Bordes 1996: 25).

39. 'Τις ημέρες μου άθροισα κι έμεινα μόνος . . .
     κι από κει που με μπόδισαν, ο αόρατος, κάλπασα
     στους αγρούς τις βροχές να γυρίσω
     και το αίμα πίσω να πάρω των νεκρών μου των άθαφτων'
     ('I added up my days and I remained alone . . .
     and from where I was prevented, I galloped invisibly
     on the fields to turn the rains around
     and take back the blood of my unburied dead') (Elytis [1959] 1989: 35)

40. To turn to another example, Pascal Quignard, one of the foremost writers currently writing in French, decided to leave Paris and the publishing microcosm more than twenty years ago. He speaks of *theosigie* or the silence of God. He also speaks of creation as the opposite of judgement. Literature is an *écart*, he says, which instead of 'gap', I would translate as 'making (taking) an ontological distance-difference'. I see in this *écart*, as the opposite of judgement, first a putting oneself in the distance, not first a putting the object that I look at in the distance, which is important because the step away transports the beholder in a space created by the step away, rather than transforming/objectifying the object. This needs to be compared with the anachoretic tradition more generally.

41. 'Μονάχη έγνοια η γλώσσα μου στις αμμουδιές του Ομήρου, Μονάχη έγνοια η γλώσσα μου, με τα πρώτα πρώτα Δόξα Σοι!, Μονάχη έγνοια η γλώσσα μου, με τα πρώτα λόγια του Ύμνου!' ('My only concern was my language on the dunes of Homer, my only concern was my language, with the very first Gloria!, My only concern was my language, with the first words of the Hymn!') (Elytis 1989: 28).

42. See Borgna (1996: 55), where he explains that in psychosis or depression, there is a *precipitation* into a *Lebenswelt* that is totally *other* and that makes us live in isolation and loneliness, in estrangement and the loss of familiarity, in unrecognisability and destroyed alterity.

43. See Zambrano (2012: 27, n.16) on Simone Weil's understanding of genius as the supernatural virtue of humility in the area of thought. This, of course, brings to mind Hannah Arendt's (1994) work concerning the pariah in 'The Jew as Pariah'.

44. We noted earlier Castoriadis's understanding of *hybris*, whose sudden feature we also encountered in Lorca's poetic fact: 'one finds oneself in hybris, which lies outside any linear continuity with reasonable or expected events. Only after transgression can human beings get to know the limits. The creation of a public space-time, that is, the creation of the polis aims to the contrary' (Castoriadis 2008: 123).

45. For example, *Teignmouth Electron* (Dean 1999).

46. As a closing remark on this section, I would like to point out that the South as exile is the converse image of the South as colony. For the purposes of this chapter, I have entirely left out the relation between colonisation – one form of which is 'settler societies', as Louis Hartz (1969) called them – and exile or the

'receiving' (or colonised) societies. This will be part of a longer effort. However, it is important to note, as I did in the very beginning regarding the question of the foreigner, that we are still talking about the same coin. Just as the river has three banks in the story by João Guimarães Rosa (1984), exile is a coin with more than two sides.

47. See the introduction of García Valdés (2005).

References

Apostolidou, Venetia (2013), *Τραύμα και Μνήμη. Η πεζογραφία των πολιτικών προσφύγων*, Αθήνα: Πόλις.

Aranitsis, Evgenios (2016), *[Νότος]*, <https://www.paradoxa.gr/P55> (last accessed 16 January 2017).

Arendt, Hannah (1944), 'The Jew as pariah: a hidden tradition', *Jewish Social Studies*, 6: 2, 99–122.

Arendt, Hannah (1958), *The Human Condition*, Chicago: University of Chicago Press.

Axioti, Melpo (2015), *Kadmo, Η Κάδμω*, Athens: Kedros.

Bauchau, Henri (2000), *L´Ecriture à l´écoute*, Arles: Actes Sud.

Bolaño, Roberto (2011a), 'Exiles', in *Between Parentheses: Essays, Articles and Speeches (1998–2003) by Roberto Bolaño*, trans. Natasha Wimmer, New York: New Directions, pp. 49–60.

Bolaño, Roberto (2011b), 'Literature and exile', Speech delivered in 2000 at a symposium organised by the Austrian Society for Literature in Vienna, in *Between Parentheses: Essays, Articles and Speeches (1998⬚2003) by Roberto Bolaño*, trans. Natasha Wimmer, New York: New Directions, pp. 38–45.

Bordes, Xavier (1996), 'Préface', in *Axion Esti*, Paris: Gallimard, pp. 7–42.

Borgna, Eugenio (1996), 'La patria perdida en la Lebenswelt psicótica', *Archipiélago*, 26–7, 53–60.

Carson, Anne (2006), *Decreation: Poetry, Essays, Opera*, New York: Vintage.

Castoriadis, Cornelius (2008), *Ce qui fait la Grèce 2*, Paris: Seuil.

Cristo si è fermato a Eboli, film, directed by Francesco Rosi. Italy: Rai 2, 1979.

Darwish, Mahmoud (2007), 'Who am I, without exile?', in *The Butterfly's Burden*, New York: Copper Canyon Press, pp. 89–92.

Dawes, Kwame (2011), 'The pleasures of exile', *Poetry Foundation*, <http://www.poetryfoundation.org/harriet/2011/04/the-pleasures-of-exile/> (last accessed 16 January 2017).

Dean, Tacita (1999), *Teignmouth Electron*, Artist's book designed in collaboration with Martyn Ridgewell, London: Bookworks.

Derrida, Jacques and Anne Dufourmantelle (2000), *Of Hospitality*, Stanford: Stanford University Press.

El Cuaderno de Barro, documentary, directed by Isaki Lacuesta. Spain and Switzerland: Tusitala PC and Bord Cadre Films, 2011.

El Sur, film, directed by Víctor Erice. Spain: Manga Films, [1982] 2002.

Elytis, Odysseas (1989), *Axion Esti, Το Άξιον Εστί*, Αθήνα: Ίκαρος.

Galimberti, Umberto (1996), 'El alma extranjera', *Archipiélago*, 26–7, 61–9.

Galitzine-Loumpet, Alexandra (2011), *Les Non-lieux de l'exil*, Working papers des séminaires 'L'Expérience de l'exil', <http://nle.hypotheses.org/> (last accessed 16 January 2017).

Ganas, Michalis (2007), *Mitria Patrida*, Μητριά Πατρίδα, Αθήνα: Μελάνι.

García Valdés, Olvido (2005), *La Poesía, ese Cuerpo Extraño*, Oviedo: Universidad de Oviedo.

Guimarães Rosa, João (1984), 'The third bank of the river', in Alberto Manguel (ed.), *Black Water: Anthology of Fantastic Literature*, London: Three Rivers Press pp. 582–7.

Hartz, Louis (1969), *The Founding of New Societies*, New York: Mariner Books.

Karagiannis, Nathalie (ed.) (2016a), *La Búsqueda del Sur*, Barcelona: Animal Sospechoso.

Karagiannis, Nathalie (2016b), *Exorismos*, Αθήνα: Μελάνι.

Kemp, Rosin and Josephine Loftus (1997), 'Beckett: portraits of the artist in exile', *Psychiatric Bulletin*, 21: 10, 656–8.

Kentridge, William (1994), *Felix in Exile*, Sandton: Goodman Gallery Proprietary.

Kristeva, Julia (1994), *Strangers to Ourselves*, New York: Columbia University Press.

Kristeva, Julia (1997), *La Révolte intime. Pouvoirs et limites de la psychanalyse II*, Paris: Fayard.

Kovats, Tania (2014), *Drawing Water: Drawing as a Mechanism for Exploration*, Edinburgh: The Fruitmarket Gallery.

Media Art Net (n.d.), 'William Kentridge, "Felix in Exile"', *Media Art Net*, <http://www.medienkunstnetz.de/works/felix-in-exile/> (last accessed 16 January 2017).

Michaux, Henri (1969), *Façons d'endormi façons d'éveille*, Paris: Gallimard.

Negroni, María (2016), *El Arte del Error*, Madrid: Vaso Roto.

Nouss, Alexis (2015), *La Condition de l'exilé. Penser les migrations contemporaines*, Paris: Éditions de la Maison des sciences de l'homme.

Pajak, Frédéric (2013), *Manifeste incertain 2*, Paris: Éditions Noir sur Blanc.

Pollock, James (2008), 'Anne Carson and the sublime', *Contemporary Poetry Review*, <http://www.cprw.com/Pollock/carson.htm> (last accessed 16 January 2017).

Said, Edward (2002), 'Reflections on exile', in *Reflections on Exile and Other Essays*, Cambridge, MA: Harvard University Press, pp. 137–49.

Sennett, Richard (2011), *The Foreigner: Two Essays on Exile*, London: Notting Hill.

Steiner, George (1971), *Extraterritorial*, London: Macmillan.

The Film-maker's Holiday, TV short, directed by Johan van der Keuken. France: Arte France Développement, [1974] 2007.

The Way South, documentary, directed by Johan van der Keuken. Spain: Intermedio, D. L., [1981] 2008.

Trueba-Mira, Virginia (2012), 'Introducción', in *La Tumba de Antígona*, Madrid: Catedra, pp. 9–120.

Vigoleis Thelen, Albert (2010), *The Island of Second Sight*, Cambridge: Galileo.

Walcott, Derek (2004), *The Prodigal*, New York: Farrar, Straus and Giroux.

Williams, Raymond (1961), *The Long Revolution*, London: Chatto and Windus.

Zambrano, María (1990), *Los Bienaventurados*, Madrid: Ediciones Siruela.

Zambrano, María (2012), *La Tumba de Antígona, y Otros Textos Sobre el Personaje Trágico*, Madrid: Catedra.

Zambrano, María (2014), *El Exilio como Patria*, Barcelona: Anthropos Editorial.

Index

Page numbers shown in italics are illustrations and those followed by an 'n' are notes.

abandonment, 195–6
Abdel-Jaouad, H., 175, 179n
Abu-Lughod, Janet, 110
acceleration of 'historical time', 168–9
Adam, 186–8, 189–91
Adorno, Theodor, 137, 177–8
'advanced industrial societies', 1–2
Africa, 53, 57, 58, 61, 107–26, 166, 205
African and Asian Non-Aligned Countries'
    Conference in Bandung 1955, 127
African Greeks, 117–18
*The African Origin of Civilization: Myth or
    Reality*, 116–17
African Pyramids of Knowledge, 117
African subjectivity, 119
Afrocentrism, 117–18
Age of Revolutions, 38, 46–7n
Algeria, 174, 180n
Almagest, 135, 156n
'alternative modernities', 5
America, 11, 34, 166, 171–3, 177, 178n, 179n
American Anthropological Association, 62
'American divergence', 173
American Societies, 173
Americans, black, 115–16
Americas, 53
Andean cultures, 138, 173
'Anthropocene' hypothesis, 26, 36–40,
    46n, 153
anti-colonial struggle, 12, 175
Antigone, 186–8, 189–91, 193, 195–6
antimonies of modernity, 55–6
apartheid, 12
Apology of the Insane, 79–80
Appadurai, 64–5
Arab League, 57
Arantsis, Evgenios, 208–9

archaelogical debts, 122–3
'area studies', 63–4
Arendt, Hannah, 21, 22, 25, 30, 119–20
Argentina, 191
Arnason, Johann, 28
Arrighi, Giovanni, 61
ASA, 67
Asante, Molefi Kete, 117
Asia, 53, 57, 58
Asian Dragons, 61
Asian Tigers, 61, 65
ASPA, 67
'assisted development', 55
Athens, ancient, 186–7
Atlantic slave trade, 118–19
Aufklärung, 141–2, 143
Australia, 2, 15–16n, 72
Axial Age hypothesis, 45n
Axion Esti, 198–200
Axioti, Melpo, 192, 200, 210n

Balandier, Georges, 68n
'banality of power', 119
Bandung Conference, 57, 57–8
Barceló, Miquel, 207
Bauchau, Henry, 202
Bayer, Johann, 135, 136–7, 140, 142, 150,
    156n
Bayly, C. A., 113
Beckett, Samuel, 208
Benjamin, Jessica, 147
Benjamin, Walter, 137, 144, 207–8
Berlin Conference, 63
Bernal, Martin, 117–18
black Americans, 115–16
*Black Athena: The Afroasiatic Roots of
    Classical Civilization*, 117–18

Black Athena Writes Back: Martin Bernal Responds to His Critics, 117–18
blindness, 186–8, 194, 196, 204
Blok, Alexander, 98
Blut und Boden ideology, 101
Boers, 146
Bolaño, Roberto, 186–8
Bolívar, Simón, 171, 179n
Bonneuil, Christophe, 39
borders, 193–4, 196, 204
Bordes, Xavier, 198
Borgna, Eugenio, 201–2
Bourdieu, Pierre, 176
Brandt, Willy, 4
Brandt Commission, 57, 58
Brandt Commission report 1980, 4
Brandt line, 15–16n
Brazil, 51–2, 52, 62–3, 66–7, 72, 132
bricology, 60–5, 65–8
BRICS alliance, 12–13, 15–16n, 51–71, 72, 104, 127, 133
British Empire, 128, 145
'Building Better Global Economic BRICs', 51
Byzantism, 92–4
Byzantism and Slavdom, 92

Caesar's Throne constellation, 137
Cape Times, 107–8
capitalism, 7, 36, 46n, 163
   semi-peripheries of, 61
capitalism, semi-peripheries of, 61
Carson, Anne, 199, 202
cartographies of time, 53
cartography, 23–4
Castoriadis, Cornelius, 22
Catherine the Great (of Russia), 75–6
Catholic unity of Europe, 79
Centaurus constellation, 134, 135, 136–7, 139, 150–6
Chaadayev, Peter, 78–81, 89
chakana, 138
Chakrabarty, Dipesh, 36, 40, 42–3, 45n, 112
The Challenge to the South, 152
Charles XII (of Sweden), 75
China, 2, 43–4n, 51, 62–3, 66–7, 72, 89, 103, 132
China and Africa, 115–16
Christianity, 29, 33, 79, 83, 85–6
chronologies of space, 53
City of the Caesars, 53
civilisation, 27, 29, 31–6, 44n
Clark, M., 157n

Clark, Timothy, 46n
climate change, 43
climate change, human-induced, 19–20
Cold War, 56, 67, 99, 102
Coleman, James S., 176
colonialism, 53–5, 57–8, 127, 157n, 175, 176
   constellations, 15–16n
   structures of power, 163
'coloniality of power', 170
Columbian Exchange, 40
Comaroff, Jean and John, 8–9
'commission on futurology', 62
commonalities, 62–3
communal land-ownership, 91–2
communication, 189–92
communism, 99, 103
Companion to Social Archaeology, A, 123
Comparison of Russian and Sanskrit Words, 82
Compendium of Eloquence, 75
'competition of faculties', 172
Conceição Tavares, Maria da, 61
Connell, Raewyn, 8, 9, 45n, 176
conservatism, 93
Conspiración de Gual y España (1979–9), 171
constellations, 127–60
consumption, 40, 153
Copernican revolution, 24
Corsali, Andrea, 137, 156n
Cortázar, Julio, 191
cosmopolitanism, 18
Crimea, 88, 102
Crimean War 1853–6, 76, 84–5, 87, 89
'crisis of civilization', 115
Cristo si è fermato a Eboli, 205–6
Crosby, Alfred, 40
Crutzen, Paul, 36–7
Crux Australis, 139
'Cruzero hispanis, at Ptolemy Pedes Centauri', 139
El Cuadernno de Barro, 206–7
Cuban Revolution, 57
'cultural-historical types', 89–92
'culture-area', 64

Danilevskiy, Nikolay, 89–92, 94, 95–6
Darwish, Mahmoud, 183, 185
Dawes, Kwame, 191
De cive, 139–40
Dean, Tacita, 203
Decembrist revolt 1825, 76

Index

Declaration on the Granting of Independence to Colonial Countries and Peoples, 127
Decline of the West, 90
decolonisation, 57, 127
Decreation, 199
democracy, 6, 18–20
democracy and totality, 40–3
demos, 41, 42
Derrida, Jacques, 200
Descartes, René, 24, 33, 170
Desde el exilio (From Exile), 192–3
Developed Countries, 53
'developing societies', 1–2
development as perpetual motion, 66
development policy, 13
development theories, 52–3
developmentalism, 61
'development-promoting policies', 55
'diatopical hermeneutics', 44n
Diderot, Denis, 75
difference, semantics of, 59
digging for class, 107–26
Diop, Cheikh Anta, 116–17
'discovery', 10
'discovery of America', 34–5
'discovery of New World', 35, 44–5n
displacements
    modern, 161–82
    between spaces, 14
domination, 10, 11–12, 28–30, 32, 40–1, 150–1, 167
    resistance against, 9, 18
Dostoyevskiy, Feodor, 95
Du Bois, W. E. B., 114–16, 122
dual spatiality, 6
dualism, 33, 45n
Dugin, Alexander, 101
Durkheim, Émile, 163–4, 180n
Dussel, Enrique, 112

Earth as system, 39
'Easterns', 99
Eberhardt, Isabelle, 164, 168, 171–8, 179n, 180n
Economic Commission for Latin America and the Caribbean (ECLAC), 57, 60
'economic development', 55, 68n
'economic forecasting', 61
'economic miracle', 65
'economic progress', 68n
egalitarianism and liberalism, 93
Egypt, 116–17

Eisenstadt, Shmuel, 28
Elisabeth I (of Russia), 75
Elisabeth II (of Russia), 75
Elytis, Odysseas, 198–200
'emerging economies', 64, 65
'empty space', 169–70
encuentros, 6
Engels, Friedrich, 96
England, 87
Enlightenment, 10, 30, 38, 45n, 75–6, 141
enlightenment, 81
Les Enragés, 173
Epistemologies of the South, 9
equal freedom, 142–3
erasure of space, 6
Erice, Víctor, 206
Erwartungshorizont (horizon of expectations), 61
Euben, R. L., 167
Eurasianism, 96
Eurasianism movement (*Evraziystvo*), 99–102
Euro crisis, 14
Eurocentric world-outlook, 72
Eurocentrism, 89
Europe and modernity, 2
European, 29–36, 166
    colonies, 56
    discoverers, 136, 142
    experience, 62
    imperialism, 120
    modernity, 10–11
    voyages, 53
European Economic Community, 13
European Management Forum, 6
European revolutions 1848–9, 84
European Union, 13, 153
Eve, 186–91
Ex oriente lux, 97
exile
    as a desert, 193, 196
    implacable promise of, 192–7
    impossible return, 189–92
    islands of, 194, 202
    as a kingdom, 193
    obligation of, 186–9
    psyche in, 201–2
    as punishment, 186–8
    South as, 183–216
exiled soul, 197–202
El exilio como patria [Exile as Homeland], 193
exotic, the, 162

experiences, 9–10, 28
expulsion, 195
'extra-territoriality', 197

Facing South to Africa: Toward an Afrocentric Critical Orientation, 117
Faiz, Faiz Ahmad, 190
Fanon, Frantz, 58, 175
FarNear, 199
Fedorov, Nikolay, 99–100
'Felix in exile', *183*, 209, 210n
Ferguson, James, 112
Fichte, Johann Gottlieb, 128, 143
film, 205–7
The Film-maker's Holiday, 206
Florovsky, Gyorgy, 99
Fonvisin, Denis, 77
foreigners, 185
Foulcault, Michel, 118, 141–2
Foundations of Natural Right, 143
France, 13
freedom, 154
freedom, equal, 142–3
French Clamart, 99–100
French colonial world, 175
French Revolution, 10, 75–6, 84–5, 168, 173
Freud, Sigmund, 202
Frobenius, Leo, 107–8, 110, 116, 123–5
From Another Shore, 94
'fusion of horizons', 23
future expectations, 61–2

G7 countries, 51
G20 countries, 131
Gadamer, Hans-Georg, 23
Gaia hypothesis, 39
Galbraith, John Kenneth, 52
Galilei, Galileo, 135
Ganas, Michalis, 191–2
GDP, 51, 52
Genghis Khan, 100
Giddens, Anthony, 169, 176
global imperialism, 31
'Global North', definitions, 1–17
'global shadows', 112
global social space, 1–17
'Global South', definitions, 1–17
global well-being, 58
globalisation, 2, 5–7, 35, 152–3
'globe', 23–24
gnosticism, 198–9
Gogol, Nikolay, 77
Goldman Sachs Bank, 51–2

Graham, Jorie, 185
Gramsci, Antonio, 129
Great Acceleration, 40
Great French Revolution, 75–6, 84–5
Great Zimbabwe, 107–8, 110–12, 124–5
Greece, 186–9, 191–2, 210n
Gumilev, Lev, 94, 101

Haitian Revolution, 143, 173
Harvey, David, 165
Hegel, Georg, 44n, 85, 113–22, 128, 143–4, 146–9, 157n
Heidegger, Martin, 21, 27, 38
Heimatlose, 179–80n
Hellenism, 33
Herzen, Alexander, 84, 85–7, 92, 94
historical injustice, 40–1
'History 1, 2 and 3', 36, 37, 38–9, 45n
Hobbes, Thomas, 42, 139–40, 144, 157n
Hondius, Jodocus, Junior, 139
Hong Kong, 61, 65
Honneth, Axel, 11–12, 147–9, 157n
horizon, 26–7
'horror', 145
human rights, 19, 130–3
humanity, 21, 40–1, 43
humans, 20–1
  away from Earth, 25
  as 'biogeochemical force', 26
  as 'geological force', 42
  as species, 42–3
Hungary, 191–2
Husserl, Edmund, 21
Hy-Brazil, 53

Ibiza, 207–8
IBSA, 52, 67
The Idea of Africa, 118–19
Imperial Russian Historical Society, 76
imperialism, 7
inauthenticity, 149
incompleteness, 65
India, 51, 52, 62–3, 66–7, 72, 82–3, 108
individualisation, 5–7, 15, 157n
Industrial Revolution, 10, 40
'industrialisation', 68n
inequality, 58, 66
inequality, semantics of, 53, 55
information and communication technology, 6
An Inquiry into the Nature and Causes of the Wealth of Nations (1776), 54–5
insiders *(entranos)*, 194

Index

'intelligentsia-people' divide, 77–8, 84, 103
interconnectedness, 19, 43, 64
interdependence and interaction, 32
'internal exile', 201
internalism, 98–9
'interrupted dawn', 194–5, 197
intra-European South, 14
The Invention of Africa: Gnosis, Philosophy and the Order of Knowledge, 118
Iran, 80–3
Iranian principle, 81–3
Islam, 174
islands of exile, 194, 202
Israel, 205

Jamaica, 171
Japan, 153
Jena Writings, 146
Jews, 172
Joyce, James, 208

Kadmo, 192, 200
Kant, Immanuel, 18, 44n, 46n, 143, 144–5
Karagiannis, Nathalie, 15
Kazakhstan, 99, 101
Kemp, Rosin, 201
Kentridge, William, *183*, 184, 209
Keynesian democratic welfare state, 13
Khomyakov, Alexey, 78, 80–3, 87
Kidnapping Caucasian Style (1967), 99
Koselleck, Reinhart, 61, 168–9
Koskenniemi, Martti, 43
Kovats, Tania, 203
Kristeva, Julia, 202, 208
Kushite principle, 81–3

'lack of identity', 60, 62–3, 64
Lacuesta, Isaki, 206–7
language, 175–6, 200–2
    Russian, 77
    Spanish, 194, 211n
Latin America, 57, 58, 157n, 173, 191
Latin cross, 135
League of Nations, 18–19
Lefkowitz, Mary, 117–18
Lefort, Claude, 46–7n
Lemuria, 53
Leontiev, Konstantin, 89, 92–4
Levi, Carlo, 205–6, 209
Leviathan, 140
liberalism, 130–1
localisation of discourse, 168
Locke, John, 14–15, 166

Loftus, Josephine, 201
logic of rights, 130
Lomonosov, Michael, 75, 103
London, 87
Lorca, Federico García, 183, 185, 197, 209
The Lost Land of Lemuria, 51
Lupus constellation, 135–7, 139

MacEachern, Scott, 122
Machiavelli, Niccolò, 141
Maghreb, 174–5, 179n, 180n
Mair, Alexander, 135, 136–7
Mali, 207
Mandelstam, Nadezhda, 191
Manifeste incertain 2, 207–8
mapping the globe, 23–4
Mapungubwe, 110–13, 119, 123, 124
marginalisation, 172
'marginality', 61, 112–13
Martí, José, 128–9, 151
Marx, Karl, 7, 30, 96, 110, 111
Marxian tradition, 11–12
Masaccio, 187
Master–slave dialectic, 143–4
'master–slave races', 145
mastery of 'nature' by humans, 19–20, 25–6
'material inequalities', 58
'material progress', 55, 68n
Maya, 82
Mbembe, Achille, 119, 120
'mechanisms of embedment', 169
Memmi, Albert, 175
Mercosur, 67, 134
Merleau-Ponty, Maurice, 21
Merton, Robert, 52, 62
Meskell, Lynn, 123
Mexico, 52
Meyesenbug, Malwida von, 94
Michaux, Henri, 199
Mignolo, Walter D., 161, 170
Millennium Development Goals (UN), 132
Mitria Patrida, 191–2
Mocovi people, 138
modernisation, 9, 10
modernities
    'alternative', 5
    'multiple', 5, 112, 121
    'vernacular', 112
modernity, 10, 27–8, 51, 53–60, 142
    antinomies of, 55–6
    Europe and, 2
    European, 10–11
    as future expectations, 61

221

modernity (*cont.*)
  narratives of, 52–3
  Russian, 103
Mongolian Empire, 100
Moscow, 74–5
Mota, Aurea, 14
mother-tongue, 200–1
Mudimbe, V. Y., 61, 118–19
'multiple modernities', 5, 112, 121
multi-polar world-politics, 13
mundialisation and globalisation, 45n

Nakaz (Instructions), 75
ñandú, 138
Napoleon Bonaparte, 76, 78, 88, 95, 144, 145, 179n
narodniki, 87, 88
nation states, 164
national liberation, 127
nationalism, 165
'natural history', 26
nature and environment, 19–20
Nazarbayev (President of Kazakhstan), 101
Nazism, 120, 205
Negroid Africans, 116–17
'neo-colonialism', 58
neo-developmentalism, 52
neolibralism, 7
Neuzeit, 168–9
'new time', 168–9
New World, 3–4, 10, 11, 133–4, 141, 166, 173, 177
Newton, Isaac, 24
Nicolas I (of Russia), 76, 79, 84
Nietzsche, Friedrich, 94
N'Krumah, Kwame, 58
Nomos of the Earth, 28–9, 44–5n
Non-Aligned Movement, 57, 58
North Africa, 175
North Atlantic economies, 52, 63
'Northern theory', 8, 161–2
'Northernness', 176
North–South cooperation, 132
North–South dialectic, 128, 150
North–South divide, 58, 128, 133–4, 152
Nuevea Granada, 171
Nyerere, Julius, 152–3

L'Observateur, 56–7
Odoyevskiy, Prince Vladimir, 76
Oedipus, 186–91, 196
Of Hospitality, 200
Offe, Claus, 177–8

oil prices, 59
oil reserves, 52
Old Believers, 74
Old World, 3–4, 10, 177
On the Postcolony, 119
O'Neill, Jim, 51–2, 56, 61–2
Organization of African Unity, 57
Organization of the Petroleum Exporting Countries (OPEC), 57, 58, 59
'Oriental' knowledge, 166
Orientalism, 54
The Origins of Totalitarianism, 119–20
Ortega, A. G., 180n
Orthodox kingdom, 74
Orthodoxy, Autocracy and Nationality, 84
Ossip, 191
Osterhammel, Jürgen, 35, 113
other, 41, 54, 63
otherness, 54, 55, 65
  of the South, 8
Our America, 128–9
outsiders (*extranos*), 194
Ovid, 188–9

'pace of change', 169
Pajak, Frédéric, 207–8
Palmerston, Lord, 87
Pan-Americanism movement, 173
Panikkar, Raimon, 44n
Panmongolism, 97–8
pan-Slavism, 90
paradigmatisation of historical events, 173
Paris Agreement 2015, 43
'party', 41, 42
Paul, Jean, 203
peasant communism, 88
'people', 41
'perdre le Nord', 204
Perote, Marguerite, 199
Peru, 171
Peter III (of Russia), 75
Peter the Great (of Russia), 74–5, 77–8, 80–1, 100
'Petersburg', 76
Petersson, Niels P., 35
The Phenomenology of Spirit, 146
'Philosophical Letters', 78–9
Philotheus of Pskov, 74
'place of utterance', 59
place-imagining, 65–6
place-making, 52–3, 62, 65–6
'planet Earth', 25–6, 36–40
'planetary boundaries', 46n

planetary society, 7
Plato, 33, 53
'The Pleasures of Exile', 191
poetry, 183–209
Pollock, James, 199
Portugal, 13, 24
Portuguese explorers, 107
Post, Felix, 201
post-Cold War relations, 88
post-Soviet Russia, 101
poverty, 58–9
power relations, 32
Preucel, Robert W., 123
The Prince, 141
processual geographies, 64–5
progress, 54–5, 89
'prosperous' nations, 54–5
Providence, 79–80
'provincializing Europe', 112
Prussia, 172
psychoanalysis, 147, 208
   check earlier, 201–2
Ptolemy, 135
Pushkin, Alexander, 74

The Quest of the South, 203, 204
Quignard, Pascal, 214n
Quijano, Anibal, 170

racism, 146
Ramaswamy, Sumathi, 51, 53, 54, 56, 59, 61
raya, 24, 31
'razon poetica', 192
recognition, 143, 145–9, 150–6, 157n
'Reflections on Exile', 184–5, 189, 190
Reformation, 34–5
'reification', 11–12
religion, 96–7
Renaissance, 10, 166
representation of a space, 163
res cogitans, 33
res extensa, 24, 33
rhetoric of emergence, 62
Ribeiro, Diogo, 24
'rise of Europe', 10–11
Rodríguez, Simón, 164, 168, 171–8, 179n
Rousseau, Jean-Jacques, 149
Royer, Augustine, 139
Russia, 2, 15–16n, 51, 62–3, 66–7, 172
   as an Asian power, 95–102
   as the Christian East: Russia and
      Slavdom, 76–95
   between East, West and North, 72–106

   as European North, 74–6
   'European Power' of 'European People',
      75
   as potential rescuer of Europe, 75–6
   Russia and Europe, 89
Russian
   as civilising power, 95–6
   European nobility, 77
   language, 77
   modernity, 103
Russian Empire, 75
Russian Revolution 1917, 78, 91, 98, 100
'Russian World' (*Russkiy Mir*), 102

Said, Edward, 54, 59, 184–5, 189, 190
Sanskrit, 82
Santos, Boaventura de Sousa, 8, 9, 129
Santos, Milton, 152–3
Sartre, Jean-Paul, 58
Sauerwald, Gregor, 157n
Sauvy, Alfred, 4, 56–7, 68n
'savage' nations, 54–5
Savitskiy, Petr, 99
Schmitt, Carl, 28–9, 34, 44–5n, 170
Science, 40
scientific interpretations, 168
scientific revolution, 10
'Scramble for Africa', 63, 68n, 115, 157n
Second World War, 54–5, 115, 120, 142, 192
self-determination, 6, 11
self-reliance, 129
semantics of difference, 59
semantics of inequality, 53, 55
semi-peripheries of capitalism, 61
Semiramis, 81
Sennett, Richard, 187
Serres, Michel, 46n
Shpet, Gustav, 77–8
Siberia, 74, 75, 79, 99, 103
Singapore, 61, 65
slavery, 172
Slavic type, 91
Slavophiles, 78–9, 80–4, 87, 90–2, 100
Smith, Adam, 54–5, 59
social archaeology, 123
social control, 142
social distinction, 107–26
social equality, 151–2
social forecasting, 62
social imaginaries, 22, 31, 165–71, 178n
social movements, 128–30, 133
socialism, 85–8
'societies', 39

'socio-cultural area', 64
Socrates, 186
Sofia, 99
Solovyev, Vladimir, 96–8
Solzhenitsyn, Aleksandr, 103
South
    as an alternative, 7–10
    dark light of the, 203–9
    as elsewhere, 14–15
    as exile, 183–216
    faraway, so close, 1–3
    as a moving target, 12–14
    origins and end of the, 10–12
    otherness of, 8
South Africa, 12, 52, 62–3, 66, 72, 120, 146
    first general elections, 184, 210n
South America, 67, 173
South Center Commission, 152
South Commission, 57, 58
South Korea, 61, 65
[South], 208–9
Southern Cross, 128, 134–56, 156n
'Southern identity', 131–2
Southern knowledge, 8
'Southern theory', 161–2
Southern Theory (2007), 8
Soviet Russia, 99
Soviet socialism, 4–5
Soviet Union, 56, 96, 99, 101, 103
'space of experience', 169
space time separation, 169
spaces and experiences, 161–82
Spain, 24, 192–4
Spanish language, 194, 211n
Spanish Republic, 192
spatialisation of epistemology, 9
spatiality, 62–3
spatiality and conceptuality, 7–8
spatio-political form, 18–50
Spengler, Oswald, 90
SSC acronym (South-South Cooperation),
    127, 131
St Petersberg, 74–5
state socialism, 5
Steiner, George, 197
'struggle', 140–9
Subrahmanyam, Sanjay, 66
Sufism, 174
Sukarno (President of Indonesia), 58
El Sur, 206
Suvchinsky, Petr, 99
Sweden, 75
Syria, 184

Taiwan, 61, 65
Tatar yoke, 74, 79, 101
technology, 54, 189–92
temporality and spatiality, 14–15
terminal loss, 189–92
territorial transformations, 165
Theory from the South (2012), 8–9
Theory in Africa, Africa in Theory:
    Debating Meaning in Archaeology,
    122
Third Rome, 74, 84
'third way', 100
Third World, 53, 56–7, 58, 65
'Third World', 3–5
'Three Conversations', 98
'Three Forces', 96–7
three-world distinction, 3–5, 30–1
time and space in moral narratives of
    development, 51–71
time and spaces of uneven development,
    53–60
time space distanciation, 169
'time-space zoning', 169
Tocqueville, Alexis de, 177–8
topology of power, 54
totality, 26–40
    democracy and, 40–3
    of human beings, 18–21
transnationalism, 129
travel writings, 166–7
Treaty of Saragossa 1529, 24
Treaty of Tordesillas 1494, 24
Trevor-Roper, Hugh, 114
Trois mondes, une planète, 56–7
Trubetskoy, Nikolai, 99, 100–1
Truman, Harry, 55
trusteeship, 55
Turkey, 52, 172
Tutchev, Fedor, 88
two worlds dualism, 33

Ukraine, 73, 88, 102
UN General Assembly, 52
uneven development, 53–60
United Nations, 18–19, 43, 127
United Nations' universal Agenda 2030,
    132, 152
United States, 56, 153, 177–8
'universal', 131–2
universal claims, 161–82
universal consciousness, 143–4
universality, 171–7
urbis, 164–5

Index

Ustryalov, Nikolay, 100
'utopian socialism', 173

Vaen, Adrian, 139
Valladolid-Salamanca debate 1550–1, 11
van der Keuken, Johan, 206–7
Vasili III Ivanovich (Grand Prince of
    Moscow), 74
Venezuela, 171, 179n
'vernacular modernities', 112
Vernadskiy, Georgiy, 99
Visions du Moghreb, 174, 179n
Voltaire, 75
Vyazemskiy, Prince Peter, 76

Wagner, Peter, 28, 120–2, 150–1
Wallerstein, Immanuel, 170
The Way South, 206
Weber, Max, 65, 110, 111, 177–8
Western democratic capitalism, 4–5
Western development, 62
'Western' social theory, 8
Westernisation, 77–8
Westernisers, 78–80, 83–4, 87, 91

White Sun of the Desert (1970), 99
Williams, Raymond, 189
Wilsonian utopia, 19
Winnicott, Donald, 147
Wollstonecraft, Mary, 130
'world', 21–3
world
    as human creation, 22
    as incomplete, 22–3
    is modern, 26–8
'world alienation', 30
*The World and Africa: An Inquiry into
    the Part which Africa Has Played in
    World History*, 114–16
World Economic Forum, 6–7
World Social Forum (WSF), 6–7, 153
world-systems approach, 170
world-view, 27
Writer's Diary, 95

Zambrano, María, 184, 186, 192–7, 199,
    201–2, 205, 210n
Zeitlosigkeit, 202, 208
Zimbabwe, 107–8, 110–12, 124–5

EU representative:
Easy Access System Europe
Mustamäe tee 50, 10621 Tallinn, Estonia
Gpsr.requests@easproject.com

www.ingramcontent.com/pod-product-compliance
Lightning Source LLC
Chambersburg PA
CBHW070406270326
41926CB00014B/2721